THE MEDIA AND FOREIGN POLICY

Also by Simon Serfaty

FRANCE, DE GAULLE AND EUROPE: The Policy of the Fourth and Fifth Republics Toward the Continent

THE ELUSIVE ENEMY: American Foreign Policy since World War II

FADING PARTNERSHIP: America and Europe after 30 Years

THE UNITED STATES, EUROPE AND THE THIRD WORLD: Allies and Adversaries

A SOCIALIST FRANCE AND WESTERN SECURITY (*co-author*)

AFTER REAGAN: False Starts, Missed Opportunities and New Beginnings

LES ANNÉES DIFFICILES: La Politique étrangère des États-Unis de Truman à Reagan

AMERICAN FOREIGN POLICY IN A HOSTILE WORLD: Dangerous Years

THE FOREIGN POLICIES OF THE FRENCH LEFT (*editor*)

THE FUTURE OF U.S.–SOVIET RELATIONS: Twenty American Initiatives for a New Agenda (*editor*)

THE ITALIAN COMMUNIST PARTY: Yesterday, Today and Tomorrow (*co-editor*)

The Media and Foreign Policy

Edited by

Simon Serfaty
Executive Director
The Johns Hopkins Foreign Policy Institute

St. Martin's Press
New York

in association with
Foreign Policy Institute
The Paul H. Nitze School of
Advanced International Studies
The Johns Hopkins University

Library of Congress Cataloging-in-Publication Data

Media and foreign policy / Simon Serfaty, editor ; foreword by Marvin
    Kalb.
        p.   cm.
      ISBN 0-312-06498-5 (pbk.)
        1. Mass media—Political aspects—United States.   2. United
States—Foreign relations—1945-   3. International relations.
I. Serfaty, Simon.
P95.82.U6M43   1991
327.1—dc20   91-4345
                                                                   CIP

First U.S. Paperback Edition: September 1991
10 9 8 7 6 5 4 3 2

Contents

Acknowledgements

The editor wishes to acknowledge the contributions of Jim Anderson, William Bader, John Barry, William Beecher, Peter Braestrup, Harold Brown, Hodding Carter, Robert Donovan, Mel Elfin, Pat Ellis, John W. Finney, Michael Getler, Georgie Ann Geyer, John Maxwell Hamilton, Richard Helms, Stephen Hess, Les Janka, Bernard Kalb, Fred Kempe, Morton Kondracke, Richard Lugar, John McWethy, Philip Merrill, Judith Miller, Michael Mosettig, Daniel Patrick Moynihan, Lars-Erik Nelson, Herman Nickel, Don Oberdorfer, Joanne Omang, Robert Pierpoint, Jody Powell, Chalmers Roberts, Morris Rosenberg, Thomas Ross, Robert Sims, Helmut Sonnenfeldt, Tad Szulc, John Trattner, and Robert Woodward. Without their earnest participation in our meetings and their thoughtful comments on the papers published here, this volume would be much less than it is.

Our work was made possible by a grant from the John & Mary R. Markle Foundation. We wish to thank the officers and trustees of the Foundation for their generous support.

Notes on the Contributors

Kenneth L. Adelman was director of the Arms Control and Disarmament Agency from 1983 to 1987, and was deputy permanent representative of the United States to the United Nations from 1981 to 1983. He is the author of *The Great Universal Embrace* (1989); vice president of the Institute for Contemporary Studies in Washington, D.C.; and national editor of *Washingtonian* magazine. Dr. Adelman teaches Shakespeare at Georgetown University and security policy at the Paul H. Nitze School of Advanced International Studies of the Johns Hopkins University.

Charles W. Bailey served as Washington correspondent for the *Minneapolis Tribune* from 1954 to 1972, then as editor until 1982. From 1984 to 1987 he was Washington editor of National Public Radio, and was chairman of the Washington Journalism Center from 1985 to 1989. He is the author of *Conflicts of Interest: A Matter of Journalistic Ethics* (1984) and co-author of several other books, including the novel *Seven Days in May* (1962).

Richard R. Burt is U.S. ambassador to the nuclear and space negotiations (the Strategic Arms Reduction [START] and Defense and Space Talks) in Geneva, Switzerland. He was director of the bureau of politico-military affairs, Department of State (1981–2); assistant secretary of state for European and Canadian affairs (1982–85); and ambassador to the Federal Republic of Germany (1985–1989). Prior to joining the Reagan administration, Ambassador Burt served as national security affairs correspondent for the *New York Times*.

Harold Evans is editor in chief of *Condé Nast Traveler* magazine. He was editor of *The Sunday Times* (London) from 1967 to 1981 and editor of *The Times* (London) 1981–82. Mr. Evans taught at Duke

University in 1983, was editorial director of *U.S. News & World Report* from 1984 to 1986. He is the author of *Good Times, Bad Times* (1983).

David R. Gergen joined *U.S. News & World Report* in 1985 and has been editor since 1986. From 1981 to 1983 he was special assistant to President Reagan for communications, and he served in a similar capacity in the Nixon and Ford administrations (1971–77). Mr. Gergen was a resident fellow of the American Enterprise Institute and managing editor of AEI's *Public Opinion* magazine in 1977–81, and was a fellow of the John F. Kennedy Institute of Politics at Harvard University from 1983 to 1985.

Philip L. Geyelin, editor-in-residence at The Johns Hopkins Foreign Policy Institute since 1980, was editor of the editorial page of the *Washington Post* from 1967 until 1979. He worked for the *Wall Street Journal* from 1947 to 1966. Mr. Geyelin is the author of *Lyndon B. Johnson and the World* (1966) and numerous articles. He won a Pulitzer Prize for editorial writing in 1970.

John L. Harper is associate professor of European studies and U.S. foreign policy at the Bologna (Italy) Center of the Paul H. Nitze School of Advanced International Studies, the Johns Hopkins University. He is the author of *America and the Reconstruction of Italy 1945–48*, which won the Marraro prize from the Society for Italian Historical Studies in 1987.

Robert J. Kurz spent nearly ten years as a foreign policy specialist working with the Congress and is currently guest scholar at The Brookings Institution in Washington, D.C., Council on Foreign Relations international affairs fellow, and adjunct professor of national security studies at Georgetown University. He wishes to acknowledge the contributions of Stephen Hess, Thomas E. Mann, Gary C. Marfin and Mark Rosenberg.

Michael A. Ledeen is resident scholar at the American Enterprise Institute in Washington, D.C., and president of ISI Enterprises, Inc. in Chevy Chase, Maryland. He served as special adviser to the U.S. secretary of state from 1981 to 1982, and was a consultant to the National Security Council from 1984 to 1986. He is the author of numerous books, including *Perilous Statecraft* (1988) and *Grave New World* (1984).

Robert J. McCloskey is editor of *Mediterranean Quarterly*. After serving in the Marine Corps during World War II, McCloskey held various positions, including two years as a journalist, before joining the career Foreign Service in 1955. He served as ambassador to the Republic of Cyprus (1973–74); assistant secretary of state for congressional relations (1974–76); ambassador to the Netherlands (1976–78); and ambassador to Greece (1978–81). In 1981 he joined the *Washington Post* as ombudsman, and from 1984 to 1989 was vice president of Catholic Relief Services.

Robert C. McFarlane was national security adviser to President Ronald Reagan from 1983 to 1986. A 1959 graduate of the United States Naval Academy, Mr. McFarlane received his masters degree in strategic studies from the Graduate Institute of International Studies in Geneva. In almost thirty years of government service, he has been a leading contributor to national policy, serving three Presidents during nine years on the White House staff.

R. Gregory Nokes is assistant managing editor of *The Oregonian* of Portland, Oregon. He was a diplomatic writer and chief State Department correspondent for the Associated Press in Washington, D.C. from 1980 to 1986. A native Oregonian, he received his bachelor of arts from Willamette University in Salem Oregon in 1959. He was a Nieman Fellow at Harvard University in 1971–72.

Robert B. Oakley has been United States ambassador to Pakistan since September 1988. He was Director of the State Department Office for Combating Terrorism from 1984 to 1986, and served as special assistant to the President for national security affairs and senior director for the Near East, South Asia, and North Africa from December 1986 until August 1988. The essay in this volume, representing Ambassador Oakley's personal views, was written during a leave of absence at the Carnegie Endowment for International Peace.

William E. Odom is director of national security studies at the Hudson Institute in Alexandria, Virginia, and adjunct professor of political science at Yale University. A 1954 graduate of West Point and a career military officer, General Odom received an M.A. (1962) and Ph.D. (1970) from Columbia University. Prior to retiring from the army with the rank of lieutenant general, he served as director of the National Security Agency (1985–89).

Stephen S. Rosenfeld is the deputy editorial page editor and a columnist for the *Washington Post*. He joined the Post city staff in 1959, moved to the editorial department in 1962, served as Moscow correspondent in 1964–1965, and then returned to the editorial page. He is coauthor, with his wife, of *Return from Red Square*, a report on Russia published in 1967, and author of *The Time of Their Dying*, a memoir published in 1977.

Simon Serfaty is executive director of the Johns Hopkins Foreign Policy Institute and research professor of American foreign policy at the Paul H. Nitze School of Advanced International Studies. Dr. Serfaty is the author of numerous books on U.S. foreign policy, including *After Reagan: False Starts, Missed Opportunities & New Beginnings* (1988) and *American Foreign Policy in a Hostile World* (1984), and is the editor of *The Future of U.S.-Soviet Relations: Twenty American Initiatives for a New Agenda* (1989).

John P. Wallach is foreign editor of The Hearst Newspapers. He is the recipient of two Overseas Press Club awards, the Edward Weintal Prize for Diplomatic Reporting, and the Edwin Hood Award, the National Press Club's highest honor for foreign policy reporting. Mr. Wallach founded the Chautauqua Conference on U.S.-Soviet Relations and is co-author of *Still Small Voices: The Untold Human Stories Behind the Violence in the West Bank and Gaza* (1989).

David Webster is senior fellow of The Annenberg Washington Program in Communications Policy Studies, and chairman of both the Annenberg International Disaster Communications Project and the TransAtlantic Dialogue on European Broadcasting. Mr. Webster was a member of the board of management of the British Broadcasting Corporation from 1977 to 1985, and was a resident associate of the Carnegie Endowment for International Peace in Washington, D.C., from 1985 to 1987.

Foreword

Marvin Kalb

An old comic once put it: "Time flies when you're having fun."
It is more than three years since three friends associated with
the Foreign Policy Institute of Johns Hopkins University—Simon Serfaty, Philip Geyelin and Joseph Fromm—convened the opening seminar of a new study on "The Media and Foreign Policy." I was then
twenty-nine years into a career as diplomatic correspondent for CBS
and NBC, when they asked whether I wished to share an experience,
or a thought or two, with a distinguished group of journalists, scholars and government officials, including several "formers," such as
Harold Brown, once a Secretary of Defense, and Richard Helms, once
a director of the Central Intelligence Agency. Thus started a series
of seminars, rooted in decades of journalistic and governmental experience, devoted to studying the interrelationship of the press (meaning newspapers), magazines, radio and television, and the making of
American foreign policy. Now, happily, the study is complete, and,
even better from the point of view of a journalist-turned-academic,
it's a book ready for publication.

At an increasing number of universities around the country, including Johns Hopkins and Harvard, the study of "press politics"
is a growth industry. More and more centers are being established.
Academics are now coming to appreciate what successful politicians
have known for decades—that the press is a key player in the process of governance. Even the journalists themselves, who quite
properly value their independence and cherish the First Amendment,
understand the importance of their role, especially in recent years.
Imagine a presidential campaign without TV! The press has become
so inextricably intertwined in every aspect of domestic and foreign
policy that Senator Richard Lugar, the Republican from Indiana,
refers to the new power game as "medialism," and David Gergen,

who served Presidents Ford and Reagan as a director of communications, calls it "teledemocracy."

The competition for names and labels is symptomatic of the widespread view that the press is, if not quite Douglass Cater's "fourth branch of government" (a phrase that ignites passions among constitutional purists), then at least so crucial and inescapable a part of governance that we are no longer faced with the unhappy choice posed almost 200 years ago by Thomas Jefferson—either a government without newspapers, or newspapers without a government—but rather government with newspapers, indeed, with the whole complex of modern-day journalism. We live in a gigantic globe-girdling, hi-tech loop that has obliterated time and space, while linking the worlds of press and politics.

During the Reagan years, the White House came to a screeching halt at 7 P.M., so everyone could watch the evening news programs, primarily to see whether their stagemanaging of the presidency had been successfully translated into the language of television. Michael Ledeen, a scholar, writer and former aide to Alexander Haig, said during one seminar that 80–90 percent of staff time was spent worrying about the press. For quite a few years now, TV cameras have been covering House and Senate deliberations. C-Span carries the British House of Commons. CNN is essential viewing in the Soviet Foreign Ministry and in chanceries—and hotels—around the globe. Soviet President Gorbachev enjoys an extraordinary reputation abroad, in part because he is a natural at caressing the TV lens during his frequent travels. Indeed, only the foolish foreign leader can any longer afford to underestimate the power of TV news. Authoritarian regimes have learned to bar coverage of embarrassing events, proving again that the old adage, "out of sight, out of mind," is still valid. The electronic press can be an ally or an enemy, but it cannot be ignored.

Former Speaker Thomas P. "Tip" O'Neill used to say that "all politics is local." Now, because of a new generation of technology—mobile telephones, fax machines, TV satellites, up- and down-link dishes, miniaturized Super-8 millimeter cameras, supersonic jet aircraft—global politics has also become local. And while there are still correspondents based abroad, the genre known as "foreign correspondent" is becoming extinct. His or her brand of expertise is now the property of the good generalist, or the ubiquitous anchor.

There was a time when foreign correspondents spoke the language and knew the history of the country to which they were assigned. They were scholars in trenchcoats. Their dispatches, carefully considered and researched, were transmitted by cable, or telephoned on a scratchy line and then retyped by someone in the home office. There was time for reconsideration of a thought, or idea. No longer. Communications are now instantaneous. The correspondent, as well as the diplomat, is denied the opportunity for reflection. Both are part of the new, global loop of information, their fortunes intertwined. They are pressured to react quickly, in some cases "live." Judgment is rushed. Copy is ad-libbed, cables dictated at top speed. The effect on the viewer, or reader, is insignificant. So accustomed have they become to seeing "live" reports from anywhere in the world, from Beijing, Moscow or a ship off Malta, that they have become blasé about the wonder of it all. If the world is their backyard, instantly available with the flip of a switch and the blink of an eye, then everything is local. And if everything is "local," then there is the risk, in this rush to judgment, of distortion, misunderstanding, blunder, and confusion of values. The joke at NBC used to be that if the network could only get a sponsor, the next war in the Middle East would be "brought to you live."

By now it is a truism of the modern age of politics that an event is not really important, worthy of attention, unless the network anchors are personally there to cover it. Accompanied by a small army of producers, camera operators, researchers and executives, each of the major TV hosts began covering East–West summitry in October 1985, when Presidents Reagan and Gorbachev met in Geneva for the first of four summits devoted, as it turned out, to burying the Cold War. The presence of the anchors assures airtime as well as a sense of pomp and theater that world leaders simply cannot resist. By playing to the cameras, they play not only to their own people but to a global audience—quite literally, to hundreds of millions of people at the same time. If they have a message, and they want to sell it, the anchors are there to provide a gallery packed with potential buyers. The competitive struggle for an exclusive foot of tape or an interview is fierce, and journalistic standards are sometimes sacrificed on the altar of TV ratings or front-page ambitions. It was a coup for CBS when Dan Rather was in Tiananmen Square to cover the massacre of Chinese students, even more of a coup for NBC, which had lower ratings, when Tom Brokaw was in Berlin at the time the Wall collapsed. East Germans, who had been watching West German television for a decade, rushed through the various gaps to check out the TV image with the real thing. There is little doubt that TV news encouraged the moves toward democratization in Eastern Europe. The press helps fashion the look and content of foreign policy, often from a traditionally adversarial position.

There was a time, pre-Vietnam, pre-Watergate, when American journalists tended to believe their government's version of events. In Moscow in the 1950s and early 1960s, it seemed to me that my colleagues and I generally cooperated with U.S. embassy, sharing information and accepting the ambassador's interpretation of Kremlin policy. There was no discernible skepticism. By the mid-1960s, Vietnam had begun to corrode this attitude, and by the mid-1970s, Watergate turned it into a sour cynicism, which has persisted to this day. But a few thoughtful journalists, including Anthony Lewis of the *New York Times*, believe that, during the Reagan Years and even now, though to a lesser extent, the White House press corps has again become "pussycats," less than vigorously skeptical about pursuing the news and criticizing the administration. It was not a White House reporter, critics often note, who broke either the Iran–Contra story or the HUD scandal, but it should also be noted that it is not the job of a White House reporter to do investigative pieces. More often than not, the White House reporter simply covers the daily, breaking story: What did the President say? What did the President do? When? Where?

Still, if there is a single red thread that runs through the "press-politics" relationship, especially at the White House, it is the government's obsession with leaks. President Bush kept the secret of the Malta summit from all but a handful of his closest advisers, even excluding Richard Cheney, his secretary of defense, because he was concerned about a possible leak. He wanted to prove to Gorbachev that his administration, unlike previous ones, was serious about secrets. When the *Washington Post* broke the story before the assigned time for its disclosure, the Russians were "relaxed" about it, if one is to believe Soviet Foreign Minister Eduard Schevardnadze, but the President turned livid with rage and imposed a draconian order that henceforth all contacts with the press were to be reported to the White House press office.

Michael Getler, foreign editor of the *Washington Post*, asked at one seminar: "My question is what are the leaks that have hurt national security?" It was interesting that government officials, as well as a number of "formers," could not—or would not—cite a single instance when a leak proved to be damaging to the nation's security. Leaks are embarrassing and probably, if you are in the government, infuriating, but they are rarely harmful. If the government has evidence to the contrary, then it would perform a real service to journalists and scholars if it would present such evidence to the public.

Simon Serfaty, who edited this superb collection of original essays, concludes with the judgment that the press is "neither hero, nor villain." So long as the press does its job without regard to offending officials or flattering them, then that is all one can ask of such a diverse, competitive, talented group of professionals. Now that the world has become everyone's neighborhood, and no event is beyond the camera's eye, the press's job is all the more vital to an informed and free electorate.

Preface

Over the past two decades the American public, government officials and members of the press have become uncertain about their respective needs, rights and responsibilities: the public's "need" to know, but what and when; the government's "responsibility" to hide facts and policies whose disclosure might harm the nation's interest, but which ones and why; and the media's "right" to report fully to the public, but how and on whose authority?

Questions that have shaped these uncertainties, and their resulting controversies, have been tied primarily to the role of the media, and ways in which this role, however defined or understood, is carried out by journalists, accommodated by the government (specifically, the executive branch), and accepted by the general public. These questions include: Who sets the agenda, the media or the government? To what extent do the media affect the substance of national policy, as distinct from its presentation? Is the media's coverage of foreign policy events and issues distorted, or even biased? Do competitive pressures cause the media to act irresponsibly on vital national security issues such as terrorism or arms control? Is the media's adversarial relationship with government officials injurious, and what, if anything, can or should be done to make this relationship more constructive? Is a code of conduct needed for either or both sides, and, if so, who is to devise it and, more important, enforce it?

In September 1986, The Johns Hopkins Foreign Policy Institute (FPI) of the Paul H. Nitze School of Advanced International Studies (SAIS) launched a three-year program designed to review and analyze some of these salient questions. From the beginning, our project was received with much enthusiasm by a remarkable and highly diversified group of reporters, current and former officials and members of Congress, and academic experts. Nearly all of the papers presented in this volume were explicitly prepared for this program;

this fact alone demonstrates the earnestness with which our group pursued its task. These presenters were aided, moreover, by an unusually dedicated panel of critics, whose invaluable participation in our discussions helped guide our effort and improved the papers presented by our authors.[1]

A special debt of gratitude is owed to Philip Geyelin, in residence at the FPI since 1980, and Joseph Fromm, a Fellow since 1985. Phil Geyelin is a Pulitzer Prize columnist whose writing on foreign policy has enlightened readers around the country and abroad for many years. And, as Robert Sims (a faithful participant in our meetings) wrote in his excellent study, *The Pentagon Reporters*, Joseph Fromm has been over the years "one of the most experienced and confident writers covering foreign affairs." I felt privileged to co-direct this program with both of them, and I am most grateful for the role they played in leading it to its final phase.

Preparation of this book also gained from the contributions made by Michael Clark, the FPI's managing editor, and Mark S. Mahaney, currently the editor of the *SAIS Review*. It benefited further from the assistance provided by SAIS students Audrey Abraham, Matthew Baum and Harrison Wadsworth. And it would not have been possible without the support of the John & Mary R. Markle Foundation, whose generous grant helped sustain our activities. For all of these contributions, and many others that go unnamed, we are deeply grateful.

SIMON SERFATY

Note

1. Between September 1986 and March 1989 the Foreign Policy Institute commissioned thirteen papers and held twenty meetings dealing with the broad issues of The Media and Foreign Policy. In chronological order those meetings were led by Marvin Kalb, Robert Oakley, Gregory Nokes, John Wallach, Robert McCloskey, Charles Bailey and Philip Geyelin (1986–87); Richard Helms, William Odom, David Webster, Richard Burt, Michael Ledeen, Harold Evans, Kenneth Adelman and Richard Lugar (1987–88); and Robert McFarlane, Robert Woodward, David Gergen, Howard Simons and Daniel Patrick Moynihan (1988–89).

The Media and Foreign Policy

Simon Serfaty

O ver the years the press in the United States has been seen as a major force that influences both the substance of national policy and the process by which it is formulated. This influence helped bring the civil rights issue to the forefront of the nation's consciousness, helped force an end to the American involvement in the Vietnam War, and helped topple one President in the course of the Watergate scandal. To the extent that the hostage crisis in Iran was a significant cause of President Carter's failure to be elected to a second term in office, media coverage also played an important role in toppling a second President in November 1980. In 1987–88, only the unprecedented popularity of then-President Reagan overcame the impact of the bitter controversy over the sale of U.S. arms to Iran.

The influence of the media as an independent force is more than an American phenomenon, however. The past many years have witnessed profound changes in the scope and reach of the international press, in the way news organizations conduct their business, and, perhaps most pointedly, in the media's relationship with national governments around the world. Technology has transformed journalism, increasing both the flow and the volume of data available to reporters. Information that once was the sole province of governments is now routinely scrutinized in real time—or its functional equivalent, the same news day—by cadres of trained and independent professionals. As explained by David Webster, for many years a member of the board of management of the British Broadcasting Corporation, the

1

impact of technological change is most apparent with—but not limited to—television, which can now beam pictures instantaneously from virtually any location on the planet, thereby "creating an instantaneous transborder imagery difficult to assess and impossible to control" across as well as between borders. "The immediate turbulence of television's constant action and interaction," adds Webster, "is real and must be dealt with, but it can be misleading."

The exploitation of technology by the news media, in turn, has been abetted by, and contributed to, the transformation of news organizations into far-flung international business conglomerates engaged in an internecine competition for global markets. Circulation figures, ratings and other indicators of corporate profitability have asserted their exacting influence over organizational, and even editorial, decision making. And as competition for "the story" has been been sharpened by the imperatives of economic survival, the natural inclination of reporters to explore every avenue for possible "scoops" has made the media adamantly hostile to various efforts to regulate or restrict its activities.

Finally, like other transnational corporations, U.S. news organizations have been generally resistant to the local interests and preoccupations of foreign national governments whose domestic environment has been internationalized accordingly. In this context, the methods used by American journalists have been increasingly viewed abroad as a model which foreign journalists attempt to emulate in order to overcome the limits imposed upon them by their own governments or national traditions. In sum, the American media has emerged in recent years as an important transnational actor in its own right.

Viewed in their totality, these changes have given rise to a novel influence in international politics: an important and powerful international communications network capable of circumventing the control of any national government and supported by its own working ideology. This new phenomenon, aptly dubbed "medialism" by U.S. Senator Richard Lugar, has been commended or blamed as it has by turns furthered or frustrated the aims of statesmen and politicians. But whether it bodes well or ill for particular national governments, medialism represents a force that political leaders ignore at their own peril.

How has the growth in the reach and influence of the media complicated the processes of formulating and conducting foreign policy?

And what, if anything, can and should be done? The papers collected in this volume do not attempt to add to the number of competent analyses now available of the impact of these changes in technology, industry structure and political environment on the behavior of the media. Instead, they focus on the neural point where the interests of statesmen and journalists intersect most acutely—the conduct of foreign policy. The essays that follow are united by the shared concern to analyze and assess the impact of the transformation of the news media on both the formulation and the implementation of policy as well as to evaluate proposed measures to resolve or contain burgeoning conflicts between journalists and government officials.

That policy makers should be sensitive to, and even fearful of, the coverage they receive in the media is understandable, but hardly new. At all times policy makers have addressed issues on the basis of questions that bear little relation to policy proper. "How do I look in the mirror of public opinion? Do I look shrewd, determined, defiantly patriotic, imbued with the necessary vigilance before the wiles of foreign governments?" This characterization of the policy process by George Kennan predates current controversies over the role of the media in foreign policy by more than fifty years. And Kennan's representation of the policy maker's response anticipates current circumstances too: "If so, this is what I do, even though it may prove to be meaningless, or even counterproductive, when applied to the realities of the situation."[1]

So it was then, and so it is now. "What too often counts," writes David Gergen, White House communications director during the Ford and Reagan administrations, "is how well the policy will play, how the pictures will look, whether it sends the right signals, and whether the public will be impressed by the swiftness of the government's response—not whether the policy promotes America's long-term interests." To address these concerns—a normal, necessary and constructive aspect of conducting public policy in an open society—government officials willingly devote much of their time to explaining foreign policy goals, methods, and constraints, up to one third, according to Kenneth L. Adelman, a director of the Arms Control and Disarmament Agency during the Reagan administration, and now a newspaper columnist. Indeed, adds Robert C. McFarlane, who served as national security adviser to President Reagan, the ability to communicate the rationale of public policy is an essential prerequisite to public office.

Carried to an extreme, however, the search for a "good" press can create, as Gergen suggests, an almost "incestuous" relationship between the White House and the press. The President's staff helps produce television coverage by arranging for the best possible sights (of Reagan's emotional stand in Korea's demilitarized zone, for example, or his tearful speech on the beaches of Normandy) or by scheduling events in such a way as to achieve maximum television exposure (of President Nixon's triumphant return from his first trip to China). More important, with information moving faster government officials, too, are often tempted to respond precipitously in order to accommodate the artificial pressure of media deadlines—before reliable information has been gathered, its implications assessed, and the appropriate policy devised and agreed upon. So it may have been, at least in part, with President Carter after the Soviet invasion of Afghanistan, for instance, and so it may have been, too, with President Reagan after the Soviet downing of a civilian plane flown by Korean Air Line.

Yet, acknowledging this influence is a far cry from suggesting that the media also determine the substance of policy or even dominate the process that shapes policy, including the formulation of the nation's agenda. Thus, in the view of syndicated columnist Philip Geyelin, the relationship between the media and the government is an adversarial relationship "in which the government, except in rare instances of scandal or malpractice, inherently holds the high ground."[2] Notwithstanding a few exceptions, Geyelin argues, the media often serves "as nothing more than a monitor—or a megaphone" to transmit "propositions that the government wants to place on the agenda and of the debate such propositions may generate."

That this would be the case should come as no surprise: the government's capacity to overwhelm the means of communication is truly awesome. As argued by Geyelin, a presumption of credibility ordinarily gives the President and his administration the benefit of the doubt in foreign policy—"unless," that is, "his administration is careless or arrogant enough to squander its credibility." Similarly, the administration's monopoly on secret intelligence and classified information, which it can release as it sees fit, leaves it with a presumption of authority that press reports alone cannot easily overcome. Examined further, even the most remarkable exceptions prove the rule. What brought Richard Nixon down, for instance, was the discovery of voice-activated tapes made in the President's office—a revelation that came not from media investigations, but from a member of the White House staff in answer to astute questioning from a staff member of the Senate Watergate Committee prior to his public appearance before the committee, where he repeated it for all to hear.

According to Gregory Nokes, a former national correspondent with the Associated Press now writing for the *Portland Oregonian*, the administration dominates the national news agenda "about 70 per cent of the time. . . . [It] determine[s] when something becomes news, and how long it stays in the news." Even without the Reagan administration's conspicuous campaign against Muammar Qadhafi, Nokes concedes, the media would have been drawn to the Libyan leader. But Reagan's prodding intensified media interest, thereby attracting coverage far in excess of what would have been given otherwise. Conversely, the administration kept the drama of American hostages in Lebanon mostly out of the headlines. In short, despite the transformations in the scope and reach of the news media, the executive branch of the U.S. government, not the media, usually sets the agenda.

Yet the press is hardly a passive transmitter of information. With its television reports watched all over the world, and with its newspaper reporters often quoted with or without attribution, the American press has formed the nexus of an increasingly integrated system of communications that can, and on occasion does, influence the course of international events. A rough foreign equivalent of the Nixon–Watergate affair may be found in the demise of Philippines President Ferdinand Marcos: in that case, the media alerted the Reagan administration to a political crisis that it had appeared to neglect, at least publicly. To be sure, the paucity of other news at the time (and President Marcos's own imprudent prodding) also helped sustain the attention of the press. Yet international, especially American, journalists quickly gained an influential and even dominant role in shaping the form and accelerating the pace of political events in that country. Initially exploited as a forum (which, ironically, Marcos expected to manipulate to his advantage), the media became sufficiently partisan as to emerge, ultimately, as a self-appointed champion of Philippine democracy, expediting the demise of its adversary and protecting the final victory of its protégé.

Nor is the flow of information and influence unidirectional. As noted by Nokes, "news abroad usually becomes news in the United States, especially when it concerns American interests." The Iran–Contra affair, which began with an article in a small Beirut newspaper, provides the most painful example of how foreign reporting can influence U.S. policy-making. The phenomenon of "medialism" produces ever larger streams of less and less filtered information that cross national boundaries. Leaders of all nations can appeal directly to constituencies in other nations: words are used to provide a "spin" that breaks down institutional and governmental controls; images are superimposed on those cultivated by local governments; and leaks from authorized or unauthorized sources expose transactions otherwise carefully concealed or disguised. The effect is to introduce new and often unpredictable forces into the policy process. Television pictures of violence and repression can be so dramatized as to make the political pressure to "do something" irresistible; this pressure is then articulated in the op-ed pages of local newspapers, where the recommendations of would-be secretaries of state or defense have been sharpened by the pictures shown on the previous days. And, finally, journalists share with their foreign colleagues information they cannot release at home, circumventing rules imposed upon them by their own government.

Although the media do not usually determine the foreign policy agenda, they clearly wield a large amount of influence. Is this influence used responsibly, or is it so intrusive as to be detrimental to national interests? In principle at least, the need to respect certain limits on the flow of information can neither be denied nor ignored. "No right," warns Harold Evans (a former editor of the London *Times*), "is enhanced by its irresponsible exercise." And while they differ profoundly (and even passionately) over the extent of media irresponsibility, government officials and journalists agree that competitive pressures encourage (and reward) the phenomenon. Many journalists see dangers, especially in the area of national security policy (whether occasionally, according to some, or frequently, according to others). Nokes states this concern most succinctly: "There is no excuse for throwing caution to the wind just because a story is hot and competitive. But many journalists do, and we do it time and again." The issue, of course, is, what is to be done? It is on this point that differences between officials and reporters are especially sharp.

Two specific problems figure prominently in this debate: leaks of classified information and the media's coverage of terrorist incidents. Admittedly, the definition of a leak is ambiguous: an apparent leak may be, in fact, the final result of tedious and enterprising investigative reporting. But, however understood, leaks may prove costly if and when they divulge information of direct relevance to national security. This, at least, is the conclusion reached by William E. Odom, a former director of the National Security Agency. According to Odom, "perhaps the most difficult problem facing the intelligence community today is the problem of leaks and the publication of information harmful to our intelligence operations." This problem directly threatens the integrity of the intelligence process. Moreover, as Michael A. Ledeen (a former special assistant to Secretary of State Alexander Haig) argues, the ability to gather information vital to national security depends upon its "right to retain secrets. . . and the need to protect" them. In broader terms, General Odom wonders whether "a democratic society's need for open and informed debate [can] be reconciled with its need for secrecy in the conduct of an effective national security policy."

Just how does the media's reporting of government secrets damage U.S. national security interests, if at all? Certainly, it would be difficult to argue that irresponsible media reporting has directly and significantly damaged, much less destroyed, the physical security of the United States. Short of such a fundamental security concern, however, there are specific areas whose coverage may hamper the ability of the executive branch of the U.S. government to carry out certain kinds of policies essential to protecting the lives and welfare of U.S. citizens. "Low intensity warfare"—or, in popular language, terrorism—is one such area. In this case, the ability of U.S. intelligence agencies to follow or penetrate foreign terrorist organizations, for example, may well be crippled by the fact or the fears of subsequent exposure in the American press. In other words, publication of the names of foreign assets anywhere makes it more difficult to cultivate and sustain relations with foreign intelligence organizations everywhere.

Writing from a somewhat different perspective, Robert J. McCloskey—a former ombudsman for the *Washington Post* who also served as assistant secretary of state for public affairs—draws attention to the costs exacted from the government by leaks: less openness among policy makers and, because of the unpredictable nature of those leaks and their consequences, a loss of control over the agenda.

The strains in media-government relations caused by leaks, and the damage done to our society by those strains, have produced a perverse situation in which the general public may credit the statements of anonymous officials whose on-the-record declarations are met with skepticism or outright disbelief. McCloskey concludes that society "would be better served by a less fractious relationship...in which the anonymous underworld of leaks had a lesser role in informing the public and in determining policy."

Interestingly, McCloskey's conclusions are generally compatible with the conclusions reached by Odom and Ledeen. Odom, who fears that "paralysis" may result from the use of leaks as "the major weapon in policy making," would favor a more intimate dialogue between government officials and the media, and a narrower definition of the kind of information that must be kept secret. Ledeen urges "some measure to call the media to greater accountability," but he too accepts the consequences of popular sovereignty and acknowledges "the public's right to be informed about the basic elements in our foreign policy."

On whom should the blame for leaks rest? According to Odom, "the primary source of leaks is the government," namely, the executive branch "first and foremost." Such leaks, adds Odom, are "a serious matter" and they should be cause for "prompt and effective action when they occur." Yet, Odom continues, even if the government is the first sinner, reporters are often willing accomplices for "trying unrelentingly to pry loose highly classified information. When they succeed, they blame the leakers, refusing to accept any personal or professional responsibility."

However, to John Wallach, foreign editor of the Hearst newspapers, the nature and the frequency of leaks are less important than the objectives that may be sought by their sources. "A great deal more classified information," notes Wallach, "is deliberately leaked by the government in its efforts to manage the news than is disclosed, on an allegedly unauthorized basis, by reporters." Wallach insists, therefore, on the reporters' right to ascertain the truth of stories apparently planted by the administration, and he urges that "whether the selective use of leaked intelligence by senior officials serves the national interest or someone's political interest" should be made part of the story.

On the question of whether the media have shown adequate restraint in dealing with terrorist incidents, Robert B. Oakley, who directed the Office for Combatting Terrorism during the Reagan administration, and John Wallach both recognize the dilemmas faced by the government and the media because of their respective commitments, in Oakley's words, to "maintain freedom of expression and satisfy audience demand." On television especially, acknowledges Wallach, terrorists obtain "exactly what they want: a global stage to publicize their demands." In so doing, adds Oakley, the media end up "playing into terrorists' schemes." Yet, however unfortunate, coverage is the inevitable result of the terrorist act itself. Providing such coverage may well provide a conduit for terrorist demands, but it also satisfies a public demand that may be defused, or dramatized further, by the administration's own actions.

Thus, from the very beginning of what he later called the "Iranian nightmare," President Carter's own decisions prompted the dramatic and sustained coverage that followed, as he postponed state visits, cancelled scheduled trips and eliminated political appearances. As written by Carter, "staying close to Washington quickly became standard policy;" simultaneously, staying close to the story became standard policy for the news media too. In the end, adds Carter, the release of the American hostages "had almost become an obsession with me." Not only with him, though, but also with the whole nation.[3]

Although real, the danger that the media may be exploited by terrorists and others has to be tolerated *faute de mieux* because the attempt to impose restraints only introduces greater dangers. For example, the restrictions sought by Britain's Prime Minister Margaret Thatcher to deny terrorists "the oxygen of publicity" on which they depend would, even if accepted voluntarily, risk handing a major victory to the terrorists by denying democracies the air which they need to breathe. Drawing upon a different experience, Professor John L. Harper notes that during the Moro affair, the Italian government decided that "there would be no real effort to control the press and that information about the case would be made available as long as the press did not compromise the government's position." That judgment was borne out by events. "There is no evidence," concludes Harper, "that publication of [terrorist] communiqués won them converts or sympathizers. On the contrary, from beginning to end [the terrorist] actions managed to generate only revulsion and helped to set in motion a campaign that led to the capture and conviction of most of the Red Brigades during the next several years."

Determining the influence of the media is one thing. Establishing how influential they *should* be and what role they *should* play is another. For, in the end, who is to determine the "standards" that should regulate the press? If not the government, should the press be the only segment of society that remains its own judge of malpractice, however defined and uncovered?

An attempt to answer these questions is found in David R. Gergen's essay. American "teledemocracy," writes Gergen, ties together the government and the media: "The executive branch has a clear-cut responsibility to explain its policies and thinking, to answer questions, and to be accountable. The media have a legitimate and important role in insisting on those explanations and in pressing for a clear public accounting." In order to carry out a policy, continues Gergen, "an administration will need to build and maintain public support." This, in turn, requires "an open dialogue with the press on its purposes and thinking." Whatever form it might take, and whatever intent it may reflect, misrepresentation of the facts by either side exacerbates the other's mistrust, and can even turn a relationship that is naturally and necessarily adversarial into a relationship that is blatantly and unnecessarily confrontational.

Preserving confidence between government officials and the press is also a primary concern of Robert McCloskey, who observes that "information will leak from the government in direct proportion to the level of secrecy surrounding policy and decision making." Yet, adds McCloskey, "the degree to which leaks command and lead the agenda is in inverse proportion to the extent to which government responds to media inquiry openly." Consequently, he concludes, the public's need to know should be satisfied on the record, so that policy can gain the respect that comes from clarity and consistency. Conversely, reports based on information provided on background tend to erode both the clarity and the credibility of public policy.

Others, however, question whether the interests of the press and the government can be reconciled. For Odom, the role of the press is not that of an "unelected ombudsman" with a mandate to extract and disseminate information on government activities. Such a role, he asserts, "has no historic or legal foundation. . . . The constitutional system of government under which we live does not envision a town meeting approach to the conduct of national military and foreign policy, such that every issue regardless of sensitivity is submitted to the public for resolution." "In certain situations," Odom concludes, "national interests can and should limit the unbridled exercise of individual rights (such as the First Amendment)."

John Wallach, on the other hand, describes the media's role as that of a "vigilant watchdog" that plays a "crucial role" as a "safeguard" against abuses of official authority. Wallach argues that "reporters provide a much-needed service by checking the government's ability to manipulate the information flow." Nokes echoes Wallach's assertions, insisting that one of the media's most important responsibilities is "to be certain of the truth of what [is] reported" and protect society from the "enormous power" available to the government. Not surprisingly, both Nokes and Wallach believe that this protective role is best fulfilled by an independent press, governed by its own interests and standards.

The decisive consideration, however, is whether any measures to limit press abuses would not themselves do greater damage to the public as well as the national interest than is currently the case in the absence of any such measures. To address this question, Harold Evans examines press regulations in Britain.[4] There, writes Evans, regulations such as the Official Secrets Act, the D-notice, and the laws of contempt and confidence have served to impair freedom. He warns, therefore, against any attempt to bring British methods to the American system as "disastrous as well as unconstitutional. . . . Even in the face of the most eloquent 'patriotic' appeals, [the First] Amendment must never be sacrificed."

Assuming that the role of the media is indeed to serve as watchdog for the public interest, just how well has this role been performed? It seems only reasonable to assume that the adversarial relationship between the press and the government is exacerbated by growing competitive pressures among news organizations. Those pressures invite reporters to search for the exclusive and enhance the attractiveness of leaks that, by their very nature, are available only to the few. In this environment, news editors may be reluctant to overrule reporters since neither the action of other editors nor the administration's own reaction can be reliably predicted. Government officials have been quick to discover and exploit the advantages in allowing information to become public through channels that it can disavow. For example, although the initial report on covert U.S. activities in Nicaragua raised much anguish in the *Washington Post*, CIA director William Casey was, according to Bob Woodward, "very moderate in his objection...[as] the White House was quite anxious to boast that this covert operation was underway because it was the delivery of a campaign promise that had been in the 1980 Republican platform."[5] The effect of such tacit collusion, as McCloskey, Geyelin, and others observe, can be corrosive. Government accountability and press responsibility are both diminished in the netherworld of unidentified sources shrouded in plausible deniability.

In recent years especially, relations between the executive branch and the media have been complicated further by the escalation of the traditional feud between the executive and the legislative branches of the government. There is "a fundamental contrast," writes Robert J. Kurz, who served as a legislative assistant to Congressman Richard Gephardt, between "the presumption of openness" made in a decentralized Congress and "the presumption of secrecy" prevailing in the hierarchical executive. This difference alone tends to create a natural alliance between legislators and journalists: they "share a common rivalry against the executive" as they all seek to "discover what the executive is up to, uncover wrongdoing, or expose inherent contradictions in policies or their implementation." Each side gets scoops from the other, translated into news headlines or congressional hearings that provide for more news headlines. But each side also uses the other as a shield—to legitimize a news story or to serve as a conduit for an attack against a popular President.

While journalists claim a responsibility to question policy in the name of the public interest—as is done in Congress, too—they usually disavow any obligation to educate the public on foreign affairs. Yet by serving as the principal means of communication between the governing and the governed, and by providing the most important source of alternative information and analysis to the public at large, the news media act as the nation's principal educator on foreign policy matters. And in this area too it is appropriate to ask just how well the press has served the public interest.

Media coverage of arms control and defense issues is singled out for criticism by Richard R. Burt and Kenneth Adelman. Burt, who worked as a reporter for the *New York Times* before serving in the Reagan and Bush administrations, criticizes the media for contributing to a "chaotic, ill-informed, simplistic national security debate." "Reporters," adds Adelman, "like most Americans, tremble at the mere prospect of sorting out the intricacies of nuclear weaponry"—or at least "the vast majority" of reporters. Among the failures that Burt cites are the press's reliance on journalists with insufficient expertise in a topic that demands in-depth knowledge, a predilection for scoops that are difficult to verify and often inaccurate, and, consequently, a neglect of substantive analysis.

Yet, such criticism needs to be qualified. First, blame for insufficient or inadequate coverage cannot be laid solely on the press. As McFarlane argues, "strategic policy is the least understood item on our national security agenda as a consequence of the failure of the executive branch for more than forty years to engage seriously in promoting public debate and understanding of the issues" involved. Second, many journalists show impressive expertise in national security affairs, including, in certain cases, an expertise strengthened during their years of public service: Walter Pincus took an eighteen-month sabbatical from the *Washington Post* to head the staff of a Senate Foreign Relations Committee inquiry on the role of theater nuclear weapons, a topic about which he reported at length in later years. Leslie Gelb, who wrote on national security affairs for the *New York Times*, worked on related issues at the State Department and on Capitol Hill. William Beecher, of the *Boston Globe*, worked at the Department of Defense. Indeed, the qualifications of journalists often exceeds that of security experts in the academic community who may lack exposure to the complexities and routine of decision making.[6]

Finally, it must be observed that the relationship between the media and the government, as some of our contributors note, is also mediated by a third group—the public at large. This point is developed in John Harper's study. Notwithstanding significant differences between American and Italian media, Harper underscores usefully the concern which editors and publishers had for public attitudes throughout the Moro affair. "The newspapers covering the crisis," he writes, "saw themselves as protagonists, not merely as passive observers." Their sense that the mass of public opinion supported a policy of firmness toward Moro's captors, Harper concludes, was one factor—through certainly not the only factor—that led Italian newspapers to compete with each other in taking a hard line against negotiations with the Red Brigades.

The influence of the public may also be felt in a very different way. Public indifference toward some issues may serve to inhibit news coverage much more than any code of conduct, and may determine the resources made available by editors and publishers. As syndicated columnist James Reston wrote many years ago,

> We will send 500 correspondents to Vietnam after the war breaks out... but we will not send five reporters there when the danger of war is developing, and, even if we do, their reports of the danger will be minimized by editors and officials alike as 'speculation', and hidden back among the brassiere ads, if they are not hung on the spike.

Instead, Reston argued, issues need to be explored as they develop and not merely after they are announced.

Granted Reston's point in theory, such reporting may attract limited and insufficient readership or audience. Nevertheless, writes Charles W. Bailey (a former editor of the *Minneapolis Tribune*), it is short-sighted of editors and publishers to underestimate the potential interest of non-specialist readers in foreign affairs. The editor, Bailey argues, must create interest with an improved marketing of foreign news. "What does this story mean to the people who read this newspaper, who earn a living in this community?" asks Bailey. The answer, he suggests, is to give the foreign news a "local angle" that transforms foreign news into local news, with an explicit emphasis on "the domestic economic impact of international developments." Local reporters and newscasters, Bailey concludes, have certain advantages in reporting foreign news "because they are part of the community they are addressing" and because they "will more than likely have greater credibility than nationally known representatives."

A final caveat may be in order. The majority of the papers in this volume draw upon the experience of the American government and news media, and this inevitably gives rise to a distortion of the manner in which the conflict between government and the media over the making of foreign policy is presented. The press has long enjoyed a privileged, almost sacrosanct position as an independent voice in the American democracy. Guaranteed by the Constitution and identified in the popular mind with the liberty of all citizens, the extended experience of press freedom in the United States is perhaps unique in history and has been conditioned in turn by a uniquely benign experience of national security. These facts alone make it difficult to generalize from the American experience.

More important, the transformation of the media has coincided in the United States with the breakdown of a national consensus on both the purposes and the methods of foreign policy. As the press has given voice to, and sometimes even exploited, popular dissatisfaction with political leaders, the normal friction between the media and officialdom has been tinged with a mutual sense of betrayal. Much of the tone and tenor of the debate between government officials and reporters thus reflects specifically American concerns raised over issues confronted most passionately in the recent past.

Yet the problems analyzed here have a more general significance, and the issues explored here largely in their American context have taken on broader relevance around the world. Medialism is a phenomenon that states can resist only at a heavy price: the worldwide exposure given to the savage clearing of Tiananmen Square in June 1989 helped set the stage for the peaceful reunions that were reported from Checkpoint Charlie four months later. In Berlin and in Eastern Europe, as in many other places and over many other issues, the media have helped avoid bloodshed, contain repression, and defuse potentially explosive incidents. And, indeed, during the coming years the success of the unfolding global trend toward democracy may well hinge on how other governments learn to accommodate the requirements of a public debate opened by a free press.

Notes

1. George F. Kennan, *Memoirs, 1925-50* (Boston, Mass.: Little, Brown, 1957), 53. Kennan was discussing an episode in U.S.-Soviet negotiations that occurred in November 1933. That episode, explains Kennan, taught him "the first of many lessons...on one of the most consistent and incurable traits of American statesmanship."

2. How the adversarial relationship between the media and the government has evolved over the years was the focus of Marvin Kalb's comments in October 1986: "As Moscow correspondent in the 1950s and 1960s, the feeling was that I was there as an American. My close friends and my best friends were with the embassy staff. I didn't think that was wrong. There was a feeling we were all in something together—us versus them. Soon after I returned to Washington in 1963, there came the Gulf of Tonkin story. My instinct from being in Moscow was to suspect anything written in *Pravda* or said by Khrushchev, but not to be suspicious of the U.S. government...."

Even though there were telltale signs that what we were being told was not true, we believed the government." After Vietnam, noted Kalb, "our collective attitude, and the attitude of the government, changed from innocence to constant testiness."

3. Jimmy Carter, *Keeping Faith, Memoirs of a President* (New York: Bantam Books, 1982), 566, 463 and 594.

4. In July 1985, Britain's Prime Minister Margaret Thatcher asked for "a voluntary code of conduct under which [journalists] would not say or show anything which could assist the terrorists' morale or their cause." Although Thatcher's request explicitly related to the coverage of terrorist incidents, it also sought to apply, more generally, to a number of other issues as well.

5. As recalled by Woodward, Ben Bradlee, the paper's editor, and he thought the Reagan administration might send FBI agents in to arrest them or go through desks.

6. Admittedly, though, such qualifications, wherever they can be found, make misrepresentation of the facts, whenever it can be uncovered, even more reprehensible.

Part I

■

Who Sets The Agenda?

1

The Strategic Defense Initiative: The President's Story

Philip L. Geyelin

It kind of amuses me that everybody is so sure I must have heard about it—that I never thought of it myself. The truth is I did.

> President Ronald Reagan in an interview
> with *Newsweek*, March 1985.

Nothing that has been said about President Reagan's Strategic Defense Initiative (SDI) better illustrates the degree to which the President's launch-without-warning of SDI in his famous March 1983 speech was, in fact, a personal, almost single-handed undertaking. And no example more clearly demonstrates the capacity of a trusted President to overwhelm the means of communication in the world's most open, free-wheeling society than the example of Reagan's SDI. The story of the selling of SDI, then, provides a telling answer to one of this volume's central questions—who sets the national news agenda?

This is a case study of how a purposeful President, with not much more than a driving dream to work with, was able, in just a few hundred words on national television, to capture the public imagination and reshape a national debate. In the same stroke he transformed substantially the course of nuclear arms control negotiations with the Soviet Union and invited the most profound questioning by allies and adversaries of the reliability of what was thought to be established and accepted U.S. strategic doctrine.

The element of surprise certainly contributed to the President's coup, together with the government's ability not only to initiate news but to manipulate its presentation. The record suggests that once the President released the SDI genie from its bottle, the debate about it, and the news coverage of the debate, were well balanced. The weight of informed opinion was clearly against the President's proposition as it was initially presented and remains so to this day even in the light of subsequent refinement and redefinition of what the President actually had in mind. The assertions of the President and his advisers were diligently investigated and reported. But there was never even the remotest possibility that the proposed defensive system could be repackaged, much less removed, in a way that would restore the status quo ante, resolve the debate over strategic doctrine, and reconcile the President's original proposal with reality.

The failure to contain the import of the President's initiative hardly reflects lack of effort on the part of the critics. Still less was it a case of the "media" (a dreadful word now so entrenched in the language that its use is unavoidable) allowing themselves to be abused by the government. The impossibility of returning the SDI genie to its bottle was due simply to the nature of the relationship between the government and the media. It is a relationship in which the government, except in rare instances of scandal or malpractice, inherently holds the high ground. Or to put it another way, the high ground in this adversary relationship is the government's to lose.

The Government and the Media

To be sure, the communications revolution of the last few decades has vastly increased the impact, influence, and, yes, power and presence of news casting in all of its contemporary forms. Inevitably, this revolution has introduced a certain heightened frenzy into the competition between the various news outlets. After all, the news business, like all other businesses, is subject to the pressures of competition, profit-making and bottom lines. And the perception of this news explosion has given rise to the conventional wisdom that the media have become too powerful; that they increasingly distort, exaggerate, sensationalize or simply miss the point of what the government is saying or what the policy makers are up to or up against; and that they abuse their use of unattributed sources.

There is some truth in this. Nonetheless, there is no reasonable basis for the conclusion that, as a consequence, the balance of power between the media and the government has been fundamentally altered. The media and the policy makers have never competed on equal terms. The range of interaction has been substantially expanded, but the rules, conditions, opportunities and inhibitions on both sides remain the same. And in just about every important respect, they continue to favor the government by allowing policy makers, not reporters, to set the news agenda.

Even when allowance is made for the fact that, more often than not, the agenda is fixed by neither the government nor the media but by events, it must be asked: which of the two institutions has the greater capacity to manipulate coverage in ways that are favorable to its purposes or interests? Or, in the case of what might be called internal events, when the government itself is the prime initiator but the consequences spin out of its control, to what extent can the media be held accountable for compounding calamity? Finally, to what extent are the media anything more than a transmitter, or trumpeter, of propositions that the government wants to place on the agenda and of the debate such propositions may generate?

The historical record contains some persuasive evidence that the government holds most of the cards. Legend has it that warmongering press lords inflamed public passions and carried the United States into the Spanish-American War. However, the record reveals that Theodore Roosevelt himself incited the press lords by exploiting, for his own purposes, the sinking of the battleship *Maine* in Havana harbor under circumstances that were beyond the press's capability to investigate at the time. The same analysis holds for the famous Gulf of Tonkin incidents, similarly exploited by President Lyndon Johnson to ram through Congress a resolution granting him sweeping authority to involve the nation in the Vietnam War. The media proved incapable of raising in any timely way still unanswered serious questions about exactly what North Vietnamese torpedo boats did, if anything, to justify the retaliatory U.S. air strikes against North Vietnam.

Legend, with a helping hand from Hollywood, again would have us believe that the media brought down Richard Nixon. Yet, the initial investigative reporting by the *Washington Post* served as nothing more than the flint that struck the sparks. The resulting fire, however hard the media blew on it, would have almost certainly gone out had not an outraged judge, John Sirica, bent the rules to extract evidence the media could not have uncovered on their own. Furthermore, the conflagration could not have engulfed the Nixon presidency without the Watergate hearings, John Dean's whistle-blowing, and, above all, Alexander Butterfield's explosive disclosure of the existence of the President's sound-activated taping system. With that disclosure, prosecutors were able to persuade the Supreme Court to order Nixon to surrender his tapes. The House Judiciary Committee finished the job. It is safe to say that if the story had been left solely to the resourceful reporting of Bob Woodward and Carl Bernstein, Richard Nixon would have finished out his second presidential term.

Finally, there remains the example of the Iran–Contra affair. The American press did not unmask the Reagan administration's arms-for-hostages trafficking with Iran. While Attorney General Edwin Meese revealed the Contra connection, the whole public scandal might not have exploded in the first place had not persons unknown planted a story in "that Beirut rag," as Reagan called it. Even so, the story might have died if it had not been confirmed several days later by the speaker of the Iranian Parliament. The ultimate source of the story, and the events to which it gave rise was a policy that was secretly set in the Reagan White House and carried forward for at least a year and a half without attracting public notice.

No doubt, one could cite genuine examples of legitimate agenda-setting by the media—some investigations or disclosures that focused public attention on particular problems and forced some positive government response to such things as racial injustice, government corruption, medical malpractice, social distress and famine in Africa. Moreover, there may have been cases of leaks and disclosures that influenced or altered a particular course of action by the government. By and large, however, there have been more instances when the press exercised self-restraint under extreme government pressure (for example, the Bay of Pigs, the Glomar Explorer, and the Pelton spy case) than there have been instances of the press running amok in defiance of national interests. And there are many more cases of the government running rough-shod over the media with regard to military interventions, diplomatic initiatives, and the launching of large undertakings. In essence, the media has often served as nothing more than a monitor—or a megaphone.

On this last point there is the example of the Reagan administration's decision to reflag eleven Kuwaiti tankers. Members of Congress and editorial writers huffed and puffed. The media uncovered all manner of evidence suggesting that this might have been a misguided and dangerous move. Nevertheless, the commitment, once made, was impossible to reverse. Congress was thoroughly unwilling to take responsibility for the consequences of reversing it by a legislative ban. The government almost single-handedly placed the Persian Gulf high up on the foreign policy agenda.

President Dwight Eisenhower did the same for the Middle East with the Eisenhower Doctrine, which was to provide the shaky diplomatic underpinnings for his decision to land the Marines in Lebanon in 1958. Just as Reagan put Grenada on the agenda in 1982, so Lyndon Johnson placed the Dominican Republic in 1965. In both cases a threat to American citizens was the pretext for a significant, geopolitically oriented action. The media found all sorts of performance flaws in both cases and in the justifications cited for both actions, but with little effect on policy.

Of course, the effort to assign reponsibility for agenda-setting is a good deal more complicated than these episodes might suggest; it is no less complicated than the attempt to establish where, when or how a particular idea was born. Presenting the issue as a struggle between the media and the government oversimplifies the process by which public opinion is shaped and inspired. It excludes the role of the academic community, private foundations and other opinion-shaping organizations. Such a simplistic view also ignores divisions within and among different branches of "government." But to begin to clarify these simplifications would to be to embark on an endless errand. For the sake of clarity it is useful to stipulate, at this point, that by "government" is meant the President, or at most the executive branch of government.

A few pertinent observations on the executive branch present themselves. First, the President's command of the high ground derives from the inherent political prerogative of the executive to create and initiate, a power which is far greater than that of the other two government branches. Second, in ordinary times, a majority of Americans grant the administration of the moment the benefit of the doubt. And third, the burden of proof that this benefit is unwarranted rests with the media unless, as has happened all too frequently in recent years, an administration is careless or arrogant enough to squander its credibility.

In short, the presumption of authority as well as credibility ordinarily gives the government the high ground. Yet another built-in advantage to the government is its monopoly on secret intelligence and classified information—its ability to say, as government officials have so often said to those in the media, something to the general effect of "If-you-only-knew-what-we-know." In any government initiative, it is the government that controls the timing and the circumstances. A President can demand prime-time media exposure with a telephone call. Thus, to the extent that first impressions matter, the government controls the first impression. The government also wields enormous influence over the packaging and presentation of news. It has not only the power to classify what it doesn't want the public to know, but to declassify whatever may advance its purposes.

The Strategic Defense Initiative

The story of the evolution of Reagan's SDI program helps to illuminate the relationship between the media and the government because it demonstrates the enormous resources available to the government. The story also speaks to the government's awesome ability to overpower the press without the benefit of a catalyzing event, a carefully considered strategy, or even the rough dimensions of a policy.

Harry S Truman had all, or most, of these ingredients in hand before George Marshall gave birth to the single most important and enduring American foreign policy initiative of the last forty years. Interestingly enough, Marshall neither sought nor wanted the support of the American media when he laid out in a few paragraphs the idea of the European recovery plan that bears his name—he wanted, first of all, the support of Europe's leaders and Europe's media. In the case of SDI, Ronald Reagan needed to skilfully exploit the media precisely because he had so little else to work with other than his own faith in a world without nuclear arms. The strengths and weaknesses of the Strategic Defense Initiative need not concern us here. In order to judge SDI's relevance to the issue of agenda-setting, one need only analyze the reasons behind and the methods and consequences of the Reagan administration's efforts to gain public support for its initiative.

Of the origins of the SDI as an idea in the mind of Ronald Reagan a certain amount is known. Writing in the *Washington Post* in March 1985, David Hoffman reported that Reagan, while preparing for his 1980 presidential campaign, toured the North American Air

Defense Command and asked one of his guides what, if anything, could be done to stop an incoming Soviet missile. Martin Anderson, who accompanied Reagan on the trip, recalled that the answer was, in effect, "nothing," according to Hoffman. "That early exchange offers a glimpse at the origins of what may be the most profound decision of the Reagan presidency," Hoffman concluded.

That same year, Edward Rowny, a retired general and veteran arms control negotiator, was one of Reagan's campaign consultants. Regularly, Reagan would ask Rowny if it were possible to develop a defensive system against nuclear weapons. Each time, Rowny told him that the technological capability was years away. And each time Reagan would reply that nothing, in his view, was beyond the capacity of American scientists. It was evident to Rowny then that what was to become SDI was already more than a dream or flight of fancy in Reagan's mind. It was an obsession, reinforced by a tiny group of conservative advisers who shared Reagan's moral quarrel with the concept of nuclear deterrence and the whole idea of American and Soviet dependence on MAD (Mutual Assured Destruction).

Reagan was strongly tempted to make this obsession a feature of his 1980 presidential campaign. Yet, according to Hoffman, his political strategists thought it would have been "political suicide"— given its controversial nature and the then known state of the art. But Reagan clung to the idea and carried it with him into the White House, where the heavy burdens and responsibilities of the presidency compounded his questioning of MAD's morality. In 1982 Edward Teller met with Reagan to discuss strategic defense, and William P. Clark, who was then Reagan's national security adviser, told Hoffman that the President was "pretty incisive in his questioning of Teller about this defense theory" which Teller had been aggressively advocating.

Reagan was also influenced by other right-wing outsiders, notably retired Lt. Gen. Daniel O. Graham. Graham had been an adviser to Reagan in the 1980 campaign and headed an organization called High Frontier, dedicated to the promotion of nuclear defense technology. But Graham's lobbying, while well received by the President, did not win much enthusiasm from the White House science adviser, George A. Keyworth II. And the idea was also getting a cold reception at the Pentagon, from Secretary of Defense Caspar Weinberger in particular. On November 24, 1982, only a few months before Reagan would announce his SDI to the world, Weinberger wrote a letter to Graham expressing appreciation for "your optimism," but stating that "we are unwilling to commit this nation to a course which calls for growing into a capability that does not currently exist." Later, Weinberger would become a loyal SDI supporter. But when the President first publicly proposed SDI, it is clear that he did not even have the backing of his secretary of defense.

Not the least of the Pentagon's concerns, apart from the technological problems, was the fear that a crash program to develop a defensive system would sop up money for offensive weaponry. There was a fear that this scenario would become more likely if the notion set in that the United States could find security on the cheap in some miraculous defensive quick fix. It is ironic, then, that the impetus for the launching of SDI came from a February 11, 1983 meeting that included Reagan, the joint chiefs of staff, Weinberger and Robert C. McFarlane, who was then deputy national security affairs adviser. The main topic was supposed to be the congressional outlook for the defense budget. The consensus was grim. Reagan was told that Congress might never again approve a new intercontinental ballistic missile program and that the one under debate, the MX, was in deep trouble. Somehow, strategic defense was introduced as an option; the President's interest was evident. He reportedly asked the participants in the meeting, "Would it not be better to defend lives than to avenge them?"

Later, some of those present reported having a sense that the President was signaling something new and important. It turned out to be just that. Shortly thereafter, the President's most intimate aides were preparing a major address to the nation scheduled for late March. It was to be a powerful pitch for the President's defense budget, especially for the controversial MX. One of the aides suggested inserting SDI into the address. What had been thought of in the Pentagon as a dangerous notion, for the adverse effect it would have on support for offensive arms spending, suddenly became in the eyes of a handful of White House advisers—and, of course, the President himself—a sweetener for the bitter pill of heavy defense spending.

Weinberger is said to have continued to argue right up to the last minute that it would be premature to make so big a deal of a project that was still in such an unproven state. The responsible experts in the Pentagon were not even consulted. Nonetheless, in an eight-page speech, seven pages of which were devoted to supporting offensive weapons, the President suddenly switched gears in the last eight paragraphs.

Even in this brief closing passage, the President crept up to the climax. At the start, he was downright cautious about the prospects and quite careful to explain the difficulties of switching from nuclear deterrence to a defensive system without seriously destabilizing the balance of nuclear power, and without stimulating an offensive nuclear arms race. Nonetheless, the final flourishes were dramatic. There was a "call upon the scientific community who gave us nuclear weapons...to give us the means of rendering these nuclear weapons impotent and obsolete." Then came the hard news: "Tonight...I am directing a comprehensive and intensive effort to define a long-term research-and-development program to begin to achieve our ultimate goal of eliminating the threat posed by strategic nuclear missiles." Finally, the closing crescendo: "My fellow Americans, tonight we are launching an effort which holds the promise of changing the course of human history."

In the next day's *Washington Post*, reporter Lou Cannon, whose contacts with the Reagan entourage stretched back to Reagan's days as governor of California, described the ground work that had been done to maximize the speech's impact. "Last night's speech was carefully orchestrated by White House officials, who have become sensitive both about news leaks and about prior lack of coordination in administration efforts to present the military budget in a positive light," Cannon wrote. He reported that on the day before the speech, several network correspondents had been told there would be "significant news" in the President's address—"news that was deliberately kept both from communications director David R. Gergen and White House spokesman Larry Speakes." On the day of the speech, the sections having to do with SDI were leaked to some of the same network reporters "in an effort to get some, but not all, of the story told on the evening news casts." The White House also invited assorted dignitaries, including prominent nuclear scientists, for dinner on the night of the speech.

Taking the *New York Times* as a reasonably good example of the media's reaction, the White House strategy paid off, at least in terms of first impressions. The *New York Times* account by Steve Weisman led the front page, and the first paragraph could hardly have been more to the administration's liking: "President Reagan, defending his military program, proposed tonight to exploit advances in technology in coming decades so the United States can develop an effective defense against missiles launched by others." The story continued, "In effect, Mr. Reagan proposed to make obsolete the current United States policy of relying on massive retaliation...to counter the threat of a Soviet nuclear attack." Not until the third paragraph did the story get around to the President's appeal for more defense spending. Moreover, inside the first section, Charles Mohr wrote an analytical piece, entirely devoted to SDI, which stated that "President Reagan is apparently seeking to begin a sweeping, long-range change in national strategic doctrine."

But the White House's free ride did not last long. Quickly, the role of the press changed from that of megaphone to that of monitor—questioning, analyzing, and providing wider and more sophisticated perspectives on the President's plan, from critics as well as supporters. Two days after the speech, Leslie Gelb reported in the *Times* the circumstances under which SDI was launched. "President Reagan went ahead with a proposal to develop new defenses against missiles even though several White House and Pentagon aides suggested that the idea had not been carefully studied," Gelb wrote, attributing that conclusion to "administration officials."

It is safe to assume, however, that the critical reaction had nowhere near the same impact nor anything like the size of the audience of the President's proposal, televised by all three commercial networks. The Democrats demanded, and were granted, equal time, with Senator Daniel Inouye their designated hitter. And while it is again safe to say that he did not reach into as many homes as the President, Senator Inouye did deliver what might have been, under other circumstances, a coup de grâce.

Picking up on Senator Edward Kennedy's apparent first use of the consciously derisive nickname "Star Wars," Inouye helped set the tone for the general line that would be used by a swarm of critics, including not just the President's political opposition but distinguished defense experts and a significant slice of the scientific community. The line was a blend of ridicule—SDI was depicted as a futuristic "Buck Rogers" fantasy—and reasoned arguments. In strictly scientific terms, the President was offering disingenuously something that could not possibly be delivered until perhaps well into the twenty-first century. To this was added the arguments of defense strategists and geopoliticians that the President was playing with fire. Merely by presenting the idea, they contended, Reagan was shaking the European allies' confidence in the reliability of nuclear deterrence; creating deep anxieties in the Soviet Union (as reflected by the violence of Moscow's first loud shout that the idea was "insane"); and leading the country into a multi-trillion dollar competition with the Soviet Union not only on defensive systems but on new and smarter offensive nuclear weapons. Critics cried out that the disciplines of the anti-ballistic missile (ABM) treaty, however controversial their interpretation, would be an early casualty; and that the prospect for arms controls negotiations that might lead to mutual reductions in offensive nuclear forces would be diminished if not done in.

A review of the news coverage at the time reveals a relatively fair and evenhanded treatment of the President's initiative. Proponents and opponents alike were given ample space on op-ed pages and full exposure on television talk shows. Any effort to score the debate is necessarily subjective. But it is hard not to conclude that the critics had the more convincing arguments, if only because the President was so demonstrably offering pie in the sky. It was obviously popular pie. The President was telling the American people that one of these days or decades (the timetable was usually lost in transmission) they would no longer have to worry about a nuclear war. The White House reported receiving the day after the speech a torrent of supportive calls and telegrams, some 2,800 in all with 80 percent in favor. Michael Deaver, who was then Reagan's senior White House adviser, called it "the most favorable response to any speech since he was elected President." One doesn't have to accept that sampling to know that the President had indeed struck a popular chord; the polls showed it.

The resilience of the President's dream owed much, as well, to his popularity and to his credibility, which had yet to be battered by the Iran–Contra affair. However, the most decisive factor behind Reagan's success in fixing SDI onto the agenda was the President's ability to mobilize and manage his campaign in a way that his unorganized critics could not. It is worth noting that four days after the speech, Weinberger was no longer dragging his feet. On "Meet the Press," he was firmly on board. While he wasn't quite ready to accept the idea of a joint Soviet–American approach to the problem of strategic defense, he did think that "for the moment the best thing we can do will be to try to develop the technologies that can insure that we would have an ability to protect the people from Soviet missiles falling on this soil."

"Protect the people" were the operative words. For as long as Reagan was able to sell Star Wars as a shield for people, he would have the public's support. Later, the administration backtracked under the pressure of the critics. There was talk of a first-phase shield to protect offensive nuclear weapons. Critics were quick to reply that this could be even more destabilizing than no shield at all. But these fine points were largely lost on a public whose support remained strong.

How, then, does one reconcile the developing congressional resistance with the continuing public glow of enthusiasm? One explanation for why Congress has regularly reduced the President's request for increased SDI funding has to do with budgetary constraints. The more interesting question, however, is why Congress, given its level of skepticism, hasn't cut even more deeply into SDI funding. The answer here says something about the power of the press in relation to that of the President. Almost from the inception of SDI, the media was its usual adversarial self. It was not just the *New York Times.* Right after the President's speech the *Atlanta Constitution* argued that "by raising the remote possibility of a Sci-fi defense against Soviet missiles, [Reagan] risks destabilizing the U.S.-Soviet military balance—already dangerously tenuous." The *Chicago Sun Times* called the speech "an appalling disservice" and the *Detroit Free Press* charged, "Reagan's vision of a 21st century in which the U.S. will be hermetically sealed against all nuclear attack provides no answer to the problem of how our national security is to best be addressed now and in the next couple of decades."

These arguments were echoed in congressional debate. Yet, it must be emphasized that Congress by no means reversed the growth of research and development of strategic defenses. It merely slowed the rate of increase. And one major reason for that was Reagan's fiercely stubborn faith in SDI and his never-ending campaign to sell it over the heads of Congress to the public. According to the polls, Reagan returned from the arms control shambles at Reykjavík something of a hero to the American public, however much of a villain he may have been in the eyes of arms control enthusiasts. He returned a hero because, even at the cost of breaking up the Iceland summit, he did not bargain away "Star Wars." Indeed, Reagan plunged quickly into the congressional campaign with SDI as a main talking point and was greeted at campaign rallies by the Republican faithful chanting S-D-I. He had a head-full of images to describe his vision of a nuclear-free world. He likened SDI to the British development of radar before World War II and shuddered at the thought of what would have happened if Chamberlain had surrendered radar as well as Czechoslovakia at Munich.

On another occasion, the President recalled telling Gorbachev at Reykjavík that SDI was like "keeping our gas masks, even though the nations of the world had outlawed poison gas after World War I." Reagan stated repeatedly, as he had in his famous exchange with Walter Mondale in the 1984 campaign debates, that once the United States had developed its own defense system, it would share it with the Soviet Union "so that we can both go down through the years without having to be suspicious of each other."

That's what the public heard and that's what the public believed, even though lesser administration figures had for a long time been publicly insisting that a leak-proof umbrella against nuclear missiles had never been contemplated. In 1984 Lt. Gen. James Abrahamson, director of the SDI project, told the House Appropriations Committee, "Nowhere have we stated that the goal of the SDI is to come up with a leak-proof defense." George Keyworth, science adviser to the President, insisted in that same year that "the SDI has never promised... absolute perfection and the President would never propose such a bold step if only perfection would suffice."

Abrahamson and Keyworth apparently forgot the President's original proposal to render nuclear weapons "impotent and obsolete." They also seemed to forget what Weinberger had said in that "Meet the Press" interview in March 1983, four days after the President's speech: "The defensive systems that the President is talking about are not designed to be partial. What we want to try to get is a system which will develop a defense that is thoroughly reliable and total... and I don't see any reason why that can't be done." Neither, obviously, did the President. Mikhail Gorbachev disconnected the issue of SDI and related questions about the ABM treaty from the negotiations on intermediate-range nuclear missiles in Europe, the debate over strategic defense gradually diminished. It is not likely, however, that SDI will remain disconnected from nuclear arms control negotiations with the Soviet Union as the negotiators focus on the subject of longer-range, strategic weapons.

This may not prevent the Bush administration from attempting in one way or another to establish the SDI as a permanent fixture. Various Reagan administration officials publicly proposed some deployment of something—nobody knows exactly just what—that would have put in place a sort of building block which no President could afford to ignore or to remove. Conceivably, Bush could succumb to the same temptation. The more likely prospect, however, is that budgetary pressures and technological constraints will combine to deny the realization of even that much of the SDI dream during the Bush presidency. This is not to rule out the possibility that the United States may not eventually develop and deploy a nuclear defense system. It is simply to say that the program will proceed at a more restrained pace. As good a measure as any of Bush's sense of the importance of the project was his early decision to hand the job of selling the SDI over to Vice President Dan Quayle.

The more likely prospect, however, is that budgetary as well as technological constraints will combine to deny the realization of even that much of the SDI dream during the Reagan presidency. This is not to say that work on a nuclear defense system will not proceed, that the United States may not eventually develop and deploy a nuclear defensive system, or that it may not someday be seen as entirely consistent with what the President was talking about seven years ago.

But this is not the point. The point is that whatever evolves in this radically new domain of scientific research would have probably moved forward in any event over the last four years at something close to the same pace as it has, but without all the controversy, the disruption of the arms control processes, and the unsettling of relations with our allies as well as with the Soviets. That "Star Wars" could have been so much a centerpiece of the national agenda over the last four years, with so little substance behind it, can only be accounted for by the power of positive presidential thinking to determine what the American public ought to be thinking about. SDI is a good example of the power of the President to set the agenda.

2
Libya: A Government Story

R. Gregory Nokes

The government, not the news media, dominates the national news agenda. More often than not, the President and his administration can determine when something becomes news, and how long it stays in the news. They can do this simply by giving an issue attention or not giving it attention.

No surprise here. A President's influence over the press occurs because of the powerful office he holds, and it is hard to imagine that he would not exercise his authority from time to time. A problem arises, however, when that influence is abused. And the potential for abuse is great.

A President and his administration can put the desired spin on a story through selective release of information to the public, emphasizing what they want to be emphasized and withholding contradictory information. Reporters under the pressure of deadline do not always have time to get the other side of the story.

A skilful administration can time events or activities to serve its own purposeful agenda. This is obviously true with scheduled events such as the State of the Union address, the release of the federal budget, summit meetings and the President's foreign trips. The President does not go overseas without a barrage of advance speeches, interviews and backgrounders by him and his aides—all designed to drum up anticipatory coverage to capture the spotlight. But this is also true of other issues, too, such as a campaign against drugs, a new policy against terrorism, and the Reagan administration's support for the Contras. As these items suggest, the President's power extends beyond timing: speaking from the bully pulpit of the White House, the President may force the press to focus on issues that otherwise may not receive front-page coverage. He can even get the press to pay more attention to him by denouncing it from time to time for not paying enough attention to him.

The art of manipulating the media was not invented by the Reagan administration. President Jimmy Carter also showed an acute awareness of the power of his office when, for example, he attempted to sooth nervous financial markets and public opinion by rewriting his 1980 budget, changing it overnight from a deficit to a surplus. Reporters had no choice but to report the revised figures, however preposterous the notion of a "surplus" appeared to be. Questions could be, and were, raised in subsequent news analyses, but such follow-ups seldom have the same impact as the initial front-page account.

Ronald Reagan, even as a candidate, proved to be especially adept at using the national media to promote his message. His 1980 campaign assertion that he would balance the national budget in three years was, given his other priorities, as preposterous as Carter's surplus. Yet reporters were able to make this point only in follow-up stories, and then only cautiously as they sought to avoid being perceived as playing favorites in the campaign.

Under certain circumstances, deliberate attempts to influence media coverage may be constructive—provided the intention is explicit and the purpose legitimate. If drug addiction is a demonstrable problem and an administration emphasizes this in order to do something about it, then the administration acts in good faith. This might be said, for instance, of Secretary of State George Shultz's attempts to convince the news media to give more attention to the problem of global terrorism. Yet the enormous power of the government to influence the media is also open to great abuse. No institution exists to guarantee that an administration will not use its credibility dishonestly and disingenuously to shape the news for ends other than those declared. And nothing so clearly illustrates the dangers of this as the Reagan administration's manipulation of the press in presenting its policy toward Libya.

Hyping Qadhafi

It was the Reagan administration and not the news media that made Muammar Qadhafi and Libya a story. Were it not for the administration's efforts to keep Libya in the news, the media surely would have paid it far less attention. What made the administration's handling of this issue distasteful was that it focused its wrath on Libya to divert attention from its failure to deal effectively with more serious problems of terrorism elsewhere. Terrorism also became an excuse to punish Qadhafi for other activities that the Reagan administration disliked.

Qadhafi was a problem for the administration. No doubt about it. But a more effective way of dealing with him would have been to ignore him or deal with him quietly, behind the scenes. This was the policy of the Carter administration, and has been the policy of the Bush administration.

Two points should be kept in mind. One is that, in spite of eight years of Reagan administration efforts to remove him, Qadhafi remains in power in Libya, with scant evidence that he has moderated his behavior in any appreciable way. The second is that Qadhafi failed to win any support among Americans—not among Democrats or Republicans, not among conservatives or liberals, and not among members of the media. No one denied that Qadhafi engaged in terrorism. No one disputed that his activities were inimical to our national interest. In fact, the virtually unanimous abhorrence of Qadhafi is probably what made him such an inviting and attractive target for the administration. Officials did not need to worry about a domestic backlash even when their actions against him exceeded the bounds of fair play.

As Sol Linowitz, President Carter's Middle East envoy, stated in an interview,[1] the Reagan administration's handling of the Libyan strongman was a patent case of "news management." As he explained, "The administration...found it suit[ed] its purpose to have Libya seen as the bête noire in the Middle East and as the epitome of the bad guy terrorist." Interestingly, some top officials within the Reagan administration have had second thoughts about the Qadhafi policy. For example, John Hughes, when he was a State Department spokesman, said that Qadhafi was "a brigand and an outlaw, and I don't have any problem about drawing attention to that fact." Yet, in a subsequent interview after he had left office, Hughes said, "Where I do think there were discrepancies is that there are other brigands and outlaws around the world, not the least of which was Syria and not the least of which was Iran, and we didn't apply the same kind of yardstick.... I always thought it was kind of unfair."

The media would have been drawn to Qadhafi, of course, without encouragement from the administration. However, the coverage would have been occasional, in response to particular events. The shooting by the Libyan embassy official of the policewoman in London's St. James's Square would have been a major story. The incursions into Chad also would have been a story, although perhaps not for page one. Qadhafi would have received some attention for his sudden merger and later break with Morocco. There would have been some coverage of the assassination attempts against anti-Qadhafi dissidents abroad, as well as coverage of Libya's role in other terrorist acts, even though it seldom played the lead role. Nonetheless, despite these events and Qadhafi's pompous posturing, the overall coverage would have been nothing like what it became with the administration's prodding.

Libya is a small country in terms of population. It has not played a central role in the Arab–Israeli conflict, or in the search for a peace, not even as a spoiler. During the Carter years, Qadhafi created an occasional big story, but never an enduring one. The Libyan government did not bother Americans who lived there. It remained hospitable to American investment. It did not seize American hostages, as happened in other countries. In fact, the involvement in Libya of Americans such as former CIA operative Edwin Wilson and Vatican ambassador William A. Wilson may be the one truly underreported story about Libya.

The Reagan administration set in motion the events that would lead to the struggle with Qadhafi in its first days in office. At a welcoming ceremony for the hostages held for 444 days in Iran, Reagan declared, "Let terrorists beware that when the rules of international behavior are violated, our policy will be one of swift and effective retribution." Similarly, at his first press conference, Secretary of State Alexander Haig asserted, "International terrorism will take the place of human rights in our concern because it is the ultimate abuse of human rights." Once the administration had made such a public commitment to retaliating against terrorism, it could not easily back away. It had set a standard against which the press and public would measure its response to future terrorist provocations.

Libya ended up paying the price for the administration's frustrations in dealing with terrorism in Lebanon, in Syria, in Iran, including the much-publicized hostage takings, and the deaths of hundreds of marines. Libya's vulnerability and isolation—more than the actions of Qadhafi—made that country an inviting target for reprisals. The administration started by taking an aggressive position in the Gulf of Sidra, which Qadhafi had unilaterally declared to be Libyan territorial waters. Washington wanted a confrontation. Geoffrey Kemp, the Middle East specialist on the National Security Council staff during the first four years of the administration, explained in an interview why Qadhafi was singled out:

> Libya is an easier target than Iran, and right after the election I think there was a general feeling that the United States had been humiliated and that something had to be done to restore some sense of American status in the world and that Iran-bashing was not in the cards because of logistics and military intervention. Libya, on the other hand, was perfectly located for a U.S. response and there was a ready-made issue in the Gulf of Sidra confrontation.

Of the several operations by American warships near the Gulf of Sidra, Kemp declared, "Sure it was a way of twisting his arm and provoking him, but in a way, from our perspective, that put him completely in the wrong." John Hughes, in a separate interview, did not agree that all of the operations were intended as provocations, but admitted that "there were many other times when we trailed our flag off Libya to see what he would do."

Similarly, Robert Sayre, former director of the State Department's Office of Counterterrorism, maintained that Qadhafi deserved what he received, but added, "I wish we didn't engage in so much public discussion of it." He said that the White House's active involvement in dealing with terrorism was probably a mistake and that it would have been better to leave it to the State Department to deal with in a lower key. "I think terrorism and navigational rights in the Gulf got kind of confused," he noted.

Reviewing the 1981 reports of the Associated Press (AP), one finds that during the first year of the Reagan presidency hardly a week went by without a major story critical of Qadhafi that originated with the administration. In most cases, the AP and other news outlets gave the stories prominent play without many questions. The stories covered, among other things, the threat of Libyan hit squads in this country, the expulsion of Libyan diplomats from this country, Libyan troops in Lebanon, the Gulf of Sidra incidents, the administration's consideration of sanctions against Qadhafi, and the administration's urging of Americans to leave Libya. Included in these stories was a stream of denunciations against Qadhafi intended to underscore the administration's characterization of him as a madman and Libya as a lawless state. The story on hit squads, widely circulated with attendant hysteria in 1981, turned out to be a fabrication based on faulty intelligence. But before the story finally was reined in, Reagan himself moved it along by saying the administration had proof that Qadhafi had sent hit squads to kill top U.S. officials, when in fact it had no such proof.

Throughout this period, however, scant evidence was presented to implicate Qadhafi in direct terrorism against Americans or anyone else, other than Libyan dissidents living abroad. Most of the accusations dealt with his financial support and training to groups that carried out terrorist acts. But many other nations, including Saudi Arabia, have also provided support to such groups. Even Libya's role in the bombing of a West Berlin bar frequented by American servicemen, an attack that resulted in the 1986 air attack on Libya, seems to have been much less than originally reported.

Some of those involved in policy making do not shy from the notion that news concerning Libya was manipulated to suit administration purposes. Geoffrey Kemp said that there was "an anticipatory string of stories that the administration certainly didn't put the damper on, all pointing to the strong feelings that one had about Qadhafi." He noted that "most of the strong feelings were based on highly reliable intelligence about what he was planning to do rather than proven events that he actually participated in." Kemp concluded, "The evidence was not particularly hard, but I think it would be wrong to rule out that this is what Libya would have done if they had the opportunity."

John Hughes asserted, "Libya was an attractive thing for Shultz to beat up on. He was in charge of antiterrorism and here was one country he could pin it on decisively and one country he could act against with very little fear of reaction or retaliation from the Soviets." Hughes cited the example of the State Department's reaction to the Libyan incursion into Chad. According to Hughes, "When the Libyans went into Chad, we were delighted. Well, not delighted, but given the fact that the Libyans had done it, took advantage of it. I think the Chad thing was given quite a run."

Disinformation

These actions of the Reagan administration toward Libya are perhaps understandable in light of the government's interest in taking some ostensible action to give substance to its commitment to combat terrorism. In its zeal to punish Qadhafi, however, the Reagan administration did more than strike at a convenient target of opportunity. As former White House spokesman Larry Speakes disclosed in an October 8, 1986, interview with the *New York Times*, the administration attempted to influence foreign events and shape the content of domestic reporting. Most notably, these efforts included an effort to feed contrived facts to the media about the Libyan government and its leader. A story in the *Wall Street Journal* on August 25, 1986, quoted unnamed intelligence sources as saying there were indications Qadhafi was about to resume his terrorist actions following a hiatus after the U.S. bombing of Libya in April. Moreover, the source suggested that the Libyan armed forces were plotting against Qadhafi. The account stated that the two countries were again on "a collision course," implying that the United States would retaliate with a new and devastating attack. But other reporters raised questions about the account after being informed by their sources that intelligence from Libya showed the opposite—that in fact Qadhafi was still lying low and seemed to be in complete control. Larry Speakes quashed such doubts, however, by insisting that while the information was unauthorized, it nonetheless was "authoritative." This put the White House imprimatur on the information, and a public which believed its government would henceforth believe that Qadhafi was planning new terrorist attacks, that his position at home was shaky, and that the United States was once again planning to retaliate.

Then, on October 2, President Reagan confirmed a *Washington Post* report that he had authorized a secret disinformation campaign against Qadhafi. According to Reagan, the campaign was intended to make Qadhafi "go to bed every night wondering what we might do" to deter him from backing terrorism, although he maintained that the strategy did not involve spreading false information through the American press. For his part, Secretary of State Shultz said he knew of "no decision to have people go out and tell lies to the media," but that, "If there are ways in which we can make Qadhafi nervous, why shouldn't we? Frankly, I don't have any problems with a little psychological warfare against Qadhafi." Shultz went on to quote Winston

Churchill as saying that in the time of war "the truth is so precious it must be attended by a bodyguard of lies." And as far as "Qadhafi is concerned," Shultz added, "we don't have a declaration of war, but we have something pretty darned close to it."

The disinformation campaign was widely condemned. For the administration to suggest that it was all right to mislead the foreign media, as long as it did not misinform the American media, was to make a meaningless distinction. News abroad usually becomes news in the United States, especially when it concerns American interests. It took less than twenty-four hours for a report in an obscure Lebanese magazine on the arms deal with Iran to explode in the American media. Certainly, new allegations that Qadhafi was preparing more terrorism against Americans, and that the Reagan administration was preparing a military response, were bound to find their way into American newspapers. And, indeed, they did.

As for Shultz's suggestion that lying about Libya was justified because the two nations were close to war, the fact remains that they were not at war. A real danger in Shultz's argument is that it could be used to justify disinformation against any government with whom we have profound differences. If it is okay for Libya, is it okay for Nicaragua, for Cuba, for the Soviet Union, for South Africa, for China? How is the media at home or abroad to know whether the information alleged in such cases is valid? After all, the administration did not voluntarily admit its campaign against Qadhafi.

In fairness, one must keep in mind that the Reagan administration was not the first to engage in disinformation. Probably most Americans old enough to remember still believe that Fidel Castro and his party roasted chickens over a fire in their Harlem hotel room during the Cuban revolutionary's 1960 trip to the United Nations, although that was disclosed years later to have been a fabrication. It would seem obvious, however, that an administration that wants to be believed ought to tell the truth.

Reporters are often castigated by critics for being skeptical of what government spokesmen tell them. Speakes himself made the point in a January 26, 1987 interview with the *New York Times*. Said Speakes:

> There is in the press corps, since Vietnam and Watergate, many times, an automatic presumption that the government is lying. And a government spokesman is forced day in and

day out to prove he isn't lying. And too much of it boils down to: How can we get 'em to say what they don't want to say? Somehow we need to get away from this 'I gotcha' syndrome.

But Speakes was begging the question. If an administration acquires a record of deceptions, no matter how inconsequential they might seem, it should expect to come under scrutiny from a responsible press. The Reagan administration built up such a record on big issues, like the disinformation campaign against Libya and arms sales to Iran, and on small ones, such as the insistence that the summit in Iceland was not a summit.

Mixed Motives

The deceptions on Libya went beyond contrived incidents and spurious information. They went to the reasons for going after Qadhafi in the first place. While the administration said Qadhafi's role in international terrorism was the issue, another interest was perhaps equally important. Qadhafi had long threatened American interests and policies in North Africa. During the Reagan administration, he had fomented instability in the Sudan, assisted rebels in Chad, worried Egypt, menaced Tunisia, and embarrassed the United States by merging with our close ally in the region, Morocco. Earlier, Qadhafi had played a major role in driving up the price of oil, contributing to all sorts of problems for the American economy. And of course, he controlled important oil reserves.

Kemp, Hughes and others have acknowledged that there were multiple motives for focusing on Qadhafi. "To put it bluntly," Kemp said, "people would not understand us getting involved with Libya because of Chad. Terrorism, anti-terrorism was a highly popular domestic event." Furthermore, Reagan was under intense pressure to do something about terrorism. He had, of course, brought the pressure on himself by announcing a tough stand early on in the administration. And by 1986 the United States had suffered several major setbacks at the hands of terrorists without the "swift and effective retribution" Reagan had promised. More than 300 Americans had been killed in Lebanon, hostages were being held there for periods longer than Americans had been held in Iran, and provocative terrorist acts, such as the TWA hijacking in Beirut and the *Achille Lauro* killing, horrified the American public. Fortunately for the Reagan

administration, there was Qadhafi to help "set us on the right path."
According to Kemp, "We were reaching the point where we had to
do something. Reagan was behind the power curve in this country."

Secretary Shultz's own frustration with terrorism also contributed to the administration's Libya policy. Shultz had become fixated on terrorism because of what had happened in Lebanon. One
State Department official involved in policy making at the time said
of Shultz that he was "warped by the Lebanon experience, particularly the embassy bombing. He [saw] terrorism as the major factor
that destroyed the Lebanon agreement. I've seen him get so worked
up on it privately that I'm sure he believe[d] it." According to this
official, going after Qadhafi amounted to "a cheap thrill" that made
everyone feel better, even though it accomplished little.

Another reason for targeting Qadhafi may have been to show
solidarity with Israel in the fight against terrorism. At least until
the American involvement in Lebanon, Israel, not the United States,
was the target of most of the Middle East–based terrorism. Now,
to some extent, we have made Israel's struggle against terrorism
our struggle as well.

Costs

What were the costs of our preoccupation with Libya? Probably
the two most important were the diversion of our attention away from
the Arab–Israeli conflict and the damage to U.S. credibility.

It is fair to say that after the failure of Reagan's 1982 Middle East
peace initiative very little senior-level attention was given to the
Arab–Israeli peace process by the Reagan administration until the
latter part of 1988. Many observers believe that if Secretary Shultz
had gone to the region to campaign actively for the 1982 initiative
soon after it was announced, it might have succeeded. But, by focusing on Libya and terrorism, the administration diverted itself, the
press and the public from the peace process. The most important
American interest in the region was ignored.

Sol Linowitz has made the point well:

> We have dillied and zigged and zagged and not done anything.
> The peace process has withered. There is an exacerbation of
> violence because there is no peace effort underway. It inevit-
> ably happens when making terrorist acts from Libya central

that you are detracting from the other side, which is moving toward peace. We gave Libya front and center and relegated the peace process to the back burner. And, as a result, nothing has happened.

President Hosni Mubarak of Egypt also faulted the Reagan administration's priorities in the region although in fairness it needs to be said that Mubarak had put considerable pressure on Washington to eliminate Qadhafi. Mubarak once complained to C.L. Sulzberger in a *New York Times* interview that the Soviet Union was paying more attention to Egypt than was the United States: "You . . . virtually ignore us. Whereas the Carter administration played an active role here, there is none now. Carter's secretary of state, Cyrus Vance, came to Cairo several times; Secretary George Shultz only once in five years." Israeli officials also complained publicly of what they perceived as American inattention to the peace process.

As for the Reagan administration's loss of credibility, it was quite apparent. In the beginning, no previous administration had enjoyed as much. Libya, however, cost the administration dearly in terms of the media's trust. It also undermined the administration's credibility with the public and with our allies. While the Iran–Contra scandal no doubt had the most devastating impact on the administration's credibility, it was the experience with Libya that helped to set the stage.

Alternatives

Our policy toward Libya, including the 1986 bombing, did provide some benefits. The United States demonstrated its willingness to act decisively and thereby served notice to terrorists that our patience was not without limits. Our policy undoubtedly made all terrorist groups more wary. Arguably, it also restrained Qadhafi, and certainly it produced greater cooperation among our allies.

Yet there might well have been a less costly way to deal with the Libyan leader. The Carter administration's approach offers itself as a model. William Quandt, the National Security Council's Middle East specialist under Carter, said in an interview that, rather than wage an international propaganda campaign, the Carter administration communicated quietly, but directly and firmly, with the Libyan dictator. Quandt reported that the Carter administration had concrete intelligence in 1977 and 1978 that Libya was planning to assassinate the American ambassador to Egypt, Hermann Eilts. According to Quandt, Carter wrote a letter to Qadhafi, declaring that we had such information and that, if anything happened, he would hold Qadhafi personally responsible. Qadhafi replied to Carter that nothing would happen to Eilts, and that was the end of it. Quandt's view is that Qadhafi wanted to be recognized as a leader, and felt he had more clout when people were paying attention to him: "Like any pseudo-leader, he doesn't want to be ignored."

As Quandt and others have argued, if the United States wanted to make a point with Qadhafi, it should have moved with sufficient force to achieve quick success. Instead, the Reagan administration's approach led to the worst possible outcome—Qadhafi remained in power and the United States appeared impotent to do anything about him. Indeed, as Sol Linowitz maintained in an interview, Qadhafi may well have been stronger at home than before Reagan set out to eliminate him. Furthermore, there were credible indications that Qadhafi's international meddling and involvement with terrorism have continued. In the month after the United States bombed him, Qadhafi was still active in Chad and continued to be active in trying to destabilize Tunisia, according to Quandt. "It's clear," he said, "Qadhafi is not out of business. We did not succeed in so intimidating him that he's pulled back."

Perhaps because it became preoccupied with other matters, the Reagan administration began to tone down its approach toward Qadhafi after the disclosure of the disinformation campaign. The administration did, of course, send help to Chad, but without the attendant hysteria of some of its previous efforts in the region. Furthermore, President Reagan eventually acknowledged late in his administration what should have been admitted from the beginning—that there are places, like Lebanon, where U.S. power and influence are severely limited. If he had admitted this earlier, he might not have felt compelled to expend so much time and energy on a minor league dictator like Qadhafi.

The Press Role

Finally, a number of things must be said about how the press handled the Libyan story. While most of the media recognized the White House efforts at news management, there was little challenge to the administration's story. The press was simply too gullible. It aggressively reported whatever information the government chose to provide, virtually without question. The Libya stories were, after all, extremely "newsworthy." While some reporters may have felt the media were falling short of the responsibility to be certain of the truth of what was reported, it was easy to fall back on the word of a very popular President and pass along a story most people wanted to hear.

Most journalists gave occasional expression to their private doubts in news analyses. However, such articles are almost always buried inside newspapers. It is the headlines that have the most impact, and, when it came to Libya, the Reagan administration dominated these.

The press fell into the trap, as it often does, of careless reporting and careless sourcing in the heat of going after a story. While the Libyan hit squad story was given credibility by the administration, we clearly embellished it with fantasy that more careful reporting would have avoided. There is no excuse for throwing caution to the wind just because a story is hot and competitive.

Note

1. Unless otherwise noted, interviews referred to in this essay were conducted by the author in the year this paper was prepared, 1986-7.

3
Diplomacy in a Television Age: The Dangers of Teledemocracy

David R. Gergen

Since the early 1970s, it has been axiomatic that television constitutes an independent force in international affairs. President Richard Nixon carefully choreographed his visit to China for prime-time viewing back home. President Jimmy Carter's administration engaged in "verbal ping-pong" with Tehran as the two sent messages back and forth through the channels of television; and President Reagan converted "photo ops" into a science in his foreign trips. And even President Bush, though lower-keyed, chose Malta as the site for his first Soviet summit, searching for the perfect visual effect.

The Television Revolution

Recognizing the camera's power, foreign leaders, diplomats and terrorists have all followed suit, tailoring their messages to television audiences in America and elsewhere. Egypt's Anwar Sadat was one of the first foreign leaders to hire American communication experts; the Sandinistas are only among the most recent. And who will soon forget the Chinese students in Tiananmen Square carrying aloft their Goddess of Liberty or the young men and women dancing atop the Berlin Wall, sending a euphoric message to television viewers across the world?

47

The stunning events of 1989 and 1990 have made the world understand how positive a force television can be in human affairs. Time and again, evidence has surfaced that televised pictures from the West were a catalyst for people in communist countries of the East to press for change and that, in turn, repressed people used the medium to build public support in the West. Were it not for modern communication technologies—from television to the fax machine—modern revolutions might never have occurred. The past two years have been the most triumphant in television's short history.

Yet there is reason to ask whether in the land that invented the cathode ray tube, the United States, public officials have learned that there are also limits to television and the role that it should play in a democracy. Too often in recent years, U.S. officials have substituted the power of television for the power of their own reasoning, believing that successful policies must first and foremost please the Great God of Public Opinion. This emphasis on teledemocracy marks a serious departure in American diplomacy. For most of U.S. history, diplomats have been guided by their own judgments and only later have worried about public reaction. Indeed, in the first twenty years after World War II, American diplomacy was conducted with the rather certain expectation that public opinion would support it. Daniel Yankelovich has found that whenever a President like Eisenhower spoke to the nation on television, half his audience would automatically grant him the benefit of the doubt on any foreign issue simply because of who he was and what his office represented. Congress also was a ready partner.

It is well understood that Vietnam shattered the postwar foreign policy consensus, leading Congress to become more obtrusive and causing the executive branch to become much more concerned with public support. It is less appreciated that changes were also taking place in television technology which brought the world more fully into American living rooms. During the 1970s, for example, television introduced the portable videotape camera (or mini-cam), which allowed editing shortcuts. Soon after, satellites were sent aloft and earth stations were built in most nations. By the end of the decade, American television was prepared to broadcast instantaneously from almost everywhere in the world. The "global village" was upon us.

Increasingly during the 1980s, government officials have shaped their policies with an eye toward generating positive and timely television coverage and securing public approval. What too often counts is how well the policy will "play," how the pictures will look, whether the right signals are being sent, and whether the public will be impressed by the swiftness of the government's response—not whether the policy promotes America's long-term interests.

Given the number of hours that Americans spend in front of their television sets and the degree to which they depend on it for information, such preoccupation with the power of the camera is understandable. The camera is an extraordinarily powerful instrument. No other technology in history has so influenced a culture. Nonetheless, there is no need for leading officials to be mesmerized or intimidated by television and public opinion.

Realities of Television

Before the world turned upside down in 1989, the charge most often hurled against the networks was that they regularly neglected international affairs in favor of domestic news, soft features and personalities. In fact, as Michael Mosettig, a former NBC producer now a writer for Public Television's "MacNeill-Lehrer Newshour," pointed out in the late 1980s, "The foreign news content of the evening programs has doubled and trebled since 1976. . . . Ten years ago U.S. network coverage consisted largely of canned film features; now it runs like a wire service, with morning and evening cycles of updated news and pictures." A study by James F. Larson of evening news broadcasts over the period of a decade (1972–81) found that on average the networks devoted ten of their twenty-two minutes—40 percent—to coverage of foreign affairs. Only the most serious American newspapers come anywhere close to that proportion of foreign news; most smaller papers give less than 10 percent of their "news hole" to foreign affairs.

Moreover, the Larson study does not take account of the foreign affairs coverage by the networks, PBS, and CNN during non-evening hours. "Nightline," for example, was born during the Tehran hostage crisis and continues to emphasize international issues such as apartheid. The morning news shows not only carry reports from overseas, but sometimes move their entire operations to countries such as China and South Korea. CNN has not only built a far-flung system of correspondents, but is broadcasting by satellite to elite audiences in many other countries. The problem, therefore, is not indifference to foreign news.

In fact, the problem with television inheres in the medium itself. By its very nature, television is an instrument of simplicity in a world of complexity. In a report of 80 seconds—150 words at most—a television reporter cannot provide context or background. No matter how many stories it devotes to international affairs, a thirty-minute news broadcast must essentially be a headline service. It cannot be educational, nor does it even attempt to be. A former network president and veteran of the industry was dismissive when I once asked him whether his network had a duty to enlighten. "We have a duty to tell people the news—period," was his response. As many old-timers in television admit, they see their task as asking each day two essential questions about the news: Is the world still safe today? Is my family still safe today? If everything is alright, they feel perfectly justified providing entertainment.

Another limitation is that television cannot and does not provide continuity in its coverage of international affairs. As a medium that depends on drama, it is drawn to conflict and crisis. It shuns the quiet periods in which most people live. For instance, in 1982, when El Salvador held a critical election, television crews descended on the country, turning it into a center of world attention. American senators and congressmen inundated the region. Within forty-eight hours of the election, however, the cameras had left to cover the Falklands War. It was as if the lights went out over El Salvador, and the country's subsequent struggle to preserve democracy disappeared from sight. Out of sight, it also passed out of mind for American viewers. Television loves sagas in which someone wins and someone loses. It abhors long, tedious, complex stories and will usually ignore them if possible.

It is also obvious that television has terrible blind spots. In his study, James Larson found that the major networks rarely cover Latin America, sub-Saharan Africa, South Asia or Australia. Canada was also lucky if it made the news. Instead, stories were heavily centered on Europe, the Soviet Union and the Middle East. The most egregious mistake made by television in the past concerned Cambodia. A study by William Adams found that during the height of the worst massacre in modern times, the networks' evening news coverage of Cambodia averaged only ten minutes a year. The carnage was virtually ignored until it was far too late to arouse world attention. Television was also slow to recognize the extent of famine in Africa. American television was eager to dramatize ethnic conflicts in

Azerbaijan and Armenia, two hotspots in the Soviet Union; should similar trouble develop in Yugoslavia, it is doubtful they will attract one tenth the coverage.

To be fair, networks are often handicapped by government restrictions on movement and coverage. For example, the Soviet invasion of Afghanistan would have caused much more of a sensation if Western television had had early access to the fighting. Many African nations are reluctant to grant visas to journalists, and the Soviet Union until recently has been highly restrictive. Restrictions on television coverage have also spread to industrialized nations such as South Africa, Israel, and Britain. The pattern is alarming because it appears to work to the short-term political advantage of the censoring nation. Should it take hold, television's "window on the world" will be even cloudier than it already is.

Room for Improvement

There was a time when observers thought that the development of new technologies would make television more thorough and complete in its coverage of the world, but the most recent breakthroughs—mini-cams and satellites—have actually been a setback to the quality of coverage. Because it is now possible to fly a crew to the scene of a crisis and instantaneously send back information, television is even more addicted to "parachute journalism" than before. "Technology has ruined the life of the foreign correspondent," NBC's Richard Valeriani has said, underscoring the point that correspondents now seem to spend more time jetsetting than concentrating on a small handful of countries. Moreover, reporting in one time zone while feeding stories to New York on another can make for grueling eighteen-hour days, hardly a lifestyle conducive to reflective reporting as Valeriani and others have admitted.

The costs of maintaining a foreign news operation has skyrocketed as the dollar has declined in value overseas. Some news organizations have found that maintaining a correspondent in Tokyo requires more than $200,000 in supplemental expenditures to meet that city's high costs of living. Cutbacks in foreign staffs have already occurred in several organizations. Between 1985 and 1989, for instance, *Time* magazine's masthead showed a cut from thirty-six to twenty-six in the number of overseas correspondents. The number of journalists sent scrambling overseas increased sharply in 1989-90, but whether that same commitment to international coverage will remain after the world calms down is highly uncertain.

Television clearly serves many excellent purposes. Yet it is a mistake to expect too much of the medium. In particular, policy makers cannot assume that television alone will ever create a public informed and enlightened about international affairs. Television can awaken people's interests, but it does not yet have the capacity to educate them.

Realities of Public Opinion

Just as it is important for policy makers to accept television's limitations, it is equally important to understand and accept at least three hard truths about public opinion:

First, even though their exposure to foreign affairs has increased, Americans in general have an abysmal understanding of the world. A number of surveys over the years have shown a startling lack of knowledge among the mass public. In 1981, for example, a *Washington Post*-ABC national survey asked the question, "One of these two nations, the United States or the Soviet Union, is a member of what is known as the NATO alliance. Do you happen to know which country that is, or are you not sure?" Through random guessing—say, by flipping a coin—50 percent should have given the correct response. Only 47 percent actually answered the question correctly. In the same survey, the public was asked which two countries were involved in the SALT talks: only 37 percent knew the answer. Another poll during that period asked for the location of El Salvador; 25 percent knew the answer. Barry Sussman of the *Post* concluded: "Whether they realize it or not, people are intentionally turning away from public affairs. It is not a lack of brains that is involved here. The little poll quizzes do not measure intelligence; they measure the storage of bits of information. A person need not be bright to avoid telling an interviewer, as one did, that El Salvador 'is in Louisiana, near Baton Rouge.' "

Second, Americans show little appetite for increasing their understanding of the world. At the elite or opinion-maker level, there is a keen interest in gobbling up new information about the world, most recently about Japan. *The Economist*, for example, has experienced its most rapid sales growth in the United States and circulation here now outpaces that in the United Kingdom. But consider a recent experience of the three major American news magazines, *Time*,

Newsweek, and *U.S. News & World Report*. These three magazines all featured on their cover the 1985 summit meeting in Geneva between President Reagan and General Secretary Gorbachev, a splashy event that attracted saturation coverage by television. Ordinarily, magazines featuring events that have received widespread television attention score well on the newsstands. Yet, for all three magazines, the Geneva cover was that year's worst-selling cover. Other covers on foreign affairs, unless they concern crises or Americans in trouble, share a similar fate. It is hardly surprising, therefore, that only a modest number of magazine covers are devoted to foreign affairs. Recent events in Eastern Europe provided further evidence that the public is not easily drawn into major international events: ratings for national news programs actually went down during the period when communism was collapsing. Polls suggested that the public felt too confused to watch closely.

Third, there is no reason to believe that public opinion will grow more informed. In early 1989, National Geographic published the results of a disappointing survey by the Gallup organization, showing that Americans know less basic geography than the citizens of Sweden, West Germany, Japan, France and Canada, and considerably less than they knew forty years ago. More distressing, eighteen- to twenty-four-year-old Americans knew less than their counterparts in any nine countries; America was, in fact, the only country where young adults knew less about geography than did adults aged fifty-five and over. There is, as Gilbert M. Grosvenor, president of the National Geographic Society, has reported, a shocking lack of geographic knowledge throughout this country. And several surveys have demonstrated that familiarity with foreign languages is also low.

These findings do not support the view that Americans are dumber than other people. It has been aptly said that while one should not overestimate the amount of information Americans have, one also should not underestimate their intelligence. On many occasions, Americans have demonstrated sound common sense. Recent polls, for example, show that while approval ratings for Gorbachev have shot upward in the United States, the public still urges caution in trusting the Soviets and in extending financial help. Clearly, the American public has not forgotten the lessons behind the failures of détente. Moreover, despite the fears expressed by some about conflict escalation, Americans supported recent government efforts in the Persian Gulf, correctly sensing that they were in the national interest.

Americans have also demonstrated that, if a strong case can be made, they are open to persuasion. The Carter administration, for example, was able to turn public opinion around on the Panama Canal treaty. The larger point, however, is that Americans do not pay close attention to foreign affairs, even if they are frequently exposed to them. As Walter Lippmann noted in the early 1920s, most citizens spend their time thinking about their jobs, their families, their neighbors and communities. They cannot and should not be expected to keep up with every twist and turn in a fast-changing world. That is the job of their elected representatives.

Lessons for Foreign and National Security Policy Making

From these realities one can draw certain obvious lessons about the formulation of foreign policy. Most important, policy decisions ought to be made with an eye first and foremost toward what is sound and in the national interest, not toward what is temporarily popular in the opinion polls or toward what will gain a quick, favorable notice on television. A government cannot make sound decisions about, for example, the use of military force based on a referendum or some theory of participatory democracy. The public simply does not know enough about the world to be able to render sound judgments on issues such as the Strategic Defense Initiative, the START negotiations, or the ABM treaty. Rather, it is entitled to expect its elected and appointed officials to act on these issues and then to have the chance to throw them out of office if they fail. Were foreign policy to be dictated solely by public opinion, several sound decisions would never have been taken. It is highly likely that the United States would long ago have canceled its foreign aid program, for instance, and it is very unlikely that we would have instituted a peacetime draft before World War II.

By the same token, it is a serious mistake for executive branch officials to make policy hastily in order to meet news broadcast deadlines. Policy makers should respect the power of television and learn how to utilize it in conducting policy. They should not be cowed by it. In retrospect, several key members of the Carter administration thought they were wrong to respond within hours to the Soviet invasion of Afghanistan, a decision based in part on a perceived need to make the evening news. A better U.S. policy would have resulted from larger deliberations inside the U.S. government. Similarly, some members of the Reagan administration believed it was a mistake to rush out with a full-scale condemnation of the Soviet shootdown of Korean Airlines flight 007. Some of the information that the administration had in hand at the time later turned out to be wrong. In retrospect, it would have been more effective to build an air-tight presentation over a period of days so that the credibility of the strong case against the Soviets could not be undermined. Officials sometimes argue that the American public demands fast answers from its government, especially in a television age. There is no evidence to support this view. On the contrary, the public seems to care more about results and consequences than about one-night headlines.

To sustain a policy, the executive branch must also have a clear rationale for what it is doing *before* it acts. It is not necessary to have public approval in advance, but if public support is needed after the fact, the government must have a persuasive case that will stand up over time. The Reagan administration blundered, for example, in failing to develop a clear rationale for sending marines to Lebanon. When there was no obvious mission that could be explained to the country, support for the exercise crumbled, and the marines eventually had to be withdrawn. Similarly, it is now clear that the administration's efforts to bolster the Contras were badly handicapped by the lack of a clear rationale for the policy. In this case, the public became confused because the administration kept shifting its argument.

Once it has adopted a policy, there is also a clear need for an administration to conduct an open dialogue with the press on its purposes and thinking. Obviously, in order to carry out a policy, an administration will need to build and maintain public support. Past administrations have demonstrated that such support can be sustained. For instance, the Reagan administration demonstrated a remarkable effectiveness in convincing the European public to accept the deployment of missiles on their soil.

There is, however, another equally compelling reason for such a dialogue: in a representative system, a government that assumes the responsibility to make decisions must also accept a high degree of accountability for its actions. We do not permit the Supreme Court to issue fiats when making major decisions. It is expected to issue carefully written opinions explaining its reasoning. Similarly, the executive branch has a clear-cut responsibility to explain its policies and thinking, to answer questions, and to be *accountable*. The

American media have a legitimate and important role in insisting on those explanations and in pressing for a clear public accounting.

Diplomacy in a Television Age II:
Lessons of Panama

These conclusions, though perhaps not the reasoning on which they are based, might be readily accepted by most policy makers. But should the same rules of open dialogue apply in the extreme case of foreign policy decision making—in the application of military force? The answer that most policy makers instinctively give is a resounding no. Since Vietnam, it has become almost an article of faith among military and defense officials that America can no longer fight a war that is not quick, almost bloodless and virtually certain of victory. As Alistair Cooke reportedly told President Reagan, the television-age public would no longer stand for another battle of the Somme.

So entrenched is this thinking in government circles that in 1984 Secretary of Defense Caspar Weinberger publicly proclaimed, as a precondition to the use of American force, that an administration must make certain the public would support it. Note that Weinberger did not say it was important to gain public support after the fact; rather he insisted that the military be assured of such support before it acted. While no other public official has spoken so boldly in public, there should be no doubt that similar sentiments exist elsewhere in government.

Weinberger's statement may have been intended to reassure military leaders who are concerned that they could be left holding the bag for a war that civilian leaders initiate but cannot justify. Certainly this is the lesson that many senior officers have drawn from the American experience in Vietnam. But Weinberger may have also been concerned that, once an intervention has begun, it becomes much more difficult to garner or maintain public support. And there are good reasons not to expect full cooperation between the press and the military once the action begins.

For both the government and the press, the critical hours of a military engagement come right at the beginning as bullets first streak through the air. Military officers have their hands full directing the action and usually regard reporters as a distraction, if not a bloody nuisance. "Keep 'em the hell out of here," is a typical reaction. Journalists, on the other hand, want to be on the front lines when the action begins, just as they went ashore with troops storming Normandy. They believe it is the military's job to do the fighting but not the reporting. Nor do most veteran correspondents accept the notion that the military should keep them out of harm's way. They have shared plenty of foxholes over the years and have left behind dead buddies on the battlefield.

A second concern for the military is to keep its plans secret. Officers in the field prefer to tell the press nothing, especially about a surprise strike. Reporters insist they can be trusted not to leak anything to the public and point to a long string of examples. When Americans were hiding in the Canadian embassy in Tehran during the hostage crisis of the late 1970s, for example, many American reporters knew of them but never breathed a public word. The press also withheld information that William Buckley was CIA station chief in Lebanon when he was held captive by the *Hizb Allah*. Barry Zorthian, chief U.S. spokesman in Saigon during much of the Vietnam War, has said that he entrusted American reporters with sensitive advance information on surprise strikes on many occasions and was rarely burned. Despite such evidence, suspicions run high among military commanders about giving the press early notice of a combat mission.

All of these concerns boiled angrily to the surface when American troops launched a surprise attack in Grenada in 1983. The commanding officer in the field and the Pentagon both agreed to keep the press off the island during the early skirmishing and President Reagan readily accepted their recommendation. The press acknowledged the government's right to keep the invasion a secret but insisted that the media had an equally important right to be on hand as soon as the action started. The commander of the operation, Admiral Joseph Metcalf, resisted and he found a stout ally in Reagan, who hated to second guess the military. Within the administration, staff aides began choosing up sides between the military and the press. Tempers flared. Eventually, White House chief of staff James A. Baker III persuaded Reagan that American forces were sufficiently in control that the press should be permitted access to Grenada. But the first reporters reached the scene fully forty-eight hours after the invasion started, an intolerable lapse by their standards.

Many reporters suspected—correctly—that some officials wanted to keep them off Grenada to pay them back for Vietnam and to prevent them from filming wounded or dead American soldiers, pictures that might sour public support for the operation. The Pentagon was also taking a leaf from Margaret Thatcher's book: the British military kept all but a small press pool at a safe distance during the Falklands conflict and the government reaped a political harvest from public support for its actions. In Grenada, as *Washington Post* columnist Lou Cannon pointed out later, advance word of the invasion leaked out anyway so that news bulletins about the American strike were being broadcast within communist Cuba before they were reaching the ears of American citizens. Bottling up the U.S. media seemed to serve no clear purpose other than the convenience of the government.

So loud were the howls from the press and so damaging were their stories about Grenada that the Reagan administration felt compelled to rethink the issue of press coverage in the months that followed. It was not lost upon the press corps that initially the public strongly supported their exclusion from Grenada, but it was not lost upon the administration that public opinion eventually began to turn against the government. Defense Secretary Caspar Weinberger asked Winant Sidle, a retired major general who commanded respect within the press corps, to head up a study commission and return with recommendations. After soliciting ideas from a wide body of opinion, the Sidle commission in 1984 proposed a pool system whereby the Pentagon would maintain a small, rotating group of reporters who would be on call at a moment's notice (they were expected to carry beepers in Washington and their news organizations were expected to keep up with them or have a substitute if they were traveling). The Pentagon was to alert the pool of an impending operation and then take them in with the first wave. While local commands were to control movements of reporters on the ground and to run facilities for sending copy, film and videotape, the emphasis was to be upon open coverage. In exchange for full access, the press promised full secrecy; or at least that was the idea.

The Pool System in Action: Panama

Weinberger not only accepted the recommendations and ordered them into action but even acknowledged that the administration had been too heavy-handed in Grenada. The new system was given a test of sorts in the 1987 Persian Gulf operation and several trial runs seemed successful, but its first serious tryout was in the December

1989 invasion of Panama. It flopped horribly. When U.S. Marines and Rangers stormed Panama in December 1989, not a single journalist went with them to cover the action. The Pentagon did organize a fourteen-member pool but it arrived on the scene four hours after the fighting started, and it was unable to file any dispatches for another six hours. "Worse," as Stanley W. Cloud reported in *Time*, "the initial pool report shed almost no light on the confused military situation, leading with the hardly titanic news that the U.S. charge d'affaires in Panama, John Bushnell, was worried about the 'mischief' that deposed dictator Manuel Noriega could cause." Complained pool member Steven Komarow of the Associated Press, "We kind of missed the story."

Frustration grew among reporters as the fighting dragged on longer than expected and General Noriega at first eluded his captors. The invasion had begun at 1 A.M. on Wednesday, December 20. Seeking to accommodate the press, the Pentagon began letting in trickles of new reporters on Thursday and allowed a chartered jumbo jet, carrying 200 journalists, to land early Friday morning. But armed U.S. security guards prevented reporters from leaving U.S. military installations on their own until Saturday.

U.S. government briefings often seemed indifferent to journalists' interests and escorted tours conducted by the military usually carried reporters to the scenes of yesterday's action or traced the droppings of Noriega's bizarre lifestyle. Both in Washington and in Panama, U.S. officials spoonfed stories about Noriega that portrayed him as a corrupt dictator who had gone mad. "We kept explaining to our escorts that we needed to see troops on combat maneuvers, military police on patrol, wounded American soldiers, Panamanians being taken prisoner, whatever was happening today that hadn't been reported or photographed," wrote one member of the pool, Kevin Merida of the *Dallas Morning News*. "Officials at the Southern Command were not interested in showing journalists scenes that would detract from what they regarded as a military triumph."

Adding insult to injury, reporters could not find enough food and, in most cases, ended up sleeping on concrete or linoleum floors. Howard Air Force Base, where 850 members of the press were housed, could provide only two phones to file stories and even those worked badly. The military did help to improve media access as the week wore on, but by the end of the week, when the press's straitjackets were finally loosened, many reporters had had enough and began heading home—only to miss Noriega's dramatic entry into the papal nuncio. Concluded one correspondent, Walter Robinson of the *Boston Globe:* the new-found freedom of the press in covering American combat "for the most part has been illusory."

The military also piled up a list of complaints in Panama. Their sharpest was that when the press pool was activated in Washington, one of its members violated a cardinal rule: not to tell other reporters, especially from rival publications. According to *Newsweek,* a magazine reporter from *Time* told a newspaper correspondent who called his editors hours before the invasion started. As it turned out, U.S. military preparations were so large that they tipped off the Panamanians anyway, so that no harm was done by the press, but the apparent leak confirmed the worst fears of the Pentagon. How could any military commander be confident about the secrecy of a future mission if the press pool were told in advance? A good question, to which there is no good answer. As for jibes from visiting reporters about their inability to cover the action, the military pointed out that a number of major news organizations already had reporters or stringers posted in Panama, and they could move about freely. "They had plenty of indication that something was happening," noted Ret. Admiral Metcalf, the Grenada commander who infuriated the press. "They could have found out days in advance. If they can't use their knuckleheads, it's their own damn fault."

Did restrictions on the press in Panama make any difference in the flow of information to the American public? On the fundamental story line, no: the reading and viewing public were clearly told from the beginning that the U.S. had launched its largest military operation since Vietnam, that it encountered more resistance than expected and that Manuel Noriega remained at large, but that the U.S. had succeeded in ousting the dictator from power. In Washington, the administration was remarkably open about operations—much more so than the Reagan administration during most of its military missions—as President Bush made a series of public statements and his top lieutenants at the White House and Pentagon answered voluminous questions from the press.

Even so, the press was unable to cover crucial elements of the story. It never had a clear picture, for example, of how well U.S. combat troops performed because it was rarely close to the action. As a result, it had to depend on secondary sources, many with a pro-military bias. It was also unable to cover the impact of the fighting upon civilians, so that days after the action stopped information was still fragmentary on how many were killed, how much damage occurred to homes and office buildings, and who was responsible. Some reports put the number of homeless as high as 25,000 and placed the blame on U.S. attackers; others said the figures were much lower and claimed that the Panamanian Defense Forces had been lighting fires and forcing the action into civilian neighborhoods.

The Press's Failures

If press coverage of the invasion of Panama was weak in several critical areas, not all the blame can be laid at the feet of the Bush administration or the military commanders on the spot. Given the initial success of the invasion and the inability of the press to cover some of its more gruesome sides, it is perhaps not surprising that the general coverage in the early days was overwhelmingly favorable for the administration. Congress and the public, which usually support a President's side during a moment of international conflict, rallied in this case with extraordinary fervor and unanimity. Jingoism ran high. The reaction of the press, however, is more difficult to explain. In the face of this broad support, the press seemed reluctant to raise vital, but troubling, issues. Some newspapers that might have been expected to question U.S. intervention in the hemisphere, such as the *New York Times* and the *Los Angeles Times*, gave glowing editorial reviews. One White House correspondent privately commented a few days later that the press felt it had severely criticized Bush for wimpishness during the failed October coup in Panama and now had no choice but to respond positively. Strong public hostility toward Noriega and his alleged drug running also helped to drive the tenor of early press coverage.

Most news organizations also wore blinkers during the invasion: with resources limited, they sent their top correspondents into Panama and failed to spread reporters throughout the rest of Latin America. As a result, they missed the sharp, bitter reaction in capitals throughout the hemisphere; Latin hostility was taken for granted and tucked onto back pages. Only later, after Noriega surrendered, did the press begin to focus on the broader international implications of the invasion. President Bush publicly acknowledged that there might have been diplomatic damage and ordered Vice President Quayle to visit Latin leaders—a signal he meant to be taken seriously but was met with mixed reviews by the press, who mostly dismiss the Vice President. As Colombia, Peru, and others began showing some resistance to the use of U.S. forces for drug intervention, the press started to question aspects of the invasion. But by then, second guessing had become seemingly irrelevant; the public had apparently made up its mind that the invasion was an American triumph, unalloyed and beyond criticism.

Lessons

The Bush administration might almost be forgiven for believing that the Panama invasion was a textbook case of how to manage a military conflict. Keep the combat short and sweet; apply overwhelming force; establish goals that are clear and attainable; and keep the press at bay until the shooting stops and blood stops flowing. Add it all up and, as Republican national chairman Lee Atwater called Panama, it can amount to a "political jackpot." It can even re-elect a President, as some Republicans believed in the aftermath of Panama. Who cares if the press grouses? That's small beer, and besides, they are notoriously crotchety.

By the normal standards of public accountability, however, the government's handling of the press in Panama—as well as the reporting by the press itself—was keenly disappointing. The government should re-activate the Sidle commission to find better ways to run the pool system. Sidle himself expressed frustration with the results in Panama: "If you're going to let the media in, you have to let them do something." As a general proposition, the Sidle commission seemed right to recommend that pools go in with the first wave. But the military failed to follow that recommendation in Panama and, despite enormous energy poured into advance planning, was unprepared to meet the legitimate needs of the press pool or the hundreds of reporters who followed. The briefings that took place in Washington were a step forward in government-press relations but were no substitute for on-the-spot coverage in Panama. Responsibility for reforming the pool system rests not only with field commanders but with their political masters in Washington.

By the same token, the press must answer to higher standards. If a reporter violates the rules of a press pool by leaking news of a pending military strike, he could endanger many lives. There seems only one answer: his news organization should fire him, and if there is a second infraction from that organization, it should be banned from pools. The press should also ask itself whether it pursued the story as dispassionately as it should have. Was it overly supportive of the invasion because it had been overly critical of the U.S. response to the coup in October? Did it feel some responsibility for goading the President into action? Did intense distaste for Noriega drive the coverage? Did intense public support make it more jingoistic? Not easy questions.

On balance, the invasion of Panama was an undeniable military victory and a triumph for President Bush in the United States, but as for journalism, there are no Pulitzers in sight. More important, the governments' assertive control over the flow of news out of Panama left bruised feelings among the press and an insistent demand that rules of coverage for U.S. combat once again be reformed. And in the wake of triumph one could only question whether the American public had received a full and balanced account of the largest mobilization of U.S. military forces since Vietnam.

4

Congress and the Media: Forces in the Struggle Over Foreign Policy

Robert J. Kurz

No analysis of the impact of the news media on foreign policy can be complete without some discussion of the role the fourth estate plays in mediating, sometimes exacerbating, and often exploiting conflict between the executive and legislative branches of the United States government. The American democracy is not a parliamentary system, but a form of representative government in which powers are divided among and *shared* by separate but formally equal branches. The national government of the United States was designed to limit the powers of government, even at the expense of government efficiency. As James Madison wrote in *Federalist* Number 10, the aim of the Constitution was first to "enable the government to control the governed; and in the next place oblige it to control itself."

Nowhere are the deficiencies or virtues of the American system more apparent or acute than in the area of foreign policy. The Constitution grants to the legislative branch the powers to ratify treaties, to confirm (or reject) all major executive branch nominations—including all military officers as well as civilian department heads, and, perhaps most important, to authorize and appropriate all expenditures. Congress thus has the power to, and frequently does, manage—some would say "micromanage"—foreign policy. Among other things, it can withhold key executive branch appointments, condition

65

foreign aid expenditures, revise or kill treaties, force changes in troop deployments, or even simply threaten any of these measures, which imposes opportunity costs on an administration with a broad agenda. All of this gives the Congress enormous leverage in the struggle to direct and control foreign policy. Seen in a more positive light, these powers also assure that the voice of the people is heard in the making of foreign policy and in checking the abuse of executive power.

Whether or not, to what extent, and how Congress will assert itself in the conduct of foreign policy are of course separate questions. The answer to each of these questions has varied widely as public support for executive branch policies has waxed and waned. Even in the late 1940s and 1950s, the so-called golden age of American foreign policy when "politics stopped at the water's edge" and party differences gave way to bipartisan consensus, Congress was rarely a compliant or silent partner. By the same token, the willingness of Congress to take responsibility for foreign policy today is easily exaggerated. For all its power to debate, oppose, reject, delay and obstruct policy, Congress cannot conduct foreign policy and so generally cedes primary responsibility for the conception and implementation of national security policy to the executive branch. Still, compared to the standards of other democratic societies, the influence of the American legislative branch on the conduct of foreign policy is extraordinary.

This influence of Congress as an independent branch of government acting as a counterweight to the executive in foreign policy places the media at the vortex of a broader relationship between the government and the governed. As Thomas Mann argues in his study of the relationship between the President and Congress:

> There is little doubt that changes in public opinion about foreign policy were the root cause of the weakening of the president's leadership position and of the chronic conflict between the executive and legislative branches that began in the late 1960's. Moreover, public opinion continues to be the prime determinant of the level of cooperation or conflict between the President and Congress. An administration that sails against the tide of public opinion invites a more active congressional role; a president who succeeds in bringing its foreign policy and public opinion into closer conformance—either

by adjusting his policy or by reshaping public opinion—will be more successful in diffusing opposition on Capitol Hill.[1]

This is not news to Presidents. More than a hundred years ago, Abraham Lincoln said, "Our government rests on public opinion. Whoever can change public opinion can change the government practically just so much."[2] Today as then the press plays a leading role in shaping public opinion. By reporting events in certain ways, by selecting or emphasizing some events over others, or by offering opinions, the press influences governmental bodies that are necessarily sensitive to public opinon.

Just as Presidents understand the power of the press, so too do members of Congress. Fated to be rivals by the Constitution in the exercise of governmental power, the two branches compete for the attention of the media. Even as they both seek to use the media to communicate their messages to the people, each is required by the court of public opinion to respond to the other directly and through the media. The multiple dialogues that result from such interaction are conditioned significantly by the profound differences that separate the legislative and executive branches, and, in turn, contribute to additional pressures and tensions between the two governmental bodies.

Decentralization vs. Hierarchy

A fundamental source of differences between the executive and legislative branches and their relations with the press springs from the way power is organized in the two branches. The executive branch is organized in a hierarchial manner. The President is the Commander in Chief. In the realm of national security, the President, although limited by constitutional checks, has extraordinary power. Power, at least on high visibility issues, naturally flows from the White House to the civilian cabinet officers, and then down the line through the executive agencies. The President possesses an unrivaled ability to freeze out an official or agency, or to unify the executive branch if he chooses to do so. Cabinet officers (notably the secretaries of state and defense) if they so choose, to a significant degree can impose their will upon (or at least ignore) dissent within the bureaucracy. Yet, especially on divisive and difficult issues, when there are divergent views among executive agencies, the President alone makes the decision, and has the ability to make it stick. "When the President says 'jump'," Richard Nixon's chief aide John Ehrlichman once observed, "they only ask, 'How high?' "

This is not to say that the executive branch operates as a highly unified machine. As any practitioner of executive branch politics will testify, there are many ways to handle orders from the top. The ability of the bureaucracy or the military services to drag their feet is legendary. Deflection, delay and obstruction are as much a part of executive branch politics as they are of Congressional politics. Intra- and inter-agency politics can consume the careers of executive branch officials. Any policy maker or political appointee who ignores the interests of the bureaucracy is likely to find that unpopular decisions are ignored, sidetracked or subverted.

Yet, even with the power of the bureaucracy to push its own agenda and spin its own orientation, as a general rule in foreign policy, information does flow up and down a line of command. There is only one President, and on major issues, what he says goes.

Congress, by contrast, is highly decentralized. The House has 26 full and select committees, with a total of 140 subcommittees. In the Senate there are 21 full and select committees, with 87 subcommittees. There are also four joint House–Senate committees. In the foreign policy arena, there are at least eight major House and Senate committees that have some form of primary jurisdiction. There are also 14 Senate subcommittees and 18 House subcommittees with direct involvement in aspects of foreign affairs. Because of the specialization of these committees and subcommittees, they are rarely all involved with any single issue at the same time. Which subcommittees and which committees are involved depends upon political power, and the definition of the issue.

The result is diffusion of power. Even when there is a consensus on an issue, it is likely to involve at least four, and often more, subcommittees. It is normal for an issue to fall within competing jurisdictions of various committees and subcommittees. And it is equally normal for these groups to compete with and contradict each other. There are, of course, institutional management agents that force decisions and enforce some degree of order. Not all subcommittees are created equal and some legislators are more powerful than others. The leadership of the two bodies also can and do impose controls, and when an issue is voted upon on the floor of the Senate or the House, internal disputes tend to be resolved, at least temporarily.

This complex power-sharing arrangement is further complicated by the two hundred years of congressional history. Congress has developed its own special language and unique rules of behavior. The distribution of power is highly dependent upon the interaction of individual personalities and therefore subject to constant change. All this is not to say that the Congress does not reach decisions, because it is a highly developed mechanism established to do just that. The point is that it operates in a manner quite different from the executive.

To those unschooled in congressional ways, particularly those on the military or intelligence side of the executive branch, the Congress is confusing and alien. Certainly there have been times when committee chairmen could work their will independently of the majority or make a decision stick in Congress. When the seniority system enabled congressional leaders to rule more or less with an iron fist, it appeared that presidential national security decisions could be coordinated quickly and quietly. Consultations were sometimes handled among a small number of individuals who often shared the same generational view or at least a common frame of reference built up over several decades.

The elections of 1974 severely weakened the seniority system and brought an end to the ability of a few individuals to act and speak for the whole. The "Watergate babies" elected in the aftermath of Richard Nixon's resignation came to Congress in sufficient numbers to alter radically the institution's procedures and priorities. As a result of reforms introduced in 1975 and passed since then, decisions that were once made on the basis of seniority, or simple agreement of the House and Senate leadership became subject to ratification or rejection by vote of the party caucuses. Votes that previously were kept secret were forced into the open.

The reformers challenged not only their elders' procedures, but their views of national security and foreign policy as well. Indeed, the desire for radical policy changes impelled the procedural reforms. The pressure led to greater diffusion of power among a proliferation of subcommittees, and as new members assumed subcommittee chairs, they were able to pursue their own agendas and develop their own power bases.

This decentralization has led many observers, particularly critics, to observe that on foreign policy matters the Congress acts as if it possessed 535 secretaries of state. However, this assertion is based on a false impression. Rather than evoke the emergence of 535 secretaries of state, it is more correct to recognize that there are twenty or so chairmen who consider themselves equal to assistant secretaries of state. This is particularly true of the subcommittees that have jurisdiction over contentious regional disputes.

The power of an individual chairman is highly dependent upon a number of factors. Primary among these is the level of interest and the knowledge base that is developed. Should they choose to, these chairmen can have access to a wide variety of information and intelligence from all parts of the U.S. government. They have the ability to visit the countries involved, and personally investigate all sides of a conflict. It is also not unusual for chairmen, even new ones, to outlast their State Department counterparts. In recent years, the time in office for assistant secretaries, particularly in areas of tension and debate, has been as short as two years.

Such events have had an impact upon the way the media covers foreign affairs. First, it has meant that the institutional power centers of Congress have been under the control of individuals who are quite willing to fight with the executive. Second, it has meant that there are often several competing groups in the Congress, one of whom will probably be willing to form alliances with reporters. Third, younger reporters find they are of the same generation as the newer congressional leaders, especially subcommittee chairmen, and that they often have a common frame of reference. Next, the younger members, especially subcommittee chairmen, actively seek out the press, recognizing that they need the press to build public opinion for proposals opposed by their more senior colleagues and the executive. The younger, more aggressive congressmen and senators being more entrepreneurial than their elders, seek to make their marks and plant their flags on the political landscape. They are versed in the uses and powers of television, understanding that they need the media. The result has been a proliferation of centers of power and information from which to challenge the President, and for the media to cover. Predictably, this has produced incentives for greater, not lesser, levels of conflict between the two branches of government, and has fueled the naturally adversarial relationship between the media and the executive.

Openness vs. Secrecy

Another major difference between the legislative and executive branches is the general presumption that governs everyday business. In Congress, all business is normally considered open, subject to

strong and vigorous public debate. It is the exceptions, mostly details of intelligence and military matters, that are handled behind
closed doors or locked in vaults. The opposite is true of the executive branch. Normal business in the White House, the Departments
of State and Defense, the CIA and other intelligence agencies is considered secret. It is the exceptions that are open.

Of course the Congress does deal with and keep secrets. And it
is equally true that the White House places considerable importance
on positive media coverage. Yet there *is* a fundamental contrast in
orientation, particularly between the executive branch agencies and
the Congress. As a norm this means that the Congress is more open
and accessible. By rule, sessions of the House and the Senate, and
virtually all committees are open to the public and the press, unless
closed by a public vote. In the executive branch, reporters are invited
into important meetings of the Cabinet or National Security Council
only for carefully crafted "photo opportunities." Otherwise executive agencies seek to limit reporters to the daily message, focusing
interchange into carefully prepared briefings, often called "feedings"
by the press, that are conducted by officials whose sole responsibility
is to manage press relations.

Congressmen and senators are more open to the press than are
executive branch personnel. Reporters can visit virtually any congressional office without an appointment, roam the Capitol freely,
and stalk a source with little hinderance. In the executive branch
reporters' access is strictly limited.

A further difference lies in the willingness of staff-level officials
to talk to the press. In Congress, even the most junior staffer regularly talks to reporters "on background." In the executive branch,
the most senior of staff officials usually avoid reporters unless the
conversation is cleared by the office of a cabinet secretary. The efforts
of Attorney General Richard Thornburgh in November 1989 to control press access in the Justice Department, prompting comparisons
to the Nixon "plumbers" unit, is but the latest of innumerable mani-
festations of this tendency.

More important, this difference in attitudes toward openness and
secrecy means in practice that almost all policy matters or events
in the world are subject to public comment or debate in Congress,
regardless of the impact on the President's agenda or itinerary. This
is not to say that the Congress can control or dominate the daily news
coverage to the degree or with the success of the White House.

Television coverage is especially sensitive to presidential management, spin control and timing. But it does mean that the Congress can offer a competing power center for the press to cover.

On occasion, the timing and openness of congressional action can upstage the executive branch or at least its press strategy. On some issues of high salience—the fights over assistance to the Nicaraguan contras, for example—the Congress, not the Executive, controlled the timing of fights. The same is true of congressional hearings, in which politically sensitive discussions often become hot news or at least "news hooks." All this occurs in the open, beyond the control of the President or the executive branch and makes a contribution to the shaping of the news and its influence on foreign policy.

Attitudes toward the Press: Allies vs. Antagonists

This leads to a third level of observations. In Congress, the media often, although not always, are seen as allies. In the executive branch, especially away from the White House political operation, the press is more often than not seen as an antagonist.

To be sure, the White House devotes a substantial amount of time and energy to managing press relations. A President's fortunes in the public opinion live or die on a positive image in the media. The Reagan White House developed press relations to a fine art. Getting a favorable daily "spin" and exercising "message control" became preoccupations, if not obsessions, during much of the Reagan era. The Bush administration's approach, while different, has been no less concerned with shaping coverage. Conversely, reporters often compete for the good will of the White House in order to gain access to powerful officials and appear successful to their editors.

Still, in the executive branch only the President and the Vice President are elected officials. They are political animals. Everyone else, from the White House staff to the Cabinet and on down the line, is an appointed or career official or bureaucrat. Many senior officials, especially those of cabinet rank, recognize the importance and power that is derived from friendly relations with the press. But that is not the general rule. In addition, the senior level officials who do understand and value the power of the press, often seek to reserve press exposure for themselves, strictly controlling access to the press for others.

Policy dissenters discover that open relations with the press can carry a high price. The bureaucracy is notorious for imposing penalties, from the cold shoulder to banishment or firing, on policy dissenters who carry their disputes to the press. Of course, dissenters will often run this risk under the protection of anonymity. The media are full of information acquired from "offical sources." And while the usual executive agency response is to seek to punish the individuals who divulge sensitive information, this does not stop leaks or allow a perfect "stone wall" to be constructed around decision-making circles. As the existence of "deep throat" during Nixon's Watergate crisis proves, an administration cannot control the media even when its own survival is at stake. The attitude of the executive branch toward the press is shaped by this atmosphere.

Thus most national security officials—the military, intelligence officers, and foreign policy specialists—avoid, even if they do not fear, the press. Reporters are seen as troublemakers or worse. Media attention can only complicate matters or hurt, not help, a career. Only upon rising through the ranks to senior office do reporters become part of their lives. Even then, the national security official who cultivates the press remains an exception.

The attitude of members of Congress toward the press is nearly the opposite. All 535 legislators, of course, are elected—and successful election campaigns almost always require good media relations. Where getting elected and staying in office is the name of the game, press relations are sure to be carefully cultivated.

In his study of the American political process Hedrick Smith provides a telling glimpse into the Congressional mind set, observing that in modern politics the campaign for office, either reelection or higher office, never ends.[3] Smith's descriptive labels—"visibility at all costs" and "playing the press and TV gallery"—epitomize the reality. In another analysis Timothy Cook has revealed how the media have grown in importance for the Congress and affected its role in policy formation. Cook puts it simply:

> Media strategies are important activities, not only to get reelected but increasingly to accomplish policy-related goals in Washington. And it matters that the media have been welcomed into the legislative process.[4]

Legislators form alliances with the press because they share a common interest, often a rivalry, against the executive. These alliances solidify during times of controversy and tension with a

President. It is not unusual for the Congress and the press to work together to discover what the executive is up to, uncover wrongdoing, or expose inherent contradictions in policies or their implementation. They share the desire for the notoriety and attention that comes with this conflict. The common perception of congressmen or senators as ready sources for news stories is certainly correct. Legislators work hard to get into their hometown newspapers and televisions news shows. And they bask in the attention they get from their colleagues after receiving coverage in Washington.

However, just as common is a reporter's collecting or ferreting-out information that is unknown to members of Congress or hidden by the executive branch. In the foreign affairs arena, reporters regularly tap sources in the executive branch who are inaccessible to the Congress, or who are unwilling to speak openly in contradiction of official administration policy. Reporters also regularly rotate, or at least travel, between Washington and foreign hot spots. This yields access to sources and information that may be unavailable even to the executive branch intelligence agencies. For example, reporters could and did travel to meet with leaders of Nicaragua, Libya, and the Palestinian Liberation Organization at the very moments the U.S. government appeared intent on destroying them.

A symbiotic relationship between the media and members of Congress often develops. Congress can provide the context for the hot news discovered by the press by calling hearings and scheduling floor action, often in direct response to press interest and attention. It is just as usual for a congressional hearing to be sparked by a news report as it is for the press to report on the congressional action. On other occasions the Congress, through hearings or public statements, provides the "news hook" which allows the reporter to push new information past their editors to the public. While these alliances may initially form as a matter of convenience, they often result in long-standing friendships. Trading information among a wide variety of sources is a vital aspect of the way business is transacted in Washington.

Another factor serves to cement the alliance between members of Congress and the media—namely, the reassurance each gets from the other. The Congress and the press provide each other with the legitimacy to challenge a President. No senator, congressman or reporter takes on the President without great trepidation. Rarely is the story complete, and usually large parts of the picture are missing. The executive branch, and the President himself, have enormous power to embarrass or politically penalize individuals who expose and pursue controversial matters. White House efforts to dissuade a publisher or an editor from developing a story not to the President's liking are very much a part of press relations. A congressional inquiry grants some, though not complete, protection from this, allowing a reporter to continue the chase.

Similarly, elected representatives, even powerful ones, are usually reluctant to challenge a popular President. Even when they have clear evidence of abuse, they seldom take independent action before they have been empowered by press reports that serve to catalyze public opinion. The mining of Nicaraguan harbors provides a good example. Although there was some official knowledge of the operation in the Congress, it took the reporting of it to produce widespread knowledge. As it turned out, then chairman of the Senate Intelligence Committee Barry Goldwater (R–Arizona) learned of it from the press, and his reaction was strong. "I am pissed off," Goldwater wrote to then CIA Director William Casey. The result of the news reports was strong opposition from the Republican-controlled Senate that led to the termination of the project. But the point is that the senator did not act until after the front-page reporting of the administration's activities.

Media Reports vs. Official Intelligence

In the interplay of relations between the Congress, the Executive and the media, information is the currency of power. Control of information, called intelligence by the government, is vital for controlling the initiative in foreign policy. The increased public availability of technology to acquire and disseminate information, called news by the media, has significantly weakened the ability of the executive branch to monopolize information. And this in turn shifts the power balance between the President and the Congress on foreign policy matters.

The collection, analysis and dissemination of intelligence by the U.S. government is an executive branch responsibility. This includes both analysis of information on events overseas as well as secretly collected intelligence. How this role is managed, and who receives this intelligence, is a critical issue in determining who makes and is involved in foreign policy decisions. In the not so recent history, the executive branch could collect and analyze information largely for itself. The U.S. government invests large sums of money to maintain an extensive network of collection platforms. In the days when large governments enjoyed a monopoly on overseas posts and the ability to transmit information quickly, they also had a natural monopoly on decisions and actions. In the United States it was the President who could decide what to share with the Congress, and when to do so. The executive determined when and who received legislative consultations. Problems, and even crises, could be anticipated and managed. During the Cuban Missile Crisis, for example, President John F. Kennedy was able to digest the intelligence and engage in almost a full week of private discussion before he placed the crisis in the public domain.

Today Presidential control over intelligence is drastically reduced. Media access to technology that was once the exclusive domain of governments has changed the nature of who knows what and when, thus altering the terms of the policy debate. The use of satellite communications allows the media to transmit information on breaking events at the same time it happens or shortly thereafter. The availability of realtime news on a crisis that comes from such outlets as Turner Broadcasting's Cable News Network and "Headline News" means that the Congress and the public can know of events at the same time the President does. It is widely known that the crisis watch centers in the U.S. government now have a televison tuned to CNN or "Headline News" at all times.

The news media can now keep pace with and often anticipate classified reporting by the State Department and the intelligence agencies. Coverage of the 1989 coup attempt in Panama and of the student demonstrations in China shaped public opinion in short order. The wide availability of computer technology also expands the availability of news. Today journalists and congressmen can sit at their desks and draw information from a number of computer data bases that allow them to compete with executive branch intelligence. Virtually all congressional offices subscribe to the Associated Press wire service, allowing the members and their staffs to stay abreast of news events without waiting for the evening television news or the next day's newspapers.

This change in the speed and quality of information distribution has the affect of accelerating the impact of world events. In the past, a President normally would have had time, days or even weeks, to reflect on events and consult experienced advisers before responding or acting. It is not uncommon to hear former CIA station chiefs remember nostalgically the days when only intelligence agencies had access to satellites. Those days are long gone, of course. During a crisis now, a Congressman can sit in his office and know just about as much as the President.

Technology has redefined what can be considered secret. News reported in one part of the world now travels around the world instantaneously. News that the U.S. government was trading arms to Iran for hostages in Lebanon, for example, was first reported not by the *Washington Post* or the *New York Times* but by an obscure Lebanese newspaper.

Communications technology allows television networks and even local stations to be on the scene with a satellite dish while events are happening. Producers seek out for broadcast the views and analysis of academic specialists who may be as skilled as those employed by the government itself. This provides the Congress, and the American people, with a competent alternative to the executive branch view.

Free Government and Effective Policy

The Founding Fathers recognized that a free and unfettered press was necessary to keep democratic institutions alive and functioning. Their commitment to press freedom reflected their profound belief in the fundamental wisdom of the people as well as the judgment that, for this wisdom to be exercised, the people need to be informed of the actions of their government. "Our liberty," said Thomas Jefferson, "depends on freedom of the press, and that cannot be limited without being lost."

The relationship between the press and the government is filled with tension and complexity. So it has been and always will be. The role of the media in foreign policy making is intertwined with the roles of the executive and legislative branches. At once, each needs and resents the others. Each is constantly building alliances and waging "war" with the others. The structural and institutional differences between the two branches of government and the media tend to shape their mutual relations and exacerbate policy differences: there is no easy escape from this predicament. Yet, it is not at all clear that resolving these antagonisms would be in the best interest of the nation. For, however irritating it may be, this competition for the "external vigilance" demanded by Jefferson is "the price of liberty."

Notes

1. Tom Mann "Making Foreign Policy: President and Congress," in *A Question of Balance: The President, the Congress and Foreign Policy* (Washington, DC: The Brookings Institution, 1990), 11.

2. Speech at Chicago, Illinois, December 10, 1856.

3. *The Power Game* (New York: Random House, 1988), 118–159.

4. Timothy Cook, *Making Laws and Making News* (Washington, DC: The Brookings Institution, 1989), 12.

Part II

■

Who Says What?

5

Leakers, Terrorists, Policy Makers and the Press

John P. Wallach

How should the press balance the interests of the nation against its own duty in an open society to report what it knows? Whose responsibility is it to determine what news shall be reported and how that news should be treated? And when, if ever, does the press have an obligation to suppress information that it has obtained through official or unofficial channels? An answer to these fundamental questions begins with a distinction between information that the government itself supplies and events and information that have an impact upon government policies and interests. The thesis of this paper is that the national interest is best served when the government and the press each attend to their own traditionally defined roles and responsibilities: the government oversteps its legitimate bounds by seeking to impose a code of conduct on the press to contain its own mishandling of information; and, similarly, the press fails to serve its own proper function as soon as it begins to worry about the impact of its reporting on policy.

Leaks: A Government Problem

Leaks are not a new phenomenon. Two hundred years ago, General George Washington entreated the delegates to the constitutional convention to "be more careful, lest our transactions get into the newspapers and disturb the public repose." One hundred years ago, Abraham Lincoln leaked his January 1862 State of the Union address to the *New York Herald,* which he regarded as a sympathetic newspaper. He also ordered the shut-down of the telegraph system so that the correspondent for the competing *New York World* couldn't alert his editors to rewrite the *Herald's* story.

Reporters have always tried to get close to their sources so that they will leak to them and not to the competition. In this sense, the background system (whereby a public official briefs the press on condition of anonymity—"on background") serves the interest of the reporter at least as much as it does that of the official responsible for the leak. Although probably self-evident, it should be noted that the official rarely consciously "leaks," that is, deliberately divulges information he knows to be damaging to a particular policy or policy maker. In a capital city crammed with almost as many journalists as sources, it is axiomatic that reporters need to cultivate ties with officialdom and vice versa. While there is no doubt that the background system is abused and that much more information should be put "on the record," abolishing the background system would probably not help guarantee a freer flow of information.

There do exist some built-in safeguards and checks. When reporters get too close to their sources, they risk censure by their colleagues. Their credibility consequently could be damaged. George Will experienced a temporary credibility gap, for example, after he helped prepare Ronald Reagan for his presidential debates against Walter Mondale. But neither is this a new phenomenon. President Franklin Roosevelt completely disappeared from public view from September 18 to October 1, 1942, travelling 8,754 miles through twenty-four states without a single word being written about his trip until he returned to the White House. The trip, which took place during wartime and was intended to raise the spirits of defense plant employees and Americans as a whole, could not have occurred without the cooperation of the three wire services. Each reporter assigned to travel with the President promised to obey the two-week embargo, although they wrote stories datelined from each city on the whistle-stop tour. One of the reporters daily showed his copy to FDR, so that the President could pencil in comments in the margins.

Although such a trip clearly is inconceivable today, the response of the press corps to a similar situation would probably be the same as it was with Roosevelt. When the three reporters returned with FDR, both the President and the reporters were castigated in *Time* and *Newsweek* for conspiring to exclude the rest of the media from a legitimate news story.

The Government and the Press

Three general points need to be made about leaks and the role of the media in American society. First, a great deal more classified information is deliberately leaked by the government in its efforts to manage the news than is disclosed, on an allegedly unauthorized basis, by reporters. And such "authorized" leaks frequently have as much impact on national security as the allegedly unauthorized ones do. Indeed, one can argue with some justification that the nature of the leak—whether it is authorized or not—is less important than the political use which is made of the information. The reporter's job is to find out whether the selective use of leaked intelligence by senior officials serves the national interest or someone's political interest. Unless an official can make a convincing case that publication of the material would damage the national interest, the reporter has every right (one could argue an obligation) to publish the story. Although no reporter obtained the story at the time, the use of intelligence information by Robert Gates to bolster the case for the Iran arms sales is an enlightening example. Did Gates provide that intelligence to the White House to assure an impartial review or to strengthen the hand of those who wanted to initiate the policy? The Tower Commission drew the latter conclusion.

Another example of the selective use of leaked information is the leaking on the night of Reagan's landslide reelection victory of the news that Soviet freighters were on their way to Nicaragua with unmarked crates presumably containing Soviet MiG fighter bombers. Taking on faith the administration's assertion that it did not know the contents of the crates, the leak nevertheless created something of a war scare inside Nicaragua and served the administration's own apparent aim of sending a timely signal to the Soviets that the United States would use force to rid the hemisphere of such an offensive threat if it were to materialize. It appears that the President has not hesitated to declassify top-secret information to support charges of Nicaraguan subversion of neighboring El Salvador or the receipt of thousands of tons of offensive Soviet-bloc weaponry by the Sandinistas.

More recent examples include the memorandum by National Security Adviser John Poindexter proposing a "disinformation" campaign against Libyan leader Muammar Qadhafi. Richard Halloran suggested that I might have been one of those taken in by the campaign when he wrote that my story about the imminent U.S. attack on Libya may have been deliberately leaked to keep Qadhafi off-balance. That is inconceivable to me, because the original source of my information was not an administration official. It was a colleague at the BBC in London who had heard rumors that Prime Minister Margaret Thatcher had forbidden the use of British NATO bases in the attack. Also, it is simply not plausible, because of the obvious danger to American lives, that administration officials would knowingly, with approval, leak the approximate time and date of a planned action, as well as the site from which it would be launched. However, no one at the White House, Pentagon or State Department would deny the story even when I asked one official whether it would jeopardize lives to "go with it." When I asked him after the attack why he hadn't cautioned me against writing the story, he replied that that would have given me the confirmation that I was seeking, something he didn't want to do.

The second point about leaks is that intelligence-gathering is an imperfect science at best (witness the administration's reliance, despite CIA warnings, on Iranian arms merchant Manucher Ghorbanifar), and reporters provide a much-needed service by checking the government's ability to manipulate the information flow. Had the media discovered Ghorbanifar's key role in carrying out the ill-conceived plans of Oliver North and others, the Iran–Contra debacle might conceivably have been avoided.

Third, the CIA and other intelligence agencies were never intended to be "supra" governmental bodies existing independent of, or above, the legislative branch. The Intelligence Oversight Act of 1980 reduced from eight to two the number of committees to which the President must report covert activities. Yet, it also granted to Congress for the first time the statutory right to be fully and currently informed of all intelligence activities. Much attention was focused on President Reagan's failure to inform Congress in a "timely fashion," as required by the Arms Export Control Act, of the supply of U.S. weapons to Iran. But the act lacked sufficiently stringent notification procedures. On August 27, 1986—six weeks before the final shipment of American weapons—Reagan signed omnibus antiterrorist legislation, which stipulated that the United States "may not export any item on the munitions list to any country which the

Secretary of State has determined" is supporting terrorism. Iran was and still is on that list of nations. The bill the President signed that summer had a specific reporting requirement allowing him to waive the legislation's prohibitions by giving Congress thirty days' notice. No effort was ever made to comply with that requirement, or even to acknowledge its existence.

The 1980 oversight law also directed the CIA to "furnish any information" requested by either the Senate or House Intelligence Committees. Policies and activities over the past seven years—in particular the CIA mining of Nicaragua's harbors, the bombing of Libya, the alleged plot to assassinate Qadhafi, and the covert arms sales to Iran and subsequent diversion of profits to the contras—all seem to point in another direction. It is as if the CIA had a mandate to avoid disclosure to the appropriate committees. Consequently, the media have a crucial role, and they have a crucial role precisely because one cannot allow the CIA to ignore its legal and other requirements to inform duly appointed representatives of the American people of its activities. This is not to suggest a public plebiscite for every covert operation. But a failure by the CIA to consult the appropriate committees and, even worse, a presidential order to the CIA not to consult the committees (as occurred in the Iran arms sale decision) only compound the problem. It permits the President to conduct policies without the authorization or even the indirect approval of the American people. The press is a safeguard against such abuse of CIA and executive branch authority.

It is worth reviewing the background to an article I wrote, using a leak concerning the CIA's plan to mine Nicaragua's harbors. It will be recalled the CIA Director William Casey only notified the Senate Intelligence Committee two-and-a-half months after the harbors had been mined. That notification came on March 8, 1984—some nine months after the initial decision was made. Casey's reference to the "magnetic mines" placed at Corinto, El Bluff and Puerto Sandino was brief, a mere six seconds during two hours of testimony. He probably would have felt no need to even mention the covert action but for the fact that two fishing boats sank after hitting mines on February 25, 1984, and for the fact that a Dutch dredging ship struck a mine on March 1. Radio Managua had been claiming the existence of those mines since January 3, 1984, but there was only scant reporting of those claims in the American press. My story on the CIA's plans ran on the front pages of most of the Hearst newspapers on July 17,

1983. I later learned that the policy had been approved barely a month earlier. It was not, however, until Senator Barry Goldwater's famous "I am pissed off" letter to Casey, in early April of 1984, that the extent of CIA involvement in the mining was discovered. A sequence of events then unfolded that eventually led in June, effective that October, to the cut off of military funds for the Contras.

Yet, almost a year earlier, my story had declared that the CIA had obtained navigational maps of the depths and channels of the ports in order to mine them. The story's source was not an official upset with the decision. Nor was it an official deliberately leaking something in order to embarrass another policy maker. Far from it. The source was, in fact, an American ambassador to a Central American nation who was upset that a liberal Democrat in Congress had discovered the plan and was allegedly threatening to vote against arms aid to El Salvador if the mining scheme was not abandoned. In other words, the leak was not pried loose from a disgruntled, disloyal official. It was almost spoon-fed to me by someone who believed he was furthering the policy. Naturally, he wanted to write what an ogre this particular congressman was in threatening Casey. The story, in his eyes, was about the disloyalty of the Maryland Democrat. That figured in my account but was hardly the lead.

The Media and Middle East Terrorism

An analysis of the media's role in terrorist incidents produces the following observation: The media, while less than perfect or uniform, are not some "evil" force that makes classified documents public simply to sell newspapers or boost ratings, although that surely is partly true. And over the past two decades, there have been very few instances where a news story truly damaged national security. In dealing with cases of terrorism since the 1979–81 Iran hostage crisis, in fact, the American press cannot be held responsible either for any particular incident, or for worsening the consequences of any incident. Furthermore, in most cases, the media has acted responsibly in weighing the terrorists' demands for publicity against the need to report the story fairly and accurately.

There are, certainly, areas where the media could improve their performance. On the whole, they have not done a very effective job of interpreting Islamic change. Representatives of the media have tended to lump Arabs and Iranians together in presenting a portrait of Islamic fundamentalism that often depicts Shi'a as madmen because they are willing to die for their beliefs. Suicide squads, allegedly attracted to martyrdom, driving explosives-filled trucks into marine barracks is not a very easy concept for the media to comprehend. We have tended to be less interested in the motives behind the acts than in the acts themselves, because the latter are so outrageous to our sensibilities.

Nor have the media, until quite recently, distinguished between, on the one hand, religious leaders such as Nabih Birri, the Amal militia leader, or Hussein Husseini, the Shi'i leader in Lebanon's Parliament, both doctrinally opposed to the Iranian model of Shi'i fundamentalism, and, on the other hand, Mohammed Fadlallah, the leading Lebanese Shi'i cleric, who champions the Iranian model. The media are prone to depicting Islamic fundamentalism as a uniform, united movement—as mainly a religious and Shi'a phenomenon cutting across sectarian and ethnic divisions and extending to Pakistan, Saudi Arabia and the Persian Gulf states as well as to Iran. Not surprisingly, the media's coverage has been influenced by the prevailing view that Islamic fundamentalism is a holy crusade, led by zealots and fanatics, that will not outlive Ayatollah Khomeini. Perhaps representatives of the media should ask themselves whether the phenomenon might not also be a social, political and economic movement spawned by the failure of the Western and Soviet social, political and spiritual models to meet the needs of the Muslim masses.

Turning now to the most commonly heard criticisms of the media, four major ones can be discerned. The first is that television, by its very nature, escalates a hostage crisis far beyond its actual importance, making it very difficult for an administration to stick to its policy of no concessions to terrorists.

In the satellite age, there is little question that the State Department is handicapped in conducting diplomacy through traditional means. It may in fact need anchormen, such as Ted Koppel or David Hartman, simply to keep abreast of the latest conditions for securing a hostage's release. Ed Joyce, president of CBS News until 1985, noted after the June 1985 TWA 847 incident: "It was obvious we had access to more information than the U.S. government." Recalls Joyce: "A State Department official reacted with horrified disbelief when told by CBS news that the hijackers had separated and removed hostages with Jewish-sounding names."

But is there evidence that television coverage actually prolonged a hostage crisis? As journalist Don Oberdorfer noted several years ago, television took its cue from the Carter administration—not the other way around. According to Oberdorfer, in the first six months of the 1979–81 Iran crisis, more than 100 meetings of the National Security Council were devoted exclusively to the hostage affair. More than 1,000 pages of cables, memoranda and reports on it were reviewed daily by the NSC staff. As a practical matter, this meant that in the national security arena, the government's attention was focused almost entirely on the Iran hostage crisis. Lloyd Cutler, President Carter's chief legal counsel, has recalled that the President spent more time watching the three television sets simultaneously beaming the latest news about the crisis into the Oval Office than he did reading CIA cables containing the latest evaluations of how to deal with it. Hodding Carter noted that "we were reminded every single day of this terrible outrage: that a little country of Muslims and people who ran around in robes and looked funny could do all this to us and we couldn't do anything about it." But again, was television coverage responsible for this?

Today, there is little disagreement that it was Carter's own "Rose Garden" strategy that made the crisis the leading news story for 444 days. The former President has admitted that he may have been mistaken in feeling the need to respond to the kidnappers' every public demand. But he also believes, and has told many colleagues, that it was the constant exposure that the hostages received that protected them from having to endure physical torture and spy trials. In short, it was the Carter administration's own obsession with preventing terrorist spokespersons from dominating the evening news that eventually allowed the crisis itself to dominate the administration.

Until the Iran–Contra affair, the Reagan administration appeared to have learned the correct lessons from the Carter administration's debacle. During the 1985 TWA hijacking, it maintained a business-as-usual atmosphere. There were no additional briefings at the White House or State Department. (During the Iran hostage crisis, there often were three or four briefings a day, and most of them were televised "live" to hundreds of millions of American homes, because the Carter administration wanted the coverage.) Reagan also received a foreign head of state and traveled to California, as had been previously scheduled. For a time, the administration was able to keep the story off page one by working primarily behind the scenes to free four Americans who remained behind after the initial thirty-five passengers had been freed. And in the *Achille Lauro* hijacking, the administration went a step further: it manipulated television coverage by successfully conveying an image of fighting back.

In none of the three major terrorist crises confronted by the Reagan administration—the TWA hijacking, the *Achille Lauro*, and the Pan Am hijacking in Pakistan—did television coverage force the administration to abandon its no-concession policy. It may very well have increased the pressure to achieve a negotiated settlement, and that in turn may have accelerated the already-planned release of several hundred Lebanese Shi'a detained in Israel. Nonetheless, television coverage did not result in a victory for the terrorists.

The second major criticism of the press is that it has become a pivotal actor in terrorist crises because of its instantaneous access to the combatants and because its self-declared air of neutrality is vulnerable to exploitation by terrorists.

Shortly after the TWA 847 incident, Secretary of State George Shultz stated that he was disturbed by the fact that reporters had trooped in to a news conference staged by the Amal militia with several American hostages and then had dutifully trooped out when the news conference was over. Shultz wondered where their responsibilities as journalists ended and their duties as Americans began? What would have happened, he asked, if the reporters had declared that they were not leaving without the hostages? The answer is that there more than likely would have been several dozen more hostages. In fact, the relative neutrality provided by the international press corps probably helps ensure that the kidnappers' demands are conveyed. More importantly, the extent to which such coverage helps terrorists obtain their objectives probably helps ensure the safety of the hostages.

Television has often been a constructive force. Walter Cronkite's simultaneous interviews with Anwar Sadat and Menachem Begin created a kind of camaraderie that certainly facilitated the peace process. Having Corazon Aquino and Ferdinand Marcos on the same show (even if they did not talk to each other) made a similarly constructive contribution. During the TWA crisis, television presented Nabih Birri for what he was—in the words of *Washington Post* critic Tom Shales, "more rug merchant than terrorist." That was neither a bad nor a dangerous move. The coverage clearly conveyed some legitimacy on him, but it also helped dissipate the fury many Americans were feeling. It certainly helped channel some of the kidnappers' own anger. Most importantly, though, the instantaneous access to Birri, and his availing himself of that access, conveyed the much-needed sense that a genuine effort was being made to resolve the crisis.

Vilifying television because David Hartman asked Birri if he had any message for President Reagan and then asked Reagan for his response is like blaming the messenger for bearing bad news. Would the crisis have been resolved more expeditiously, or with less loss of life, if Birri had been denied access to the media? The answer is most likely no.

A third commonly heard criticism of the media is that they provide terrorists with exactly what they want: a global stage to publicize their demands. This is an unfortunate but inevitable byproduct of the terrorist act itself. Indeed, the real question is not whether the demands should be publicized, but whether and how those demands should be satisfied. That is the policy maker's dilemma. This also suggests a good reason why there cannot be a uniform antiterrorist policy. Demands change with every incident and with every group. Some of them may be worth satisfying, particularly if large numbers of lives are at stake. Since in almost every recent terrorist incident, the U.S. government has negotiated with the captors, and, moreover, since the government continues to negotiate with groups holding Americans today, wouldn't it make sense to adopt a flexible public policy that conforms to this reality? The almost complete loss of credibility caused by the Reagan administration's trading of arms for hostages might have been mitigated somehow if U.S. policy had not been perceived to have been so inflexible on the issue of negotiating with terrorists.

The media have improved their performance in responding to terrorists' demands. During the Iran hostage crisis, the networks almost fell over each other trying to secure interviews with Iranian militants. On occasion they even paid for the interviews or offered the militants valuable airtime in which to make unedited, propaganda statements. Ford Rowan, a former NBC State Department correspondent, says he quit in part because the network wouldn't allow him to air a response by the State Department spokesman. Recalls Rowan:

> The deal that was offered [for the 'right' to interview Marine Corporal William Gallegos] was...you've got to interview the

hostage they pick, so it's a hand-picked hostage. No pre-taping of the interview...they control the switch. It's got to go out live from Iran, and they added, well, no U.S. spokesman during the body of the show can appear.

Such checkbook journalism has largely disappeared. Excepting the final news conference in Damascus after the TWA hostages were freed and David Hartman's live interview with Nabih Birri, none of the networks have carried interviews or press conferences without videotaping and subsequently editing them since the Iran hostage crisis. There certainly are valid moral issues raised by NBC's interview with Mohammed Abu Abbas, the mastermind behind the *Achille Lauro* hijacking. But it is inevitable that television will continue to be exploited as a propaganda forum by all kinds of groups, including terrorists. The networks have a clear responsibility to identify the use of their airwaves for such purposes, to edit the interviews, and to provide equal time to those who hold opposing views as well as to those who don't believe the interview itself should have been aired. Nonetheless, as is the case with the government, there can be no official policy to control or regulate the media when it comes to dealing with terrorists. White House or State Department officials should be consulted in every case. However, the final decision must remain with the networks themselves.

The fourth and final major criticism is that the media irresponsibly report on U.S. troop movements and consequently limit the government's options. In the *Achille Lauro* case, overflights by network helicopter were dangerous and conceivably could have interfered with retaliatory action. Yet, it is also worth recalling that at one point during the crisis, the Pentagon temporarily lost the cruise ship on its radar screens and required the networks' cooperation to relocate the vessel. Moreover, plans for retaliatory action often are deliberately leaked to the media in order to send a message to the hijackers. When an NSC staffer leaked word to the *Wall Street Journal* that naval maneuvers off the Gulf of Sidra were in preparation for another U.S. attack, that constituted disinformation. The official, acting on the basis of a memorandum approved by NSC adviser Poindexter, knew that there were no plans to attack. The government has a right to plant stories. But at the same time, reporters have the right to ascertain the truth of these stories and the motivation behind a particular policy. Moreover, any administration should be

aware that it damages its own credibility when it deliberately lies
to the public. There is, in short, a need for a vigilant watchdog press.

Cooperation between the government and the media, when required, is improving. There was, for example, no premature disclosure
of the plan to pirate the EgyptAir 737 jet and kidnap the *Achille
Lauro* kidnappers. The government, furthermore, retains the option
it exercised in Granada to limit news coverage. A system has been
devised under which a "pool" of reporters will accompany U.S. troops
on future invasions. Members of that "pool" have agreed, in return,
that it will withhold news of troop movements until a mutually agreed
time.

Government and the Media: Different Roles, Different Responsibilities

There is a crucial and legitimate role for the media to play in the
national security sphere. The challenge remains for it to maintain public pressure on the government to devise the most effective strategy
against terrorism. Since the Iran hostage crisis, the media have con-
structively carried out this role while checking the CIA's and the executive branch's abuse of their authority. A review of the major terrorist incidents over the past eight years shows that the American
press has not been responsible for exacerbating these incidents, much
less for creating them—two commonly heard criticisms of the media.
In fact, a convincing case could be made that the media have helped
facilitate the resolution of these incidents.

Still, the media's performance could be improved. To begin with,
it must acquire a more sophisticated understanding of Islamic change
and terrorism itself. Furthermore, in dealing with specific terrorist
incidents, the media should be more responsible. They must refrain
from certain actions, such as allowing unedited, prime-time exposure
to terrorists and recklessly interviewing grief-stricken relatives,
thereby whipping up emotional public frenzy. Finally, the media
should be more responsive to government requests for cooperation
so as to avoid telegraphing military moves that might interfere with
retaliatory or rescue operations.

In the final analysis, though, the primary responsibility for dealing effectively with terrorists lies with the government. And, the
truth be told, the government shares as much, if not more, of the
blame as the media for escalating hostage crises far beyond their

actual importance. The government must realize that by diminishing the rights of its own citizens to be well-informed and by circumventing the necessary executive and legislative branch policy channels, it risks handing a major victory to the terrorists.

Alexander Bickel, the constitutional scholar, declared in the Pentagon Papers case that the presumed duty of the press is to publish and the presumed duty of the government is to govern. They are not the same, he wrote. One of the guarantees explicitly not written into the Constitution is that the press will interpret its responsibility in the same way that the government does. That separation was one of the main objectives in establishing the First Amendment's protection of freedom of speech. Hodding Carter II places this point in a relevant contemporary context:

> When the press starts thinking in terms of the government's obligation, or the government starts thinking in terms of the press' necessities, you've got real problems. Why? Because there are societies in which the press constantly thinks in terms of what's good for the government and the country, and they publish newspapers such as *Pravda*.

6
Terrorism, Media Coverage and Government Response

Robert B. Oakley

The Iran–Contra debacle, which resulted from the Reagan administration's attempt to defuse political criticism through a secret
arms-for-hostages deal diametrically contrary to its oft-repeated public policy of no deals with terrorists, underscores the media's crucial
role in foreign policy. The intensive coverage given the American
hostages in Lebanon, including family interviews and videotapes of
hostages attacking the administration for doing too little, was a pre-
lude to revelations of what was being done behind the scenes to obtain their release. The intensity of the coverage was the primary reason for undertaking the extraordinary secret diplomacy in the first
place: to minimize the powerful, negative political impact upon the
administration of the media's coverage of terrorism.

Other governments have been gored on the horns of a similar
dilemma. In France, media reports that focused on French hostages
in Lebanon, bombings in Paris, and the respective actions of President François Mitterrand and Prime Minister Jacques Chirac generated considerable political heat, led to secret dealings with the terrorists and, when these dealings failed to pay off and were exposed
to the French press, weakened Mitterrand's Socialist Party in the
National Assembly elections. In Italy the government of Prime Minister Bettino Craxi fell as a result of public controversy over its role
in the *Achille Lauro* hijacking in late 1985. The major role played
by the Tehran embassy hostage crisis in President Jimmy Carter's
1980 defeat by Ronald Reagan cannot be forgotten. Revelations of

95

the so-called disinformation campaign against Libya and the secret exchanges with Iran of arms for American hostages also caused severe damage to the Reagan administration.

As the preceding examples indicate, terrorist events tend to be more publicized and emotion-laden, and generate greater political heat, than other developments. Perhaps it is the impact of television—the viewers' horrified fascination with terrorism's drama and their sympathy with the families of victims—that accounts for the enormous impact of terrorist-induced crises on the actions and even the fate of governments. Perhaps it is the deliberate, often skilful, efforts by the terrorists to manipulate media coverage. Whatever the reason or reasons, this phenomenon has become increasingly important in recent years and figures to remain so in the near future, given the prospects for a continued high level of terrorist activity. Therefore, it merits examination.

The interactive relationship between terrorism, media coverage and government response poses particularly acute problems for democracies, whose strong traditions and institutionalized processes of free dissemination of information and responsiveness to public opinion render them much more vulnerable to media-generated pressures than less open societies. Most terrorist activities have political objectives, and the magnified political impact which publicity imparts is well understood by those behind these activities. It is also understood by the media decision makers, who find themselves caught between the goals of maintaining freedom of expression and satisfying audience demand, on the one hand, and playing into terrorists' schemes, on the other.

Governments also struggle with the desire to control media coverage in order to curtail terrorism's influence, the need to turn the coverage to their own advantage, and the tricky politico-legal problems posed by any attempt to restrain the press. The controversy over these dilemmas has been substantial. Some have gone so far as to call for direct government control of the media on the grounds that various forms of terrorism are influenced and even produced by spectacular mass-media coverage. Others have attacked the mention of even voluntary guidelines as unconstitutional, undemocratic and un-American.

The TWA Hijacking

The seventeen-day drama of the June 1985 TWA hijacking catalyzed and starkly revealed the differing interests in this debate. From the outset, it was evident that the terrorists and their supporters saw international publicity and the public pressure it could generate against the U.S. and Israeli governments as the major element in their strategy. Flying back and forth between Beirut and Algiers heightened the highly publicized drama, as did the cleverly worded communiqués, the phased released of all but male American passengers in exchange for terrorists held by Greece and Cyprus, the shock of the killing of seaman Robert Stethem, and the moving letter from the remaining passengers to President Reagan. By the time the plane returned to Algiers, the terrorists and their mentors in Beirut had reason to be pleased and to accept the proposal of the International Committee of the Red Cross and the Algerian government to remain there and negotiate. Then, suddenly and unexpectedly, the plane took off to Beirut shortly after American television and radio stations broadcast news that the Delta Force was flying to Algiers.

The hijacking's first phase ended in Beirut with the passengers removed from the aircraft to hideouts beyond the reach of military rescue and with the Reagan administration and the American public seized by the need to bring them back. President Reagan rejected the terrorists' non-negotiable demand for the release of prisoners held in Israel while the terrorists worked to satiate the TV networks' appetite for maximum coverage. Responding to the unrealistic public and political exhortations for urgent action resulting from this coverage, the President bought time and eased pressure by announcing a boycott of Athens airport, as well as a series of long-term measures to strengthen civil aviation security, and appointed Vice President Bush to head a task force on terrorism.

During the two-week Beirut phase, the TWA hijacking became even more of a media event, rivaling the Tehran embassy hostage crisis. Film crews and correspondents rushed to Beirut where special events were arranged for them: an exclusive television network interview with Amal leader Nabih Birri; another dramatic exclusive of TWA captain John Testrake in the cockpit with a hooded terrorist holding a pistol to his head; live briefings by terrorists, Amal representatives and hostage spokesman Allyn Conwell; a press conference featuring many of the hostages; and a surprise dinner hosted by the terrorists for the hostages at a beachfront hotel with TV coverage to dramatize the event. Family members were interviewed extensively and some were flown abroad by media outlets to act as surrogate correspondents in obtaining information on their loved ones.

Describing the role of the press as a "bloody circus," David Martin and John Walcott in their book, *Best Laid Plans: America's War Against Terrorism*, noted that the press had become a participant in the hostage situation. David Hartman called Nabih Birri each morning to negotiate the day's news story, asking, "Any final word for President Reagan?"

In response to the hijacking and the accompanying media blitz, there were numerous high-level meetings in Washington. President Reagan and Secretary of State George Shultz made several television appearances to reiterate their rejection of any prisoner exchange. Public and private debates ensued between Washington and Tel Aviv over whether, when, and under what circumstances Israel should resume its previously interrupted program to release the prisoners. There were also numerous exchanges between other governments and the Reagan administration, often initiated by the former who wished to play (and be seen to play) a role in the prisoners' release. Both the Syrian government and Nabih Birri, in response to international pressures, rather unexpectedly found themselves pulled into the orbit of those who sought an early solution to the crisis. Thus, when the Syrian government failed to produce any released prisoners at a scheduled press conference in Damascus, it turned in hasty embarrassment to Tehran in order to get Ayatollah Khomeini's followers in Lebanon to remove the remaining obstacle. This was done and the hostages were freed without any prior Israeli release of prisoners and without any definite promise of when the release program would be resumed or completed.

Debate over the Role oı the Media

Following the resolution of the TWA incident, considerable attention was given to establishing the media's proper role in covering terrorism. This included discussion at the July 1985 annual meeting in London of the American Bar Association, hearings by the House Foreign Affairs Committee on July 30, 1985, and the work of the Vice Presidential Task Force. The initial impulse of policy makers was to seek official media controls on the grounds that unrestrained coverage encourages future terrorism (by making it appear powerful and romantic) and frequently aids terrorists during an ongoing incident (for example, by revealing military movements). Scholars, lawyers, members of Congress and others offered opinions, and some suggested voluntary media-wide guidelines. Intra-media criticism was often tougher, more revealing, and perhaps more effective in curbing excesses. However, the focus of this criticism tended to be individualistic rather than general, and temporary rather than permanent.

Katherine Graham of the *Washington Post* summed up the prevalent media view in a December 6, 1985 lecture defiantly opposing even voluntary general guidelines. Graham argued that media leaders can and should handle the recognized problems, but admitted that intensive competition, especially among the electronic media, resulted in the "lowest common denominator factor" whereby the "least responsible person involved in the process can determine the level of coverage for all."

The Vice President's task force devoted a great deal of attention to the media issue, and the Vice President personally discussed it with a distinguished group of media representatives. The task force eventually decided against recommending guidelines per se, given the formidable media opposition to them. Instead, it identified specific "media practices that can lead to problems during an incident" (such as live interviews of terrorists and hostages) and appealed to the media to formulate their own means of remedying these practices.

The Beirut Hostages

The Beirut hostage crisis during late 1985 and 1986 raised issues similar to those in the TWA 847 and Tehran embassy incidents. It also revealed still more about terrorists' attempts to manipulate the media. The captors skilfully used the media to play on the natural anxieties of the hostages' families and to increase public pressures on the U.S. and French governments to accede to their demands. By dictating the substance and controlling the timing of letters and videotapes from the hostages—using emotion-charged language, accusing governments of abandoning them or saying execution is imminent, interspersing long periods of non-communication with bursts of public appeals and/or threats at what they considered to be politically opportune moments—the terrorists tried to sustain public interest and pressure. As *Newsweek* magazine pointed out in its October 20, 1986 edition—subsequently confirmed by released hostages—there was no question that the terrorists fully controlled their prisoners' access to information and their ability to communicate with the outside world. This obviously gave the captors a high degree of influence over their hostages' judgments, perceptions, and statements. David Jacobsen's effusive praise of the Reagan administration upon his release pointedly contrasted with his videotaped criticism of the administration while in captivity.

The freeing of the Reverend Lawrence Jenco in July 1986 produced a great deal of international sentiment for the liberation of all remaining hostages, including appeals from the Pope, the Archbishop of Canterbury and other prestigious leaders. Obviously seeing the opportunity to revive public pressures upon the Reagan administration, the terrorists broke a long period of silence with a flow of communiqués, messages from the hostages and videotapes from others. Some of these communications were clearly prepared under duress. France, too, was subjected to a campaign of released messages and videotapes. After a few weeks, the threats gave way to more subtle appeals.

When the imprisonment by the Soviet Union of *U.S. News & World Report* correspondent, Nick Daniloff, became a major issue for President Reagan, there was almost immediately a call by some of the hostages' families for similar administration attention and effort toward freeing the Beirut hostages despite the dissimilarity of the two situations. This emotional line was picked up by the captors and played back within thirty-six hours in an Islamic Jihad announcement from Beirut. When Daniloff was actually released, a videotape was rapidly produced in which two of the hostages (David Jacobsen and AP correspondent Terry Anderson) pleaded with the President to arrange their liberation and accused him of deliberate neglect. Anderson's appearance was his first on videotape. This was obviously intended by the captors both to reinforce the involvement of the American media and to accentuate the superficial parallels with the Daniloff affair. Interestingly, network commentators, even while noting the increased pressure the tapes would place upon the President, played them repeatedly and avoided any comment on possible terrorist manipulation.

Pressure upon the administration from the hostages' families, the media, public opinion and Congress increased considerably. In response, the administration provided additional details of its policy and its efforts to free the hostages within the limits of that policy. But no panic resulted, and the administration maintained its public opposition to a prisoner exchange.

By minimizing visible reactions to the public pressures, President Reagan tried to avoid actions, such as pledging to stay in the White

House until the hostages were released, or undertaking urgent, highly visible negotiations with the captors, that would have encouraged the terrorists to believe their bargaining position was strong. But neither did he slam the door on dialogue as President Nixon had done with fatal results during the 1972 Khartoum hostage crisis. In that incident, when the terrorists heard over the radio that the President personally had ruled out any negotiations whatsoever and a special team was being dispatched from Washington, they promptly killed their prisoners, the U.S. ambassador to the Sudan, Cleo Noel, and his deputy, Curtis Noone.

In other terrorist operations, including some hijackings, the perpetrators' motivations and use of publicity have been different. Operations such as the November 1985 EgyptAir hijacking, the almost simultaneous attacks on the Rome and Vienna airports in March and April 1986, and the September 1986 attacks on a Pan American plane in Karachi and a synagogue in Istanbul were carried out quickly with the obvious intention of delivering intimidating shocks and demonstrating the terrorists' capabilities. The terrorists made no attempt to engage in a public opinion battle or to seek a quid pro quo such as a release of prisoners. Their communiqués hinted only obliquely at their identity and made no specific demands. In some cases the Palestinian cause was introduced, but only to add a general rationale for vengeance. The terrorists' primary purpose, it seemed, was simply to demonstrate their ability to wreak death and destruction upon their enemies, whomever and wherever they happened to be. Vivid post-mortem media coverage of these bloody incidents, particularly by television, served to buttress the terrorists' claims.

In Western Europe and around the Mediterranean, as well as in the United States, concern over terrorism surged. Abroad, governments were criticized for doing too little to keep it in check, and the United States was castigated for its perceived impulsiveness in retaliating with force. The initial reaction of West European governments tended to be one of caution, confusion and inaction. In the United States, the reaction to the EgyptAir, Vienna, and Rome attacks was a mixture of fear, anger, a desire for retribution, and intense resentment of European governments for not providing better protection. Popular and political opinion was fully behind President Reagan's January 8, 1986 decision to impose full economic sanctions upon Libya, held to be behind the terrorists responsible for the recent incidents.

Colonel Muammar Qadhafi's high-visibility threats against the United States in response to the January 8, 1986 sanctions accelerated these developments and generated strong support for the administration's charge that Libya was directly responsible for the subsequent La Belle Discotheque bombing in Berlin. Public opinion polls and editorial comment solidly supported President Reagan's bombing of Libya on April 15, and Americans, incensed over European criticism of the raid and fearful of further terrorist incidents, canceled travel plans to Europe.

A brief statistical review of terrorist incidents during that period, however, shows the American public's anxiety to have been inordinate. During 1985–86, Americans were not the principal targets of terrorism in Europe. They were, in fact, victims of less than 5 percent of the total incidents, and the number of Americans killed, fewer than twenty, was derisory in comparison to the number violently and suddenly killed in domestic traffic accidents—more than 43,000. However, the televised images of American victims and terrorist statements, and the absence of any serious effort by either the administration or the media to calm and impart perspective to the public produced a sort of anti-European hysteria for a period of several months. To some in the administration, this seemed a useful way to vent their own frustration at European uncooperation. By the fall of 1986, the belated efforts of various Western governments to harmonize their tougher antiterrorist policies with those of the United States, plus a sharp diminution in terrorist incidents, restored a measure of mutual comprehension. Still, the underlying suspicion and latent tension across the Atlantic did not return to their previously low levels. In short, Middle Eastern terrorists had demonstrated what long-term political damage they could do, even in the absence of short-term success in achieving their specific demands.

Recognizing the political impact of press coverage and frustrated by its inability to obtain institutionalized controls over this coverage, the Reagan administration during mid-1986 threatened both media representatives and government officials with strict application of existing laws against the unauthorized disclosure of classified information. This threat was accompanied by high-level dialogue with top media policy makers (including Benjamin Bradlee of the *Washington Post*) and stepped-up FBI and internal agency investigations of suspected leaks, with at least three mid-level officials punished.

Understanding terrorists' keen interest in media reporting, the administration began to give numerous interviews on and off the record and took other actions to reinforce its public policies, such as its refusal even to consider an exchange for prisoners in Kuwait, and to throw the terrorists off stride through tactics such as the use of deliberate leaks of military movements to intimidate Qadhafi. By deliberately disclosing sensitive information (intercepts of Libyan communications regarding terrorist attacks, for example), the administration attempted to win public and political support for its anti-terrorist policies.

At the same time that the Reagan administration publicly struggled with the terrorists for popular opinion during 1985–86 and showed its muscle against Libya, it was focused upon two intensive secret approaches to resolving the increasingly painful hostage crisis: collecting intelligence and preparing contingency plans for military planes to rescue hostages, and opening indirect and direct contacts with Iran to determine what combination of pressure and incentives would lead to a long-term improvement in relations and the short-term release of the hostages.

Very little of this activity was picked up by the media and the few inevitable leaks which did occur were not subjected to serious investigative reporting—until the exposure of dealings with Iran by an obscure Lebanese newspaper in early November 1986 unleashed a firestorm of media attention and a series of Congressional investigations that exposed the administration-shaking Iran–Contra affair.

The administration set up a highly restricted all-agency, all-source, intelligence collection unit and an equally secretive process for examining military hostage rescue possibilities. A number of particular plans were drawn up at various times for various situations, but each was eventually disapproved because the uncertainties and risks were considered too great and the likelihood of safe rescue too small. Syria lacked enough influence on the terrorists to bring about release of the hostages. This left Iran as the only means of release, yet economic and political pressures were having no effect. Thus, over time the strategic focus in U.S. dealings with Iran gave way to bargaining over arms for hostages. The activity surrounding this effort became almost frantic as the 1986 Congressional elections approached.

Recommendations

The potentially disruptive short-term and corrosive long-term impact of terrorism upon both foreign relations and domestic politics has become all too obvious, particularly to terrorists. The ability of the media, especially television, to magnify that impact is equally evident, as much to senior media representatives as to government officials and terrorists. As Brian Jenkins of the RAND Corporation has noted, the publicity accorded terrorist actions creates alarm out of proportion to the damage those incidents cause. And the potential of media magnification will increase significantly as technological advances bring about a freer and even more fiercely competitive flow of televised information, with satellite transmissions easily cutting across national boundaries and governmental restrictions. In order to deal with this problem, senior media and government officials should meet, separately and together, for as long as it takes to establish formal or informal guidelines or other arrangements which will protect the national interest as well as the public's right to know.

Media representatives should reconsider their blind obedience to the principle of free information exchange and work out a set of guidelines for covering terrorist incidents, keeping in mind the differences between print and electronic media. These could draw upon the in-house guidelines already in effect at a number of TV and radio networks, magazines and newspapers. Useful work on industry-wide guidelines has also been done by, among others, the Task Force on Terrorism of the National Advisory Committee on Criminal Justice Standards and Goals, the Vice President's Task Force, and the American Bar Association and its joint panel with the Newspaper Publishers' Association. Helpful suggestions can also be found in a recent study prepared for the Twentieth Century Fund by Michael O'Neil, who strongly urges controls over television coverage.

The establishment of some sort of standing media panel to deal with these media–terrorism problems (O'Neil proposes reviving the National News Council) would be an excellent complement to guidelines and could make them effective. Recognizing the vagaries and loopholes of guidelines and the problems of adapting them to different incidents, such a panel could loosely monitor compliance and, if necessary, issue reminders or warnings. These could be strictly private and informal for first or minor offenses, but public and formal for blatant offenses or repeat offenders. In the highly competitive media environment, with an issue as sensitive as terrorism, voluntary guidelines with a system of warnings should be sanction enough, with no need for governmental regulation or legislation.

Administration representatives need to consider seriously the following observations of the Vice Presidential Task Force:

> It is essential...that the government and media cooperate during a terrorist incident....
>
> One difficulty for the press is that it cannot provide accurate coverage that takes into account risk to government action unless it has some accurate sense of what the government is attempting. Governments can assist by providing as much timely, factual information as the situation allows....
>
> The government has a responsibility to maintain effective communications during a terrorist incident. Officials should keep their comments within cleared guidance, avoid sending inadvertent signals, or leading other governments astray....
>
> Interagency working groups should provide specific guidance to all spokespersons on coordinating public statements. Without coordination, inaccurate information may result....

In addition to public statements by the administration, off-the-record communications, whether on-the-record or on background, should be maintained. Administration-media relations would benefit greatly, as would the coverage of specific terrorist incidents, if a small pool of media representatives could be briefed in confidence regularly as well as during terrorist incidents. The United Kingdom has long had such an unannounced, but mutually accepted, arrangement for national emergencies. The objective would be a frank off-the-record discussion of terrorist threats, U.S. and other governments' attitudes and actions, plus the public's need and right to know. Unless the ground rules were changed by mutual agreement, all those present would agree not to publicize *details* of any sensitive information not made public by the government, although they would be expected to share the information with their colleagues. Government officials, for their part, would need to be much more forthright in divulging information to the media. Obviously any "disinformation" or "spin" not fully supported by the facts would kill the media's confidence and vitiate the usefulness of the process.

Postscript

Since this paper was first written in late 1986, there have been major changes in the media's handling of terrorist incidents. Coincident with the appointments of Frank Carlucci and General Colin Powell as President Reagan's national security adviser and deputy adviser in January 1987, and Marlin Fitzwater's appointment to handle the media for the White House, deliberate government deception disappeared and lingering media doubts gave way to credibility at home and abroad. At the same time, there was a conscious decision within the administration to reduce the impact of media coverage of terrorism and consequent public clamor on policy, and to ensure that terrorists, states supporting them, our allies and Congress all understood this to be the case. The policy of no deals for release of hostages was strictly applied. The administration projected an image of calm concern and commitment despite the pressures generated by the taking of four Americans in Beirut in January 1987, the capture of Colonel Higgins in South Lebanon in 1988, and other incidents. Terrorist threats, appeals from hostages and media hype did not throw the Reagan administration off balance as had been the case during its earlier years. As a result, media coverage of terrorism was gradually reduced in scope and intensity, although there was no movement on developing general or specific guidelines. Nor did the issue of media coverage of terrorism arise in any serious way during the Congressional hearings on Iran–Contra.

The Bush administration was tested on the terrorist issue in late July 1989 by the announced "execution" of Colonel Higgins, threats to kill Joseph Ciccipio, the usual barrage of terrorist communiqués, videotapes and hostages appeals, and a resurgence of intensive media coverage and public clamor. In response, the President took a number of steps to deal with the events themselves and the public pressure. He actively and visibly involved himself in a series of diplomatic activities and contingency planning for possible military action, consulted Congress and used the media to keep the public informed in general of what was being done. At the same time, he and his aides made it clear that they would not be panicked by public pressure, nor reveal the details of the administration's plans and action.

The media initially reacted in almost Pavlovian fashion to the cleverly orchestrated, publicity-oriented moves of the terrorists and the Iranian government, eagerly awaiting and broadcasting every utterance, and arranging innumerable programs to advise the new administration on how to handle the situation. Some television networks exercised more self-control than others, as did some newspapers and news magazines (for example, ABC refused to broadcast the terrorist-produced shock videotape purporting to show the execution of Colonel Higgins, while others featured it prominently just as they had done when Higgins had been captured). After the first couple of weeks of near-frenzied media attention and administration steadiness, press and television coverage tapered off. There was a feeling that President Bush had easily passed his first terrorist test.

As R.W. Apple, Jr., wrote in the *New York Times* on August 17:

Unlike Mr. Carter and Mr. Reagan in similar circumstances, Mr. Bush has refused to allow the current hostage crisis, as embodied in the threat by terrorists to kill Joseph J. Ciccipio, to dominate his attention and the public agenda.... 'In the past the terrorists could be forgiven if they got the impression that they could bring the American government to a standstill whenever they wanted to,' a Bush aide said, 'The American people sometimes got the same idea. We're determined not to make that mistake.'

7

The Care and Handling
of Leaks

Robert J. McCloskey

On January 17, 1981, when I was the U.S. ambassador in Athens, I received a secure telephone call from Washington informing me that the American hostages in Iran would probably soon be released and that their first stop would be Greece. Secrecy was vital, I was told.

The following day passed with no word, and I began to fear that a hitch had developed. On January 19, I was called again and informed that the release was still anticipated. If everything went as planned, the caller added, two Algerian aircraft would be involved and would require refueling. Again, I was admonished to keep all information to myself.

At that point, I made two decisions: to inform the deputy chief of mission and, provided I heard nothing to the contrary by the end of the day, to inform the Greek minister of defense in order to obtain approval for the planes to land. That evening I drove an unmarked car to the minister's home, where he showed "pleasure" in granting advance approval. It was important, I told him, that the planes transit Athens without publicity. January 20 was, of course, Inauguration Day in Washington, and tension over the hostage issue was running deep. I recall feeling impressed that in the transition commotion information on the hostages' release was still under wrap.

On the morning of January 20, I received an "eyes only" telegram stating that the Americans would depart Tehran that evening. It included a manifest of their names and an instruction to board the planes to confirm that all were aboard. Less than an hour later, embassy press attaché John Swenson received a call from CBS New York inquiring not whether the hostages were coming to Athens, but whether an "English-speaking journalist" would be available to do "a voice-over" when the planes landed at Hellenikon Airport.

Ten hours later, when the planes landed, the airport scene was uncontrollable. Scores of camera teams and newspaper reporters had arrived from other countries. Algerian officials were so unnerved that I was barred from the planes by armed security. I did succeed, however, in getting a message to Bruce Laingen, the senior American diplomat, who assured me in a written note that all hands were accounted for. After considerable delay, the aircraft were refueled. They departed for Algiers, and the rest is history.

Was the leak deliberate or accidental? At my end, the result was damned irritating but not seriously damaging. Secrecy had been maintained through the hostages' departure from Iran, the crucial phase. From that point on the information was increasingly perishable and, in any event, already intended for official announcement. National security had not suffered, nor were the Americans placed in any further jeopardy.

What Gertrude Stein once said about a rose cannot be said as unequivocally about a news leak. Just as there is disagreement over what makes news, there is disagreement over what constitutes a leak. Both government officials and news professionals abuse and misuse the term. Not surprisingly, there is misunderstanding in the body politic over its meaning.

The *Times Mirror Company*, reporting in 1987 on a Gallup study it had commissioned on public opinion and the news media, found strong evidence of this public confusion over news leaks: 45 percent of the people surveyed either did not know the term, could not define it, or defined it incorrectly. Times Mirror also reported that among those able to define news leaks, 51 percent think they rarely compromise national security; 41 percent think news leaks frequently do; and 8 percent did not know.

In defining leaks ordinary dictionaries refer to the "accidental" disclosure of confidential information. Columnist and etymologist William Safire settles on the "disclosure of information, usually concerning government or political activity, through unofficial channels or what some consider improper means." In his *Political Dictionary* Safire cites an early example of a "sensational" leak from 1844, when

Senator Benjamin Tappan of Ohio gave a copy of the secret treaty annexing Texas to the *New York Standard*. The *Standard* printed it and set off an uproar. Tappan subsequently admitted to being the source and was censured.

Well before leak became a buzzword here, administrations contended with a House of Lords of sorts among Washington journalists. Preeminent was Walter Lippmann and included were columnists and reporters such as Arthur Krock, James Reston, Marquis Chils, the Alsop brothers and Roscoe Drummond. The relationship between policy maker and newspaperman was cozy and, in some cases, grew out of having attended the same schools or belonging to the same clubs. Officials were open to suggestions and advice from journalists. Lippmann has been credited, for example, with the successful proposal that the Europeans submit their own plan for postwar recovery in order to help assure success in Congress for the Truman Doctrine. Reporter and diplomat frequently debated policy issues while entertaining one another. Reston often met with Dean Acheson at the Metropolitan Club, where both were members. This atmosphere carried over into the Eisenhower administration and led to Reston obtaining the exclusive release of the Yalta Papers.

Those clubby days preceded the exponential growth in the foreign affairs agenda and in the size of the press corps. Today a larger number of officials compete for power, while more reporters compete for stories. The results are more unsanctioned sieves of information and an increasingly vulnerable ship of state. Nonetheless, there is evidence that the practice of leaking is no more widespread today than in previous periods. *Impact: How the Press Affects Federal Policymaking*, a Harvard University report by Martin Linsky, concludes that the frequency of news leaks has not changed in more than twenty years. Forty-two percent of 500 respondents—including former Cabinet secretaries, other executive branch officials, and members of Congress—whose experiences span the period from the Johnson to the Reagan administration, admitted "leaking confidential information" to news correspondents. "Some who did," Linsky writes, "would presumably not admit it, and others would define leaks narrowly enough as to exclude their own practice."

Again, there is the problem of definition. In *The Government-Press Connection*, Stephen Hess argues that "the leak deserves a better fate than to share a common definition with rumor, gossip and other back-channel exchanges." Consequently, Hess has constructed a comprehensive list of leaks and the various motivations and rationales behind them. He includes:

- The Ego Leak, giving information primarily to satisfy a sense of self-importance;
- The Goodwill Leak, a play for future favor and an attempt to accumulate credit with reporters;
- The Promoter Leak, a straightforward pitch for a proposal or a policy;
- The Trial Balloon Leak, revealing a proposal that is under consideration in order to assess its advantages and disadvantages;
- The Whistle-Blower Leak, perhaps the last resort of frustrated civil servants, who feel they cannot correct a perceived wrong through regular government channels; and
- The Animus Leak, used to settle grudges and to embarrass another person.

An example of the last, the Animus Leak, involved former Secretary of State William Rogers. Rogers, the first senior American official to meet with Egyptian president Anwar Sadat, was informed by Sadat that the several thousand Soviet troops which had been in Egypt for several years would be sent home "within months." Within twenty-four hours of reporting this "simply as fact" to President Nixon and the National Security Council, the information was leaked from the White House. Rogers is convinced that the motive was to demonstrate the State Department's naïveté in taking for granted Sadat's word. As it turned out, the Soviets were removed as Sadat had predicted.

Appearances can be deceptive, however. Former secretary of state Cyrus Vance had reason to suspect that the disclosure that King Hussein and other Jordanian officials had been on a CIA payroll was designed to embarrass him, since it appeared on the *Washington Post's* front page the day Vance arrived in Amman for an official visit in 1979. Hodding Carter, the State Department spokesman at the time, was later told by the *Post's* executive editor, Benjamin Bradlee, that this was not the case. According to Bradlee, he had held up the story for twenty-four hours at the personal request of President Jimmy Carter in order to give the Jordanian government advance warning. The President was apparently unaware that, as a result, its publication would coincide with Vance's arrival.

Hess's list also includes "the daring reverse leak—an unauthorized release of information apparently for one reason but actually accomplishing the opposite." Former Secretary of State Alexander Haig provided an instructive example of this type. An advance of Jack Anderson's column in the *Washington Post* one day stated that Haig was one of President Reagan's "top disappointments" and "could skid right out of the Cabinet before summer." Haig subsequently called Anderson twice, complaining that he was being subjected to a "guerilla campaign" from the White House. With this angle, the Anderson column, which is regularly run with the *Post's* comics, became page-one news and was picked up internationally.

Motivated leakers, as UPI diplomatic reporter Jim Anderson notes, "want to make a thud in Washington" and in most cases go to the newspapers that are widely read there—the *Washington Post*, the *New York Times*, and to a lesser extent the *Los Angeles Times*, the *Wall Street Journal*, and the *Boston Globe*. If the material interests them, the papers will give it space. Networks are also regular recipients of leaks, but time constraints impose limitations on how much they can report in one broadcast. Furthermore, sources usually prefer to read the reports on their leaks in black and white.

A presumption in government that the leaker had some responsibility for the matter being aired is often unfounded. An experience of *New York Times* reporter Leslie Gelb illustrates the point: A caller to the paper's Washington bureau one evening asked for "the State Department desk." Gelb explained that there was no such thing at the *Times* but that he covered the Department. With that, the caller began to read from a telegram signed by then U.S. Ambassador to the United Nations Daniel Patrick Moynihan, who argued that Washington was not being "tough enough" on Third World governments. Saying that he was having difficulty writing down the message over the phone, Gelb persuaded the caller to come to the *Times* office. The caller, still unidentified, came and allowed Gelb to make a copy of the message.

Gelb later determined that the source had absolutely no role in either Third World or U.N. affairs and to this day is not certain what the man's motive was. Gelb is persuaded, however, that the subsequent front-page publication of this story contributed significantly to Moynihan's resignation from the post.

The Fourth Branch of Government, written almost thirty years ago by Douglass Cater, contains a "Disquisition on Leaking" which couples the word leak with "cloaked news." The phrase illustrates the origins of the now commonly accepted background briefing for individual reporters (invariably at the latter's request) or for groups (often at government initiative) in which reporting is paraphrased and the administration source is cloaked as "U.S. official(s)."

The "backgrounder" and its offspring, "deep background," have periodically been attacked by journalists—chiefly editors—as simply a variation of calculated leaking. They are, in other words, a way for the government to take a position while being able to disown it. One can easily agree that backgrounders have been overemployed and that the covers for official sources rightly deserve scorn and skepticism such as that found in the *Washington Post's* editorial by Ward Just: "Walter and Ann Source," he wrote, "had four daughters, 'Highly Placed, Authoritative, Unimpeachable and Well-Informed.' The first married a diplomat named U.S. Officials and the second a government public relations man named Reliable Informant." This was, the editorial explained, "the family tree...the wellspring of news" in Washington. Whether it realized it or not, however, the *Post* editorial was also mocking its own news department, whose reporters were quite anxious to protect their sources while in hot pursuit of exclusive stories.

One of the most significant backgrounders that affected me directly was one which I did not even attend. At Guam en route to an extended East Asian trip in 1969, President Richard Nixon suddenly summoned reporters and began talking extemporaneously. Before he had finished, he had created what was later called the Nixon Doctrine—henceforth, the United States would no longer provide troops for regional conflicts, although it remained prepared to supply money and material. It was a major story aimed obviously at Vietnam and subsequently taken as a forerunner to the opening to China. Reporters smarted from not being able to identify the President as their source.

Nixon also concluded the backgrounder with the promise that, at his next stop, State Department officials (who turned out to be Assistant Secretary Marshall Green and me) would develop further the "thinking" that went into this new policy. Since neither one of us was at the backgrounder, the briefing transcript, which became available at midnight, was our only guide. We were able to flesh it out after Secretary Rogers and Henry Kissinger talked further with Nixon the following morning. By the time we reached Djakarta, the next stop, we had developed more thinking and could authorize attribution to the President for the follow-on stories. It was neither an enlightened way to articulate policy, nor an intelligent way to conduct press relations.

For strict constructionists, a background briefing does not meet the criteria for a hardcore and unadulterated leak. A leak must be exclusive, include information that is new and classified, and be volunteered by a source that remains, at least initially, obscured. These criteria were met in the following incident.

At a Washington dinner party on March 1, 1968, Townsend Hoopes, then an Air Force undersecretary, told college classmate Edwin Dale, a *New York Times* economic reporter, that a big debate was underway in the government over a new request from General William Westmoreland for substantial troop increases in Vietnam. Within a few days, the *Times* had determined from various sources that the request was for 206,000 men. When the story appeared, it was under another reporter's byline. Except for Hoopes, no one in government had any idea how the story had been developed.

It is no exaggeration to say that the story directly contributed to sapping what public support remained for the Vietnam policy, and, in turn, led to Johnson's startling decision to not stand for reelection. Johnson later complained to Henry Kissinger that he had been "destroyed, in part...by systematic leaking."

The "tilt to Pakistan" leak during the 1971 India–Pakistan war likewise caused serious policy repercussions. Kissinger had told an interagency task force that he was "catching hell every ten minutes from Nixon" for not being tough enough on India. The rationale behind White House sympathy for Pakistan lay in that government's role in preparing for Kissinger's secret trip to China the year before and in its support for Nixon's upcoming visit. The State Department, on the other hand, was unsympathetic, seeing a parallel interest with India in the creation of an independent East Pakistan (Bangladesh). Nonetheless, under White House orders, Assistant Secretary Joseph Sisco and I convened a special Saturday briefing to inform reporters that India was to blame for prolonging the war. A few days later, amid swirling congressional criticism, Kissinger said the same things in a "backgrounder," and before the day was over, a transcript of his briefing was leaked and put into the Congressional Record. As a result, U.S. policy toward the Asian subcontinent was in tatters, and the administration's prestige damaged.

In *Lyndon Johnson and the World*, Philip Geyelin cites LBJ's law, "Don't tread on me," in connection with events leading up to the controversial Tonkin Gulf Resolution in 1964. Tread on him is unfortunately what I figuratively did in early June 1965, when I officially and publicly confirmed a major escalation in the Vietnam war—that is, that American marines were involved in combat missions. This disclosure prompted the *New York Times* to declare that "a minor official of the State Department told the American people that the U.S. is at war." My statement, however, came not as a "leak," which was LBJ's initial and furious characterization of my remarks, but as a response to several days of repeated questions from reporters who had suspected as much or who had been given eyewitness material from counterparts in Saigon.

James Greenfield, then assistant secretary, and I spent several days ferreting out information, which Johnson was determined to withhold, on how the marines' assignment had expanded, and we decided, without further authority, to release the information. Dean Rusk ultimately persuaded Johnson that the administration's credibility would be better served by my remaining on the job than by my head being placed on a platter.

The incident highlighted what former *Washington Post* diplomatic correspondent Murrey Marder was first to call a "credibility gap." As a consequence, the press turned more towards advocacy journalism, and government decisions concerning the war had to be made within a tighter circle, usually limited to the President, the secretaries of state and defense, the national security adviser, and one or two others.

The inclination of Presidents and others to see leaks everywhere often demonstrates an ignorance of how the news process in Washington actually works. After he left office, Dean Rusk offered one realistic account of the process:

A reporter is leaving the State Department at the end of the day, when he sees the Soviet ambassador's car drive up. Figuring that the ambassador has brought a message, the reporter gives the machinery a chance to work, then starts calling around. After being told he's on the wrong track at several offices, he gets to the fellow on Berlin, who has been told to never lie directly to the press. The reporter says, 'John, I understand that the Soviet ambassador has just come in with a message on Berlin.' So the man says, 'Sorry, I can't say a thing about that. Can't help you on that.'

Aha, he's got it. In the absence of an absolute denial, he's on track. He figures out what the Berlin problem looks like and then calls a friend in the Soviet embassy. 'By the way,' he says, 'what's the attitude of the Soviet Union on this particular point on Berlin?' He listens for a few moments, then writes his story for the next morning on the message the Soviet ambassador brought in. Chances are that the President will call the Secretary of State and ask, 'Who the hell has been leaking news at the State Department?'

This scenario is more real than imagined and demonstrates what is invariably omitted in presumptions about leaks—that reporters have brains as well as eyes, ears and feet, and are not sitting around waiting to be called by "Leak Central." Officials can be woefully ignorant of how journalists work, how sources are cultivated and worked against each other, and of how reporters on their own can construct intelligently a plausible story about what happened or will happen in a certain area. After a while, an official's gesture may be all that a reporter needs to confirm a lead. Furthermore, some officials still tend to assume mistakenly that the executive branch is the single repository for national security information and do not realize that news organizations can and do assign squads of reporters to cover major stories. In short, stories that at first glance appear to be based on outright leaks are as likely to have been pieced together from enterprise and native intelligence. I learned this the hard way.

As ambassador to the Netherlands in 1977, I was initially convinced that *Post* reporter Walter Pincus's story on the "neutron bomb"—the bomb that leaves "buildings and tanks standing, but the great quantities of neutrons it releases kill people"—was a flat-out leak deliberately designed to scuttle the program. Like other colleagues in Western Europe, I had been under instruction for months to urge the Dutch government to accept the basing of the weapon on its soil. Following Pincus's story, demonstrations occurred, and it was virtually impossible to receive a public hearing—particularly in the news media—for our official rationale for the neutron bomb. It was much later that I realized that Pincus, knowledgeable in this field, actually constructed the story using information from earlier congressional testimony.

What no one saw coming was the ultimate leak in this story: that Jimmy Carter was canceling the weapon. Even now, the source for

Richard Burt's exclusive in the *New York Times* remains unidentified. Indeed, there is still uncertainty whether the story provoked or simply confirmed the decision that had already been made. It surely put the administration's credibility in NATO into serious question.

The episode had several peculiar turns: Burt has said that his source was "non-American" and that the information was offered in "a normal passing encounter." Pincus had received a parallel tip from a *Post* editor (who got it from a congressman), but declined to use it because he "just couldn't believe that, after all these months with everybody saying everything was go, Carter was going to cancel." And there was one final twist: at the State Department, Burt succeeded Leslie Gelb, himself a former journalist, whose task it had been to explain this confusing and aggravating reversal of national security policy.

No policy over a period of years has been at the mercy of leaks to the extent that nuclear weapons strategy has. Through successive administrations, negotiating options became the stuff of alley fights in the executive branch, with outcomes at times dependent on the number of column inches one or the other side obtained. Once the province of relatively few officials and of interest to even fewer journalists, the subject of nuclear strategy has now become a mainstream news story. Information is readily available on it, and ideologues are quick to refer to it. To what extent the news media is used—or permits itself to be used—in the debate over nuclear strategy is an interesting question.

Ronald Reagan spoke for his predecessors, though not as cataclysmically as Lyndon Johnson, when he declared that he had had it up to his "keister" with leaks. Most Presidents in recent history have resorted to desperate measures in the hope of stanching them by using wiretaps and polygraphs, restricting official information, and conducting investigations to locate the source of leaks. Very rarely, however, do any of these measures succeed.

Somewhere in the Iran–Contra swamp an "involved" and unnamed American official was reported to have said, "We thought it would be unlikely for an Iranian to leak the story, because the Ayatollah would have him killed. That's a real deterrent to leaking." This is precisely the type of sloppy thinking that invites trouble for the government. For even though the American media did not pick up on the initial leak in an obscure Beirut publication for almost a week, it was only a matter of time before the operations being run from the White House basement would have been exposed.

McCloskey's Law

It is predictable that information will leak from the government in direct proportion to the level of secrecy surrounding policy and decision making. Consequently, administrations with a passion for secrecy and for manipulating the flow of information (including disinformation campaigns) set themselves up for trial by leak. Fear of leaks exacts its price on government because, as Henry Kissinger among others has observed, "There is less openness among officials...consequently people don't know how and when decisions were made." Furthermore, adds Kissinger, "Excessive secrecy in some cases causes government to default on control of the agenda."

Serious people, journalists among them, do not argue that government does not have the right and the responsibility to maintain secrets, particularly in national security affairs. News organizations have, in fact, responded positively to government officials' requests to withhold information on the grounds that its disclosure could jeopardize national interests. The problem, however, is that administrations frequently invoke executive privilege to cloak in secrecy affairs that are of legitimate public concern.

At the same time, the degree to which leaks command and lead the agenda is in inverse proportion to the extent to which government responds to media inquiry openly. Consequently, the more substantive the government's public record of actions, the less incentive there is for anyone to indulge in leaks or to be scared by them.

The press, of course, cannot escape criticism. Its obsession with exclusivity—driven by fierce competition and a desire for recognition—compels an excessive reliance on leaks. In pursuit of stories, reporters will often not raise questions at official briefings in order to keep attention away from the topic they are investigating independently. This is especially frustrating for official spokesmen who work hard to prevent leaks, partly out of self-interest (because they want to be the recognized authoritative voice) but, more important, also because they believe that the public interest is best served on-the-record, where policy can gain the respect that comes with clarity and consistency. Given the opportunity, this objective can be achieved without impeding the freest flow of information.

These are not First Amendment issues, and the Constitution is not being violated by the disorder and confusion that leaks sometimes create. At the same time, the people's "right to know" is not a constitutional provision. But a need to know is fundamental to our society, and the latter would be better served by a less fractious relationship between the media and government—one in which the anonymous underworld of leaks had a lesser role in informing the public and in determining policy.

8
Secrets

Michael A. Leeden

We Americans are intensely ambivalent about secrecy.[1] We know that any country, even the most "open," must be able to keep secrets from its enemies in order to survive, yet we fear that secrecy may undermine democratic society: if we do not know the full truth, how can we be expected to make informed and intelligent decisions about our future? Our antipathy to secrecy is embodied in Woodrow Wilson's call for "open compacts, openly arrived at." This bit of conventional wisdom remains strong, even though many of the most successful foreign policy actions in the recent past—from the Nixon-Kissinger opening to China to the Camp David talks—would have been impossible without secret contacts and discussions.

The most recent appeal to "openness" in foreign policy came from Representative Lee Hamilton of Indiana, the ranking majority member of the House Foreign Affairs Committee, and co-chairman of the Iran-Contra Investigation, who declared that policies made in secret are inevitably inferior to policies that emerge from full, open debate. It is all wonderfully high-minded and unexceptionable; it is also unworkable. These abstract principles are in conflict with a world where secrecy makes its own demands. If secrets—of various sorts—cannot be kept, good policy and good relations are impossible.

The American distrust of secrecy is unique even among societies that share our commitments to democracy and freedom. The great chasm between the United States and other democratic countries is nicely illustrated by an exchange between Alexandre de Marenches, former head of French Intelligence and Christine Ockrent, in their recent best-seller *Dans le Secret des Princes*:

(de Marenches): . . . the sensation-seeking press cannot resist scoops. . . because it has found through more or less honest methods (who knows where?), let us say documents alleged to have come from the Pentagon. The press then prints things that only help the enemy and damage the United States. I find that totally irresponsible.

(Ockrent): In other words, the American press, which one tends to elevate to the status of a model, would be, in your opinion, an irresponsible press?

(de Marenches): No. I am much more nuanced. But certain elements in the American press are dangerous because they work against the interests of the United States. . . .

What makes Americans' attitudes toward secrecy so different? First of all, there is our unique notion of popular sovereignty: Americans believe that authority flows directly from the people to elected officials, and that the elected officials should be continuously accountable to the public. There is very little room in this political universe for the notion of "reason of state": the idea that the state itself has interests that may, on occasion, supersede those of the citizenry. For most Americans, the very notion of "state" is a virtually meaningless abstraction. For even our closest democratic allies, *raison d'etat* is a thoroughly acceptable justification for action.

Our elected officials do not swear an oath to defend the national interest; they swear to uphold the Constitution, which in turn defines the rights of individual citizens. Elsewhere, leaders swear to defend the interests of the nation. We believe that all citizens are politically equal, and therefore entitled to the same information; in most other countries it is taken for granted that the political elite is entitled to know far more than the public at large.

This is not to say that there is not a demand for greater openness in other countries (there often is, and the United States is often held up as a positive example by those fighting against restrictions on the flow of information), nor that there are not Americans concerned about excesses of information-sharing in the United States. But there is no other nation in which the antipathy to secrecy is so strong and the tension between secrecy and openness so intense. Even Great Britain, in so many ways the model for our own political culture, has an Official Secrets Act—and libel legislation—that makes the British government—and media—far more close-mouthed than ours. The willingness of the British government to wage an extensive legal battle against the publication of—and quotation from—*Spycatcher*, a recent memoir by a former British intelligence official, would be unimaginable here.

The Requirements for Secrecy

Good policy depends upon both good information and good judgment, and good judgment is best achieved through candid discussion within the policy-making community. If our policy makers cannot openly speak their minds to one another, their errors in judgment are less likely to be discovered and corrected. And they are not going to speak openly if they fear that their remarks—complete with undeleted expletives—are going to be revealed to the world at large.

The requirement for candor in the policy-making community is often mischaracterized, as if secrecy were inevitably the enemy of open discussion. While that may be true if the insistence upon secrecy is carried to such an extreme that our top policy makers no longer listen to the full range of opinion on the issues, or withhold information to which the public is entitled, it is important not to confuse the two sorts of "openness": one refers to candor, the other to the number of participants. We need candor, but we do not need large meetings or a large number of participants, or full public debate *at every stage* of the policy process, or even of every aspect of the policy.

The matter is clearer still with regard to relations with foreign leaders. In most cultures, it is taken for granted that it is sometimes necessary for leaders to do things which they would not wish to admit in public. Yet it is urgent for the government of the United States to know these leaders' real desires and intentions—as opposed to their public posturing. These real intentions can be discovered only through private conversations—if they are really private. For if the contents of private conversations leak out to the public, foreign leaders will cease to be candid with American officials, to the great detriment of the American national interest.

Some years ago, when the debate over SALT II was raging in Congress, I was present at a discussion between a top European leader and two extremely influential former American officials. The European—who had publicly called for the ratification of the SALT II treaty—was imploring the two Americans to do everything possible to defeat the treaty. One of the Americans wryly said to the European, "and if we succeed, will you not denounce the United States for failing to support the negotiating position of our President, and for being unreliable allies?" "Quite so," replied the European, "but you must try to block the treaty nonetheless."

Americans are often shocked by this sort of hypocrisy, and our instinct is to demand it be exposed. Yet this would only make matters worse, for exposure has the sole effect of depriving us of the honest thoughts of foreign leaders, and their knowledge as well. In the 1970s, following the exposures involving the CIA and White House, foreign leaders concluded that the American government could no longer keep secrets, and thus a considerable volume of knowledge was withheld. Foreign governments shared their knowledge of sensitive subjects like terrorism with a handful of trusted American friends, some in government, some outside. But the American bureaucracy never acquired the information, and thus when people like Secretary of State Alexander Haig—who had learned a lot from the Europeans during his stint as commander of NATO—asked that information on the Soviet role in international terrorism be brought to the attention of Congress and the public in the early 1980s, he discovered that the information was not available inside the American government. This made the quest for a rational counterterrorist policy all the more difficult.

Our own elected officials have reached similar conclusions about the discretion of the bureaucracy, and this has led to the use of outsiders as "back channels" between top American officials and their foreign counterparts. The most famous of these cases is the ABC newsman who was the secret intermediary between President Kennedy and Soviet Communist Party leader Khrushchev during the Cuban Missile Crisis. In such cases, it is convenient to use a single intermediary, without having to go through the usual bureaucracy. In addition to the convenience (decisions can be made by a handful of persons rather than innumerable officials), it is easier to keep the entire affair secret as well. Finally, if our interlocutors attempt to exploit the contacts for their own purposes, an outsider can very easily be denied. It is far more difficult to wash the government's hands of a full-time official. Interestingly enough, in almost all cases these channels function well, with maximum security.

The pattern, then, is the opposite of that claimed by the conventional wisdom: secrecy actually encourages the free flow of information and candid expression, while exposure limits the flow of knowledge and forces top officials to speak guardedly, if at all.

If secrecy is important in the free flow of ideas both within and among governments, it is absolutely vital in the area of intelligence. For there is far more than embarrassment at stake: we are dealing with human lives. In many countries in the world, we badly need people to commit treason in the name of *our* interests, and much of the information we need to defend ourselves can only come from individuals who risk their careers or even their lives to tell us the truth. They are most unlikely to do so if they fear they will be exposed by us; a handful of such cases will deter a far larger number of other people from cooperating with us, both now and in the future. This is precisely the position in which we find ourselves today, for the torrent of revelations that has emerged from the various investigations into the Iran–Contra affair has reinforced the fears of the mid-1970s. As the *New York Times* reported in August 1987, once again our allies restricted the flow of sensitive information to the American government.

The need for secrecy applies to all clandestinely gathered information, whether it involves human sources or more mechanical means of gathering data. Some years ago, the intelligence community was shocked to discover that a low-level CIA employee named William Kampiles had sold to the Soviet KGB (for the paltry sum of $4,000) data about the capabilities of the most secret American spy satellite, the KH-11. The loss of secret information about the KH-11 threw into question the accuracy of the "information" gathered by such satellites, for once the Soviets knew what the KH-11 could "see," they could take steps to deceive it, or to conceal things from its field of vision. And it is not even necessary for information to be given directly into the hands of a hostile intelligence organization for such damage to be done to the national interest: every time a journalist reveals the "discovery" of some kind of clandestine information-gathering program, whether it be a surveillance satellite, electronically equipped aircraft or seafaring vessels, or a working relationship with a foreign government, we pay a heavy price. And, paradoxically, the risk is run whether the journalistic "revelation" is true or false, for it invariably puts the targets of information-gathering operations on greater guard, thus making it more difficult to learn things about them.

The Search for a Workable Policy

Is there some way to balance the demands of a democratic society—above all, the requirement that the public know what leaders are doing—against the imperative of secrecy?

The "solutions" that we have adopted are embodied in two acts of legislation: the Freedom of Information Act, and "oversight." This curious term—which technically means something quite different from the process it is meant to describe—refers to the use of small groups, whether in Congress or in the courts, to monitor the ongoing behavior of the executive branch, in order to ensure that no violations of due process or the intent of Congress occurs. There used to be no less than eight such "oversight committees" in Congress, but in recent years the number has been thankfully reduced to two: the Select Committees on Intelligence in both the House of Representatives and the United States Senate. The "oversight process" is hailed by its defenders as an advance for "openness," but in reality it is simply a method for Congress to expand its territory. The legislators are expected to keep the secrets secret, just as if they were members of the intelligence community. The public only comes to know about the secrets if someone violates his vow to maintain secrecy. Thus, "oversight" merely expands the number of people who are in the know; it does not enhance the public's ability to evaluate the performance of the government.

On the other hand, "oversight" has a limiting effect on the executive branch, for in practice there are certain kinds of secret actions that invariably leak when they are shared with Congress. Some years ago, I heard Bobby Inman—then deputy director of Central Intelligence—argue against a proposed covert action on the grounds that "this sort of thing always leaks from the oversight committees." The proposal was scrapped, just as others were when Senator Joseph Biden threatened to "leak" them if, against his recommendations, they were put into effect. So, by bringing Congress into the act, some secret actions are blocked, and others are sabotaged by leaks from hostile legislators.

In a more serious effort to ensure that the public is reasonably informed, Congress a few years back passed the Freedom of Information Act (FOIA), which makes it possible for interested persons (they need not be citizens of the United States) to demand that the executive branch release previously classified information.

The FOIA is on balance a good thing, although not nearly so good as it ought to be. To the extent that information can be declassified and released to scholars, journalists, and even businessmen, we the people are better off for it. However, the shortcomings of the act are considerable:

(1) The decisions on declassification are sometimes made by people who are not in a position to be able to evaluate the sensitivity of the information. Thus, information damaging to American national security has been released.

(2) The act applies only to the executive branch, not to the judiciary or to the Congress (probably because congressmen wrote the act in the first place). Thus, it is hard to view matters in full context, since in many policy matters the documents from a single branch of government may be incomplete and even badly misleading. If we are concerned about "the public's right to know," we should ensure that the public obtains the fullest possible picture of events. FOIA should apply to Congress as well as to the executive branch.

(3) The declassification procedures are often exasperatingly slow, and reflect the basic principle that it is far more difficult to correct an original error than to avoid the mistake in the first place.

(4) The most devastating consequence of the FOIA is that officials of the executive branch, fearful that anything they write may be dragged into public view at some later date, take care to craft their written documents in such a way that they cannot cause future embarrassment. This means that many of the most crucial decisions cannot be documented—officials either do not write it down, or write it down in a way to place themselves in the most favorable possible light. Thus the historians of the post-FOIA world are going to have an extremely difficult time reconstructing contemporary events. No less a personage than Dr. Henry Kissinger has said that, henceforth, the crucial exchanges between government officials will be spoken—either face-to-face or on the telephone— rather than written.

So once again, efforts to make government more open to public scrutiny end by producing the opposite effect.

The Media

Many violations of secrecy occur through the media, which are used by those who hold the secrets to convey secret information to the public. Since the media play such a central role in the conflict between openness and secrecy, they are invariably at the center of the debate. This is sometimes unfair, for the major burden for keeping secrets should fall upon those who hold them: officials of the American government. And in cases where abuses of power are occurring, there may be no other way to call the practitioners to account, other than "leaking" the facts to the media. But this does not mean that the media should be exempt from accountability, even though some American media spokesmen have made claims that verge on such a position.

In extreme cases, the media have claimed for themselves the rights and privileges of a secret intelligence agency: total protection of sources and methods, a unilateral right to decide whether to pay for information and when or whether to release it, and a refusal to subject their analyses or even claims as to matters of fact to outside authority for evaluation. In essence, such a position amounts to a total right of secrecy for the media, with all the attendant risks of abuse that exist in other institutions. Democracy needs a free press, but it also needs a responsible press. If, as media spokesmen constantly argue, government can only be made accountable if it is open, why should the media—unique among all major American institutions—avoid accountability by being granted the right of total secrecy?

The media respond by stressing the importance of protecting their sources, arguing that if journalists were routinely required to identify them, there would undoubtedly be a shortage of "inside" sources. There is something to this; people are more likely to provide explosive information behind the shield of anonymity than to go "on the record." And an open society needs to encourage people to tell the truth to the public, even when the truth is terribly embarrassing. Thus it is essential that sources be protected whenever possible. But should this protection extend to cases where journalists hold information essential to the identification of criminals? Should it apply to cases where information clearly damaging to national security has been supplied to the media, and through them to our enemies? If, as Justice Holmes put it, a man has no right to cry "fire" in a crowded theater, do the media have the right to jeopardize the national security because sensitive information has been placed in their hands?

If it were agreed that the media do not have an absolute right to reveal secrets, and formalized into law, some of the information currently reaching the public would remain secret. Contrary to the claims of the advocates of ever-greater openness, this might actually help the policy process. For one thing, members of Congress would not be able to blackmail the executive branch by threatening to "leak" information about actions of which they disapprove. If legislators disagreed with proposed actions, they—like others charged with responsibility for foreign policy—would have to make a convincing case within the policy-making fora. Furthermore, without the constant threat of secret information finding its way into the media, candor would increase, thus making it more likely that good policy will emerge. And finally, as foreign governments come to realize that secrets can be kept in the United States, they will share a greater quantity of sensitive information with us, to the greater benefit of our policies.

Veil, by Bob Woodward, shows all the flaws of the current state of affairs. Woodward presents dozens of stories about alleged CIA operations, some true, some false, some half-true, as is inevitable with a person writing under pressure of a deadline about highly complex matters. There is little concern for national security (indeed, if he is telling the truth, he has almost certainly doomed several foreign citizens who made the mistake of cooperating with the government of the United States), and in one major respect the damage exists whether or not the book is accurate. For anyone contemplating bringing sensitive information to an American government official, a book like *Veil* will freeze the blood, since it shows both that American officials talk about subjects that are properly secret, and that American journalism will write about anything, whatever the potential cost of life, limb or the national interest. In my view, such a book ought not to be published.

It will be objected that this is a call for censorship, no matter how limited it may be. This is quite true, but other democracies' experience with the censorship of sensitive national security information should encourage skeptics to conclude that the gains will outweigh the undeniable losses.

Americans are usually surprised to learn that even in countries where the national interest is explicitly held to be superior to the requirements for free speech, journalists often find the arrangements quite satisfactory. I attended a seminar three years ago in Israel on the role of military censorship; the participants, to a man, were highly critical of the Begin government in office at the time, and could have been expected to attack the practice of military censorship. I was amazed to hear that all of them—including the editors of the leading newspapers in the country—agreed that they had never been prevented from publishing a story which they felt urgently needed to be told. In fact, several of them said that they wished the censor had been more active in certain cases, because they had published stories which, in retrospect, they wished they had not.

Israeli journalism is every bit as aggressive and rough-and-tumble as the American variety, and the reaction of the Israelis should give us all pause. On the other hand, there are clearly dangers of excess in the practice of censorship, as I believe has occurred in the British efforts to suppress *Spycatcher*, a book which provides very little new information (most of it had appeared in books published in Great Britain), and reveals nothing of any sensitive activities in the past fifteen years. We need to find a reasonable middle ground between those who think that secrecy is solely the responsibility of the government (and hence the media alone should decide whether to publish or broadcast anything that comes into their possession), and those who believe that anything "classified" should remain out of public sight.

Towards a Fair Balance

The demands of secrecy versus openness bring into conflict two legitimate, but opposed interests. Good policy, good relations and successful operations all require at least a certain degree of secrecy, and it will not do for the advocates of openness to demand that all or even most classified information become public knowledge. On the other hand, the public is entitled to reasonably complete information.

The ideal solution is for the executive branch to explain its policies, and the thinking that went into their formulation, as fully as it possibly can, so that the public can at least follow the analytical process. No one can reasonably demand that the government share its secrets with the world at large, but it is certainly reasonable to expect our leaders to explain to us what they are doing, and (to the extent possible) why. Thus, while the public is not entitled to know what foreign leaders said to our officials in private conversations, our top policy makers should be able to give the American public the "lessons learned" from such conversations. The same principle applies to other areas where secret information plays a role in policy: the secrets should remain secret, but the consequences of the secrets should be shared.

To be sure, this ideal is far more easily stated than practiced, for even with the best will in the world, governments must sometimes withhold information from the public. But this almost always attaches to operations, and not to overall policy. The exception to this rule is the case of a secret operation, which, if successful, would lead to a substantive shift in overall policy, as in the case of the secret diplomacy that led to Nixon's démarche to the People's Republic of China. Since most Americans approve of the results of the secret diplomacy, there has been little criticism of the way in which it was conducted. But many of the stinging attacks that have been directed at Reagan's handling of the Iran–Contra initiatives can just as easily be aimed at Nixon and Kissinger for the China policy, or, for that matter, at Roosevelt for his covert assistance to Great Britain in 1939–41. Both were in conflict with the publicly stated objectives of American foreign policy; both were carried out behind the backs of Congress. The difference between these initiatives and the Reagan debacle is that they achieved their objectives before they were discovered. Here there is no formula for salvation: successes are applauded, and failures condemned, and that is that. But in both the Nixon and the Roosevelt cases, had the policy been made public at the time it was being conducted, the national outcry would have been deafening, and the policy would have been wrecked. Would Messrs. Inouye and Hamilton retroactively approve a full investigation into both affairs, complete with public exposure of the role of foreign agents (like Intrepid) and private American citizens in the operations? Would Mr. Hamilton have lectured FDR about the superiority of publicly debated policy over secret operations, when it is quite likely Great Britain would have foundered without the secret American support?

Whatever the evaluation of a given policy, there is nothing to be said for the shocking disclosure of secrets that has accompanied the debate and investigations. Much has been made about the conflict between Congress and the executive branch during the Iran–Contra hearings, but in fairness to the legislators it must be said that by far the greater leakage of secrets has come from the executive branch. From the very beginning, the White House, the State Department and the CIA have shown a remarkable insensitivity to the requirements of secrecy. The names of sensitive foreign contacts have been revealed, the formats of secret American documents (such as presidential "findings") have been made public (thereby enabling the KGB to make better forgeries), methods and names of secret communications have been published, and the inner workings of the intelligence community have been held up for public examination. In short, those who wish to obtain our secrets have been provided with many of them, and given a road map to those they may wish to acquire in the future. While much of this information has emerged from the testimony, depositions and documentation released by the various investigatory committees of Congress, the bulk of it was unilaterally made available by the White House, and much was published by the Tower Commission, which was appointed by the President.

Some feeble case might be made for the astonishing refusal of the White House to assert any degree of "executive privilege" in this matter (although those foreigners who cooperated with us in the belief we would never reveal their identities would no doubt disagree), there is even less to be said for the wholesale delivery of secret documents to the "independent counsel," Judge Walsh. The members of his staff obtained instant clearances, and could not have received the sort of exhaustive background investigations to which the authors of the secret documents were subjected. Unlike the officials of the government itself, the Walsh people were not required to demonstrate a valid "need to know" the contents of, for example, all of the NSC documents concerning international terrorism and the steps taken by this country to combat it. There are many foreign governments who would love to know the contents of those documents; have steps been taken to ensure the full security of the Walsh operation? One can only say, on the basis of a few trips to their offices, that there is little sign of thoroughgoing physical security. But that is not the central issue here; the point is that the executive branch quite quickly abandoned the fight to keep its secrets secret; thereafter, many national secrets were in the hands of a variety of people, many of whom were reading their first secret document. Thus did the Reagan administration demonstrate its lack of seriousness in the defense of its own secrets?

If there is to be any hope for a reasonable approach to the question of secrecy, the executive branch will have to do far better. It must fight for the right to retain secrets, at the same time that it shows greater sensitivity to the public's right to be informed about the basic elements in our foreign policy. It must initiate the national debate on the need to protect secrets, including some measures to call the media to greater accountability. And it must engage the Congress, the courts and the media in such a way as to produce a workable compromise between the two legitimate demands—for secrecy and openness—that are today so violently in conflict in our society. Since the Reagan administration clearly lacked the vision and the will to embark on such a challenging enterprise, we can only hope that its successor will be capable of doing so.

Note

1. This essay first appeared in *The National Interest* 10 (Winter 1987–88); it is reprinted with permission.

Part III

■

Do The Media Matter?

9

The News Media and National Security

Richard R. Burt

The public debate over national security has become more compli- cated and more important. Yet the media have failed to keep pace in explaining defense and arms control issues to a confused Ameri- can public. Indeed, the performance of the press and broadcast jour- nalism in reporting and analyzing these issues is *one* reason why the national security debate in the United States (and the West more broadly) has become increasingly chaotic, simplistic and ill-informed.

This is a provocative thesis and some qualifications are in order. The media, like other major institutions in American society, not only effect change but also reflect broader cultural and political trends. Thus the decline in the quality and coherence of the media's treat- ment of national security must first of all be seen against the back- drop of more general developments within the American political sys- tem, U.S. foreign policy and the media themselves.

One important change, which has been noted by political analysts ranging from Pat Cadell to Lee Atwater, is the growth of populism in American politics over the last two decades. This has not only meant that the "smoke-filled room" has been overtaken by primary elections and techniques of mass advertising, but that political issues themselves have been popularized with the paradoxical and perni- cious result that the influence of small, but motivated interest groups has grown.

The popularization of politics has had an important impact on the national security debate. Traditionally, core U.S. national security questions—nuclear doctrine and deployments, arms control goals and objectives—were addressed among a limited community of government officials, interested politicians and academic think-tankers. This community has grown larger, with the profusion of new think tanks and the acquisition by many congressmen of their own national security advisers. And, just as national political parties have steadily lost power in a populist period of American politics, so has the traditional American national security community. The result has been a decline in understanding and support among Western publics for concepts like extended deterrence and their replacement with more popular, anti-nuclear solutions ranging from the freeze on the left to a "Space Shield" on the right.

The debate in recent years over "strategic defense" illustrates the point. Since the 1960s, the national security community has addressed the pros and cons of ballistic missile defense, including its technical feasibility, its impact on deterrence and the deeper problems of what constitutes adequate deterrence. The 1969–70 Senate debate over ABM deployment with its extensive and thoughtful testimony from analysts on both sides of the issue, remains to this day the classic exposition of the issue. The debate over the Strategic Defense Initiative has had none of the rigor, coherence or clarity of these deliberations. Instead, it has largely degenerated into a popularized contest between interest groups and passionate minorities who have depicted SDI, on the one hand, as the nation's only chance to escape the threat of nuclear devastation or, on the other, a sure way to make such devastation possible. Political action committees espousing one or another of these points of view have been formed, films have been produced and pedalled to local TV stations, and ardent speakers have criss-crossed the country with their emotional and simplistic messages.

These groups have clout. In the run-up to the Iowa Caucus, for example, an anti-SDI group, STARPAC, succeeded in getting most Democratic presidential candidates to endorse a platform that not only opposed SDI research, but the MX, the Midgetman, the Trident II and all testing of ballistic missiles! It is not surprising that the media have reflected the simplistic public debate over SDI while passing over a key question of whether, in the light of the Soviet build-up of prompt, hard-target kill capability, the acquisition by the United States of some level of strategic defense would bolster deterrence.

The impact of populism on the media's coverage of national security is reinforced (and related to) another long-term development: the failure of the United States in the postwar era, but especially after the turmoil of Vietnam, to establish either a durable consensus over strategy toward the Soviet Union or a conception of U.S. commitments and presence abroad. In the case of the Soviet Union, American policy and public opinion has oscillated sharply between undue optimism and unwarranted pessimism. In the past fifteen years, we have seen the grandiose hopes for U.S.-Soviet détente in the early 1970s replaced by growing fears of Soviet military dominance which, in turn, have now been replaced by "Gorbomania."

Our conspicuous failure to construct a policy framework able to accommodate U.S.–Soviet competition and limited cooperation has led the media to exaggerate every twist and turn in the relationship. The same lack of constancy can be seen in the area of U.S. commitments abroad. There is clearly a growing necessity for the United States, in a resource-constrained era, to engage in a "burden-sharing" dialogue with key allies. But this important issue has been distorted by neo-isolationists and unilateralists on both ends of the political spectrum. In 1988 the result, again, was that a calm assessment of a substantial and credible U.S. posture abroad was overshadowed in the media by an emotional, shallow electioneering featuring the presidential candidate warning of "American blood in the Persian Gulf" and congressmen smashing Toshiba ghetto-blasters on the steps of the Capitol.

Broader changes within the "media culture" of the United States have also had an adverse impact on the serious coverage of national security. Television has contributed to a decline in the attention span of viewers, especially young people. Despite the profusion of news programming on television, the quality and comprehensiveness of national security coverage has declined. The in-depth documentary, pioneered by CBS during the Murrow–Friendly era, has all but disappeared, replaced by short, snappy reports on breakfast television. The traditional Sunday interview programs, which gave officials and reporters time to explore issues, have evolved into "mediagenic" confrontations in which the views and antics of news entertainers, like Sam Donaldson, are thought to be more interesting than the officials and experts they interview. The competition created by syndicated and cable news programming has probably accelerated the merger of news and entertainment on television. "The McLaughlin Group" and "Crossfire," with their "inside baseball" gossip, are enjoyable programs, but they contribute little to a real understanding of SDI, U.S. policy in Central America, or the future of the strategic triad.

As TV has emerged as the main source of news for most people, newspapers have had to hustle to redefine their role. Some changes have been positive—for example, the growth of commentary and analysis in newspapers as exemplified by the op-ed page. Generally, however, the trend has been toward "McNews" coverage epitomized by *USA Today*: a heavy emphasis on leisure, sports, and entertainment with hard news boiled down to capsule coverage. Worse, the "McNews" phenomenon has affected all newspapers and magazines, including the most serious. During my tenure at the *New York Times*, for example, the space allocated for so-called hard news reporting and analysis shrunk substantially with the decision to move the paper's layout from eight columns per page to six (to make the paper more "readable") and, more importantly, to free up space for special sections covering lifestyle, sports, food and recreation.[1]

These broad trends in American politics and the media help explain why coverage of national security issues has become more superficial, trivial, and sensational. But they don't tell the whole story. Individual news organizations and the reporters, editors, and managers that comprise these organizations are also responsible. Reporters and editors, individually and as a group, need to address what might be termed shortcomings of "tradecraft" in covering national security.

Lack of Substantive Expertise

Although it is true that there are examples in which individuals with some expertise in security and arms control issues have been recruited to cover these topics, the fact remains that the large majority of reporters who report on these issues do not possess the background to write or speak coherently and authoritatively. Too often, reporters lack the necessary conceptual and historical framework to fully understand events and place them in the proper context.

Examples of this are almost too numerous to cite. There is, for instance, a journalistic "crisis industry" in covering developments within the Atlantic Alliance. Almost any time that differences emerge within NATO, journalists on both sides of the Atlantic seem impelled to suggest that a crisis is at hand and it could threaten the very underpinnings of the European–American relationship. Thus, when many Europeans expressed misgivings over the 1986 American raid on Libya, it was reported several times in both the U.S. and the European press that this was "the worst crisis in the history of the Alliance." Not only is this short-lived dispute hardly remembered today, but its coverage at the time seemed oblivious to the long history of European–American differences over the use of force in the Third World (Suez, Vietnam, Iran, and Afghanistan). There appeared moreover, to be little understanding that as important as these differences over "out-of-area" contingencies are, they must be seen in the context of a long-standing consensus within NATO over its core strategy of deterring aggression in Europe.

The media's treatment of the infamous "neutron bomb" is another example. The issue was made to hinge not on whether the deployment of a more discriminate nuclear weapon would or would not have enhanced NATO's strategy of flexible response (although I think it would have). The media never discussed the issue in these terms. Instead, the press focused on the incorrect claim that the weapon destroyed people, not things, and thus was the ultimate "capitalist" weapon. Perhaps the height of alarmist, superficial coverage was achieved by the *Washington Post*, which, in an editorial, called the weapon the "killer warhead," as though the tens of thousands of other nuclear and conventional munitions then in the U.S. inventory lacked this attribute.

Coverage of the MX and the 600-ship navy debates has also had a ludicrous quality. The MX issue was mainly presented in terms of whether a new, more capable missile should be procured. The desirability of maintaining the strategic triad and enhancing U.S. countermilitary strategic capability and the MX's relation to these issues were not explored. In the 600-ship navy debate, coverage focused mainly on the cost involved and not on the question of naval roles and missions, including the doctrinal issue of "horizontal escalation."

Although it is probably true that there has been a gradual increase in overall expertise on national security within the media as a whole, the people who have studied and followed security issues most closely are often not those who get to report on important developments. By this I mean that the small cadre of specialists who are able to prepare analytical "think" pieces are very rarely the journalists who are actually assigned to cover newsmaking events. It is the White House correspondent who covers the most important stories, the Reykjavík summit, for example, or President Reagan's March 1983 SDI speech.[2]

The effort to achieve greater expertise must contend with a countervailing tendency in journalism—the declining, but still entrenched view that the best reporters are "jacks of all trades." There is still a strong belief on the part of editors that the "tradecraft" skills of reporting take precedence over subject-specific expertise or, as one editor told me years ago, "If you know how to cover a major fire, you can cover anything." In fact, there is a tendency for editors as well as fellow journalists to be skeptical of a colleague with special expertise on the grounds that he or she has somehow been coopted by the people or institutions they are assigned to cover. Thus, sheer ignorance often masquerades as "professional distance."

Herd Journalism and Competition

It is difficult for non-journalists to understand the terrific competitive pressures of journalism, especially in Washington. The competition, in my view, is responsible for the now-familiar phenomenon of herd journalism: the tendency of the media to cover the same events in much the same way, ignoring other developments and other issues. At the White House, the State Department, and other departments, the press corps often attempts to decide in collective fashion what the "story" of the day will be. The reason, of course, is that reporters do not want to be caught off guard (and thus have an angry editor on the phone) when a colleague suddenly develops a story that they missed. It is safer to agree in advance what the story is and run with the herd.

Ironically, herd journalism offers government spokesmen enhanced opportunities to define the news by steering them toward the story of the day. More important, it means that many important stories never get covered. It also leads to a "sequential" approach to the news—a stream of different stories from day to day and week to week, reported without context and perspective. The consequence is that some stories, such as the "nuclear winter" debate, are reported only briefly and dropped. Other stories, like deployment of INF and arms control, are reported only in pieces, so that it is difficult for the public to establish a connection between NATO's 1979 double-track decision, the actual deployment of missiles in 1983, and the achievement of an agreement four years later.

Scoop Journalism

The competitive pressure of Washington journalism means that "scoops" take precedence over policy analysis. This leads to several problems. First, the competitive environment promotes leaks that can damage sensitive operations and negotiations with friends and adversaries. Simply put, there is information that U.S. officials should not divulge to the press and if it is divulged, should not be published. Revelations about U.S. clandestine operations are an example. But it is extremely difficult to dissuade a news organization from running with a juicy news leak.

Second, many scoops are not entirely accurate, but because they pertain to sensitive policy or intelligence issues, it is difficult, if not impossible, to set the record straight. As a State Department official in the early 1980s, I read many accounts in the press of National Security Council meetings which bore little or no relation to what had actually transpired.[3] But for obvious reasons, there was little the administration could do to set the record straight. Third, the "scoop mentality" of many reporters and editors can distort the very definition of news. The fact that some piece of information is "exclusive" sometimes seems of greater importance than the content of the information itself. During the Nixon–Ford and Carter eras, for example, the press placed a great premium on finding out the details of U.S. negotiating positions at SALT and the developments within the negotiations themselves, which were closely held. The Reagan administration, on the other hand, has tended to take a more public position on arms control developments, to the point of unveiling U.S. positions in presidential speeches and briefing reporters in detail afterward. Not surprisingly there was far greater press interest in the nuances of U.S. positions when that information was more difficult to obtain than at present.

Finally, scoops have a perverse impact on how the government itself handles information and makes sensitive information available. As was the case in earlier administrations, scoop journalism and the threat of leaks led the Reagan administration to progressively narrow the circle of people engaged in decision making and analysis. Thus issues that were thrashed out by the full National Security Council in 1981 were later decided in much smaller National Security Planning Groups. This reduced the potential for leaks, but it also reduced the diversity of opinion and the amount of special expertise that could be brought to bear on a problem. This certainly is one of the roots of the Iran–Contra affair.

The "People Magazine" Approach to National Security

Perhaps with the "lessons" of Watergate beginning to fade, there has been a decline in scoop journalism. But there is a danger that it will be replaced by a *People Magazine* approach focusing on personalities and bureaucratic in-fighting while ignoring the substance of policy issues. There has always been a fascination with going behind-the-scenes in covering Washington, and such reporting is often helpful in understanding how and why decisions are made. Many of the "tick-tock" pieces describing the formulation of President Reagan's March 1983 SDI address were useful in portraying decision making within the administration. But the growing emphasis on highlighting personal and institutional conflict in Washington reporting often means that real issues are forgotten.

The advantages and limitations of this approach are tellingly revealed in Strobe Talbott's two books (*End Game* and *Deadly Gambits*) and his many *Time* magazine pieces on U.S.–Soviet arms control negotiations during the 1970s and 1980s. Talbott's earlier work is remarkably thorough and well-researched. And it is, in the main, accurate. But there is something missing. By boiling down this immensely complex experience to tales of individual egos and bureaucratic in-fighting, the opportunity to explore the larger lessons of what arms control did and did not accomplish during this period are lost. Talbott's most recent arms control work—*The Master of the Game*, a description and analysis of Paul Nitze's career and views—makes up for these shortcomings. While maintaining a bureaucratic focus, it does provide a thoughtful, analytical context for judging the contribution that arms control can make to national security.

Being There

Both "scoop" and "People Magazine" coverage of national security are merely reflections of the growing role of the media and their ability to achieve greater access. The news media today are larger; they can communicate more information more quickly; and people and institutions, here and abroad, are ready and able to provide them with more information. These trends have generally positive implications for individual Americans and the United States as a whole, but they do raise difficult questions in the area of national security.

One of these issues has already been alluded to: Where should the line be drawn between press freedom and the protection of sensitive national security material? Since the publication of the *Pentagon Papers*, most news organizations have felt free, on most occasions, to report whatever information they were able to obtain. Moreover, they have criticized government efforts, such as giving lie-detector tests to suspended leakers, to stem the flow of classified information. Is this a tenable position over the long-term? Should *The Nation* be permitted to publish technical aspects pertaining to the assembly of weapons? Should Bob Woodward, as he did in *Veil*, report that former Egyptian President Anwar Sadat, former El Salvadoran President José Napoleón Duarte, and the current Prime Minister of Dominica, Eugenia Charles, served as CIA "assets"? Should newspaper reporters provide their readers detailed information on U.S. intelligence capabilities used for arms control verification?

Equally difficult questions are raised by press coverage of the use of U.S. military force. There is now a voluminous library on the role of the news media in the Vietnam conflict in shaping (or misshaping) U.S. perceptions of the war. One question, posed by Peter Braestrup in *Big Story*, is whether the news media, particularly television, are capable in complex and confused combat situations of providing the *real* story. Braestrup details how the Tet offensive was universally depicted as a major American military debacle when, in reality, it resulted in a U.S. victory. There is a saying in U.S. government circles that when an international crisis breaks out, "the first reports are always wrong." But these are often the only reports many people read.

Another question is whether the news media should always and in all circumstances be permitted to cover, first-hand, the use of U.S. military force. Obviously, there are circumstances in which even the media respects the right of U.S. military secrecy. No one (to my knowledge) has argued that reporters should have been invited along to cover the ill-fated U.S. hostage rescue mission in Iran. But when the Reagan administration, following Mrs. Thatcher's lead in the Falklands, shut reporters out of the early phases of the Grenada action, there was a terrific hue and cry.

The British, of course, have a very different tradition in handling (and muzzling) the press, but British military history does raise intriguing questions. British World War II archives released in recent years reveal that the evacuation from Dunkirk in 1940 was in many respects a sorry operation. Not only did British troops on the beach fire on their French allies to prevent them from joining in the evacuation, but Churchill, to the last minute, denied to the French that an evacuation was even contemplated. With the help of the BBC, the government was successful in depicting the evacuation as a magnificient rescue operation undertaken by a flotilla of private boats, manned by eager sailors. In fact, many British boat owners refused to make the voyage and had their ships commandeered. It is understandable that Churchill and his colleagues, in this moment of crisis, needed to construct the Dunkirk "myth." The interesting question, however, is what would have been the impact on British morale and the course of World War II had there been TV crews on the beach? Might Dunkirk have had the same effect as the Tet offensive?

Government by Press Release

Perhaps one of the most interesting issues flowing from the news media's greater role and access is the impact this has on national security decision making itself. One thing is clear: U.S. officials spend far more time worrying about what the news media is saying about them and their decisions than is commonly understood by either the public or the media themselves. Early morning staff meetings in government departments focus as much on press problems as "real" problems; as much on how to depict a policy to the press as on what policy should be in the first place. And the higher one goes within the bureaucracy, the more time is devoted to press "spin control" and damage-limitation.

The result is that public affairs staffs have grown and spokesmen wield greater influence. "Good" news is released to coincide with the evening news shows, while the "bad" news dribbles out late Friday night or over a holiday weekend. Abroad, U.S. efforts to influence foreign press have been stepped up, and at home a large "public diplomacy" bureaucracy has come into being, which not only draws on the United States Information Agency, but also the State Department, the Pentagon, the intelligence agencies, and the NSC staff. In the media age, these steps are not only inevitable, they are useful. But there is a danger of making policy exclusively through press release, of basing decisions on the arguments of media specialists rather than those of policy analysts. Thus, the next step from a news media that simplifies complex issues like SDI or MX deployment could be a government (the executive branch and the Congress alike) that does the same.

The Impact of Television

I have already referred to the possible role of television in reshaping the national security debate—how the TV generation's shortened attention span and the visual requirements of the medium can contribute to the trivialization of news. But the news media, especially television, creates news itself. Edward R. Murrow's famous "See It Now" broadcast in which he excoriated Joseph McCarthy is considered to have constituted the turning-point in the controversial senator's career. But in more recent years, television's ability to generate news events has depended less on its persuasive powers and more on its entertainment value.

In 1983, as the nuclear freeze movement approached its height in the United States and protesters marched against INF deployment in Europe, the movie *The Day After* was aired. This was truly a modern-day media event, with news organizations covering the controversy created by a second-rate, made-for-TV movie. No doubt the producers believed they were making an important statement about the dangers associated with the arms race. This is certainly how the news media described the program. But the ultimate impact of the program was probably different.

In the United States, after receiving considerable hype, *The Day After* was quickly forgotten within policy circles in Washington. In Europe and particularly West Germany, where it was shown many times, it probably bolstered the determination of the peace movement. Among the American public, the program, in providing a highly emotional and inaccurate picture of how nuclear conflict could start and what its consequences would be, contributed to a growing antinuclear bias which complicates the task of maintaining support for deterrence.

Some Proposals

Because many of the problems I have outlined here reflect deeper trends within the news media, government and U.S. society, it is difficult to suggest any comprehensive solutions. Indeed, it is questionable whether any solutions are desirable. While the multifaceted "information revolution" does pose difficulties for addressing public policy issues in a sober and responsible way, it also, over the long term, might contribute to U.S. security because of the even greater challenges it poses for more closed societies like the Soviet Union.

Nevertheless, the news media, whether they like it or not, have become a participant in national security decision making and we therefore have the right to demand improved performance on their part. The following suggestions are offered with this in mind.

First, news organizations and individual journalists should work to improve their understanding of national security problems. There are a number of obvious ways this can be done, ranging from making an effort to recruit reporters with specialized knowledge in this area, as the *New York Times* has done, to making it possible for nonspecialists to acquire greater expertise. The John F. Kennedy School of Government at Harvard has an international security program for mid-career government officials. Why not expand this program and others like it to accommodate several reporters? Government can also play a helpful role. In the Reagan administration, the Arms Control and Disarmament Agency (ACDA) sponsored a weekend seminar away from Washington which permitted senior officials to talk and mingle with reporters who regularly cover arms control. These seminars should be institutionalized and other agencies should follow ACDA's lead. The State Department could convene conferences on the Soviet Union or Central America, for example, while the Pentagon could hold retreats with reporters on the defense budget and the military balance.

But the government should also examine its own methods of talking to the press. In my view, the era of the spokesman is waning. While public affairs officials will still be necessary, the best spokesmen on national security are the policy making officials themselves, from the President and the secretaries of state and defense on down. This does not mean that TV anchormen should be chosen to fill these jobs (although it does not hurt to have a former actor as President). It means that senior- and middle-level officials must become more conversant with the media and how to use them. This must go beyond knowing what "deep background" means to actually understanding how to present complicated problems coherently and intelligibly, thus avoiding distortions and simplifications. In the media age, nearly every national security official is likely, at one time or another, to appear on television. It is surprising how many are totally unprepared to do so. While Strobe Talbott in *Deadly Gambits* was most impressed with Richard Perle's bureaucratic skills, I am more dazzled by his mastery of television. In other words, my advice to national security officials about television is "if you can't beat 'em (and we can't), join 'em."

I have the same advice for think tanks, universities and foundations. The United States is almost unique in having a large "private sector" in the national security field. Since the foundation of the RAND Corporation in the 1950s, most of the original contributions to thinking about defense and arms control have come from this sector. But it, too, must adjust to the media age. It is ironic that lobbying groups, like the Arms Control Association or the Heritage Foundation, that do the least in-depth work on national security issues are the most successful in getting their views across to the press. While more research-oriented institutions may think it unseemly to work closely with the press, this is a mistake. I am glad to see that at least some institutions recognize this. Under the leadership of Peter Tarnoff, for example, the Council on Foreign Relations has begun a series of projects designed to increase the Council's activities in television.

Finally, there is the troubling question of leaks and the news media's competitive incentives to run with them. The government can help with this problem by punishing those leakers it manages to catch, but this is hardly the answer. The news media must recognize their responsibility in this area. An Israeli-style censorship system is out of the question, but a measure of self-policing might be possible. I doubt that major news outlets would participate in some form of press council arrangement which would comment on whether previously published reports had damaged national security, but the idea could at least be discussed. Another idea would be for news organizations to hire former senior officials as consultants for their expert advice on whether and how to report potentially sensitive stories. Networks and newspapers now retain legal consultants to advise them on potentially libelous reports. And while the national security area is much less clear cut, the potential damage is greater. As a former reporter, even these modest steps make me uncomfortable. But as somebody once said, the First Amendment is not a suicide pact.

Notes

1. My predecessor at the *Times*, Les Gelb, tells me that his reports averaged roughly 1,200 words. When I came to the *Times*, I was told to keep an average story to about 900 words. By the time I left, reporters were urged to keep their pieces below 750 words.

2. My own experience is instructive here. Although I covered, almost continuously, the negotiations leading to the SALT II treaty for the *Times*, I was not permitted to cover or even attend the 1979 Carter–Brezhnev summit in Vienna. The reason was that the other correspondents, especially at the State Department and the White House, had stronger "turf" claims to cover the event.

3. Earlier, as a journalist, I found that much of the "leaked" information I received was essentially disinformation: inaccurate information provided by axe-grinding and disgruntled officials designed to distort, undermine, and change a real decision that had been taken.

10
Woefully Inadequate: The Press's Handling of Arms Control

Kenneth L. Adelman

George F. Kennan correctly told how the press furnishes "hasty, disjointed and staccato" reports—what he called "offerings"—on foreign affairs. The "low educational level" of most reporters, he added, inclines them towards "overdramatization" and "overcoverage of the peregrinations and utterances of senior figures and undercoverage of the deeper trends of international life."

Nowhere does this critique cut more sharply than in arms control. Reporters, like most Americans, tremble at the mere prospect of sorting out the intricacies of nuclear weaponry—submarine-launched cruise and ballistic missiles, SS-18s, Backfires, circular error probabilities, and so on. It is tough to understand all this and tougher yet to put it into intelligible English for the average—even the average educated—reader. Some reporters succeed in doing so, but the vast majority do not. To paraphrase Dr. Johnson, for the press to report so often and at such length on arms control is like a dog walking on his hind legs—it is not done well, but you are surprised to find it done at all.

Yet it is done. And done. Reams of copy in the print media; endless specials and Sunday interviews in the electronic media. The amount of coverage on arms control is astonishing; its quality is shocking.

Media-Tending and Media-Pandering

Top administration officials—of any administration, on any key topic—devote up to one third of their time on media affairs. In part, this helps educate the public and moves public opinion towards the administration's views.

And, in part, this helps feed egos. Most presidential appointees relish becoming a "public figure"—one of the few benefits government or, more accurately, reporters can bestow. Sidling up to journalists helps when they write a personality profile and when they file daily copy highlighting the official's role as "a big player."

This game is fueled by that most corroding of Washington institutions, press clips. Each morning each government agency photocopies articles from major newspapers on its work of subject matter. The Pentagon runs a staggering 5,000 copies of its "early bird" morning clips and another 5,000 of an afternoon edition with still more articles from yet more newspapers in still more parts of the country.

During my tenure, ACDA's clips were smaller, both in pages and number of copies, but no less destructive. For the clips helped fashion the agency's agenda for at least every morning, if not the entire day. They prod otherwise groggy bureaucrats to scramble for explanations—how some fresh disaster could ever have happened, what the boss should say about some burning new issue they never addressed before.

Just as damaging is their effect on the boss, who comes to believe that his or her agency's service and problems are forefront on the minds of every American. Reading fifteen to twenty pages of arms control articles day after day—unrelieved by other sports or entertainment news or underwear ads (all carried in normal newspapers)—can convince the most balanced of individuals that Americans everywhere are pondering SLCM verification over breakfast that morning.

Press Deficiencies

Thus for "the good guys" in government. Now on to a critique of the working press. (Note: In case you missed it, "working press" excludes columnists who, by this author's definitions, are very much "good guys.") Let me count the ways the working press mishandles arms control issues. Five are particularly egregious.

1. *The Scoop is All:* Leaks are treated as bigger news than straight news. What the government does not announce gets more prominent play than what it does announce.

For example, the press buzzed for months after the October 1986 Reykjavík summit about how President Reagan surprised the world by proposing to eliminate all ballistic missiles. He had proposed such a thing (which, indeed, was unfortunate—but that is a tale for another day), yet it should not have come as any surprise. A month before the summit Reagan had proposed the same idea in his address to the United Nations General Assembly.

The lesson seems evident: the best way to keep an arms control proposal secret is to have the President announce it before the U.N. in a televised address. The worst way is to have negotiators describe it before the Soviets in the private negotiations. To be fair (for a moment), the U.N. address made the notion seem indefinite in time and scope; the Reykjavík offer made it more concrete and part of a grander discourse on the elimination of all nuclear weapons, which set off alarm bells across America and Europe. Still, the public was not prepared for the "zero ballistic missiles" idea, however vague it was originally, so it came as more of a shock than was necessary.

Another, less important but more evident, example occurred during the heated SALT II debate of 1986. A prominent story by Walter Pincus in the *Washington Post* (April 19) tells of unnamed sources reporting that the President had tentatively decided to move to "put the United States in technical violation of...SALT II for the first time." Three days later, another *Post* story, coauthored by Pincus, tells of the United States making moves "to stay within the SALT II treaty limits." The first story, the scoop, was given front page coverage; it was wrong. The second story, the factual one, was relegated to page A-20, amidst grocery ads; it was correct.

2. *Any Proposal Gets Big Play:* A new Soviet arms offer, or even the possibility of one, gets top billing—regardless of its worth, regardless of its likelihood to lead to a safer world. News of more Soviet military aid to Nicaragua or Angola or Vietnam, news of VOA broadcasts into the Soviet Union or Radio Free Liberty into Eastern Europe—all this is relegated to the back pages, even though it has much more to do with world peace.

This syndrome is most evident during the press's pre-summit foreplay. Then, the U.S.-Soviet relationship gets covered as if it revolves almost exclusively around arms control. There ensues an endless succession of stories pondering whether the Soviets would or would not propose such-and-such, causing the U.S. negotiators to counter with such-and-such, to which the Soviets would probably react with a such-and-such trump.

This scene was played out with Cecil B. De Mille grandeur before the first Reagan–Gorbachev summit in November 1985. A researcher scanning the front pages of the *Post* during the two weeks before that meeting would be surprised at the number of such stories. None of the speculation was based in fact. None of it happened. None of it would have mattered much even if it had been true and happened.

The press is forever addressing one question in this field: Will we have an arms control accord to sign at this summit, or at least at next summit? It is like a reporter asking a senator: Will you have a bill to sign before the recess? The real question is not whether there will be a bill, but what kind of bill? With what intended effect? With what unintended effect? These questions are typical of the energetic reporting which is standard for Capitol Hill reporters; this is the kind of reporting which is rare of arms control reporters.

Instead the summit-time gaggle is fixated on arms control, up or down? Too little on progress on regional issues, the real pathway to any U.S.–Soviet confrontation, which in turn is the pathway to any conceivable nuclear exchange.

In a nutshell, the stampeding herd of the working press inverts its priorities of what is most important to peace and freedom. And getting such priorities right is, after all, the press's prime responsibility.

3. *The Historical Memory Gap:* The press seldom, if ever, furnishes a historical context for its stories. With most stories, this is tolerable. But with arms control stories, it is not. For this allows the Soviets to sell the same proposals time and again without the American people being told that the proposals are nothing more than warmed-over mush.

The clearest example of this failing occurred on January 15, 1986, when Gorbachev made his "mega-proposal"—the one advocating the total elimination of all nuclear weapons in three stages by the turn of the century. This offer received blaring headlines around the world, as one could have expected knowing the "any-proposal-gets-big-play" syndrome described above.

Yet Gorbachev's proposal was nearly identical to Nikita Khrushchev's September 1959 U.N. "mega-proposal" that also advocated the total elimination of all nuclear weapons, and ultimately all conventional and chemical weapons, in three stages. Though Gorbachev's plan was to be implemented over fifteen years, Khrushchev, who was either more ambitious or less honest, needed only a decade. (Ironically, Khrushchev's proposal would have had its most significant impact in 1962, just as he was actually sneaking missiles into Cuba.)

Despite the near identity of the two proposals—even the wording of key passages was similar—none of the press referred to Khrushchev's previous offer. More telling was the attendant press response to Gorbachev's offer: the enthusiasm for the more recent proposal contrasted sharply with the glacial indifference and hostility that greeted Khrushchev's.

A quarter century ago, *Time* carried a photograph of the Soviet leader with the caption "Taking the World for a Moron." The 1986 *Time* featured a flattering photo of the new Soviet leader with the caption: "Gorbachev: Disarming Proposal." *Time's* 1959 article was unabashedly critical:

> The response in the U.N. hall to Khrushchev's oratorical whopper was stunned silence, broken only once or twice by incredulous laughter from the press gallery.... The fact remained that Nikita's demand for total disarmament was so absurd and impractical as to be insulting.

This article concluded on an even more downbeat note:

> A grandstand display, capitalizing mercilessly on the lurking fear of nuclear holocaust, Khrushchev's brash maneuver might win him some propaganda advantage with plain people around the world.... But in blasting off so crudely from his U.N. launching pad, Nikita had displayed a brute cynicism that repelled responsible statesmen everywhere. 'It sounds so easy,' said an Asian delegate to the U.N., 'I think he must take us for morons.'

Time's 1986 article treated a remarkably similar speech rather kindly in an article entitled "A Farewell to Arms," calling it "a bold schedule for making the world nuclear-free." Sure it had some flaws, but was still a "tantalizing mixture of the old and the new."

Time of 1986 made no mention "of the old," as did *Time* in 1959.
Then, when folks cared more about history, *Time* told how Khrushchev "had only refurbished an old Soviet plan for total disarmament
that Russia's late Maxim Litvinoff first proposed in 1927" and, to
whack a bad idea once more, featured a separate box mocking even
that plan.

In the 1986 article, the Gorbachev plan was described as a "sweeping and unexpected new arms control proposal [which] startled. . .offi-
cial Washington. For all its ambiguities and propagandist sweep, the
plan hints at enough concessions to spur serious negotiating."

Actually, it spurred nothing of the kind. Within days it was summarily brushed aside by the U.S. negotiators. Within weeks, it was
forgotten by the Soviet negotiators. It has since dropped into the
historical memory-hole, there to lie until resurrected and sprung on
an unsuspecting world as new and intriguing a few years from now.

This lack of perspective and even short-term memory sometimes
afflicts the same reporter on the same issue. For example, on January 13, 1983, Dusko Doder of the *Post* wrote a prominent article entitled "Andropov is Said to Offer to Destroy Some Missiles," speaking of the SS-20s. A few months later, on August 27, 1983, Doder wrote
another prominent article entitled, "Andropov offers some Dis-
mantling of Missile Arsenal," making precisely the same point but
without any mention whatsoever of his previous article.

Even the most conscientious reader would reasonably assume that
Andropov made yet another move for peace, not having been told
that the Soviet leader was merely selling the same "concession" twice,
much less having been told that none of these "offers" meant anything at all. It was not until Reykjavík in October 1986 that the
Soviets became serious on INF, and not until a year afterward did
they move close enough to our position to strike a deal.

4. *The Linguistic Tilt:* The cherished conservative accusation of ideological bias in the press is wrong where commonly applied, in terms
of news stories. It is, however, correct where seldom applied, in terms
of language choice.

Pitched in the press against us "right-wingers" in the arms control battles are the "moderates." No one is a "left-winger" these
days—not Senator Alan Cranston, not even Paul Warnke (who
presumably would not mind the label). I cannot recall seeing "left-
winger" in print. On the other hand, those who battle these same

"moderates" are invariably described as conservatives. And we "hard-liners" never oppose "soft-liners;" I never saw that phrase once in print, but "hard-line" appeared almost daily, especially as a description of Reagan administration officials and policies.

Similarly, the President's research program on strategic defense is labeled "Star Wars" as often (if not more often) than SDI, even though that term is loaded. Who is for any "wars," in the stars or on earth? No wonder opinion polls find that the public supports SDI but opposes "Star Wars."

5. *Sensationalism:* The press most egregiously sensationalizes and personalizes arms control, treating this field much like *People Magazine* treats the world. The stakes could not be higher, the combat could not be fiercer (even if most of it takes place within the U.S. government).

In few publications has the hype been higher than in *Time*. Nor could the personalization of policy be greater than in the reporting of its former Washington bureau chief, Strobe Talbott, probably the most prominent author on arms control.

The January 31, 1983 *Time* cover was typical. It brandished a U.S. Pershing II missile—not a Soviet SS-20 missile, which had been deployed six years before and which presumably was more of a threat to *Time* readers than the Pershing. The cover caption "Nuclear Poker: The Stakes Get Higher and Higher" gave the gist. Its lead article, written by Talbott, was as sensationalistic then as it seems ludicrous today: "The Year of the Missile is barely a month gone, yet already the sense of urgency is intense, the diplomatic activity frenzied.... 'Arms control is the next big issue,' said a senior White House aide. 'It has to be faced.' If anything, he was understating the case."

By August 22nd, the stakes had risen even higher, if such is possible. *Time* and Talbott then warned: "Now it looks as though the Soviets may be bent on turning the Year of the Missile into a replay of the Cuban Missile Crisis, at least in its symbolic dimension, as a clash of wills between the superpowers."

The situation *was* serious in 1983. But in no way can it or could it have been accurately portrayed as equal in gravity to the Cuban Missile Crisis. Then, the U.S. and USSR did go to the brink of nuclear confrontation. In 1983, the two waged a confrontation, all right, but one which merely played out a NATO decision made four years before.

In 1979, lest one forget, NATO made a commitment to deploy the INF missiles in Europe if arms control efforts were not successful. And, in 1983, they most evidently were not.

Talbott's book *Deadly Gambits*, such a rage at the time, is outdated today. For its central thesis, that the "zero-option" was a nefarious American proposal no Soviet leader could conceivably accept, has been proven wrong. Were there any accountability in this field, or in foreign affairs generally—any tallying of whose analysis and prediction was right and whose was wrong—hopes for better reporting might increase. But there seems to be little prospect of this.

The Remedy

How to remedy these and other press failings? Over the past five years, officials at ACDA made several efforts to work with the press to improve public discussion of arms control issues (though with little success). For one, the top staff made themselves available to responsible reporters—of which there are many—to explain the general outlines and arguments of the issue at hand. I refused to give "scoops," details of our negotiating positions (unless otherwise known), or detail the bureaucratic politics of who stood where on the issue. Members of the press could get all that from others in the administration, and did. I concentrated on the pros and cons of the issue and tried to explain its overall importance.

And I played favorites. For a responsible journalist, with a track record of fair reporting, I was readily available on the phone or in person. For others, I would let them be; after a while they stopped calling. The cost of doing so—nothing is achieved in Washington without some cost—was being criticized or ignored in those reporters' stories, becoming a "bad apple," or, just as bad, a "non-player."

In addition, ACDA and the Aspen Institute sponsored a press seminar for top print and media journalists covering arms control. Each spring we would "retreat" to the Wye Plantation for a day and a half to discuss the important issues with administration officials, outside experts, and even opponents. In 1984 we included a presentation on Democratic presidential candidate Walter Mondale's approach to arms control by one of his advisors, Walt Slocombe, and in 1986 John Rhinelander debated the ABM treaty interpretation issue. In all of these meetings we discussed in some depth nuclear testing and compliance, gave a status report on each of the nuclear negotiations and on SDI, and attempted to give a historical perspective. Efforts such as this need to be continued and the press needs to probe deeper into both the intricacies of arms control and especially what arms control can really deliver to make the world safer.

11

U.S. Intelligence: Current Problems in Historical Perspective

William E. Odom

The Congressional hearings on intelligence in the mid-1970s raised troublesome questions for legislators, the executive branch, and, to a lesser degree, the media. Can a democratic society's need for open and informed debate be reconciled with its need for secrecy in the conduct of an effective national security policy? And can this be done within the precise guidelines established by statutory enactments? For two hundred years the executive branch and the military in particular have engaged in intelligence activities, but without a specific statutory basis. During and after World War II, Congress consistently funded these activities. Yet many in both houses of Congress and in both parties considered some of them inappropriate, even illegal. Moreover, without specific laws to authorize, guide and govern these activities, it was often difficult to determine which intelligence community actions were legitimate. In short, there was an urgent need to establish a better legal foundation for intelligence activities.

Finding that legal footing, however, proved difficult. Like acts of war and aggression, intelligence activities by their very nature contravene the normal practices of states; the accepted rules of behavior are bent; laws are sometimes broken. Successful intelligence requires secrecy and deception. But such requirements are seldom compatible with the rule of law. The failure of efforts in the late 1970s to draft effective intelligence charters reflects the difficulties posed by this dilemma.

This is not a trivial issue. Intelligence officers, sworn to uphold the Constitution, are also citizens who value their constitutional rights. They do not wish to undermine the laws, even if an activity seems in the immediate context to serve the national interest. The notion of "national interest" is notoriously slippery when defined by individuals with a personal interest in defining it loosely. Intelligence officers, therefore, must take care to avoid expedient definitions—definitions that are too facile in setting legal limits. One must consult history, precedent, and the changing executive and legislative roles to manage this dilemma, because it is unlikely ever to be fully resolved by interpretations of statutory law alone.

History provides many useful guideposts for assessing the need and appropriateness of intelligence operations. George Washington directed an excellent intelligence operation. His remarkably successful spies included Alexander Hamilton, Benjamin Franklin, and others engaged in black propaganda (that is, misinformation intended to mislead the British through the open press) and the interception of British naval communications. Some of General Washington's agents chose to die publicly disgraced in penury rather than disclose their true identity.

While Washington conveyed to the Continental Congress a great deal about the monies he spent, he never revealed the details of his intelligence operations. The issue never seemed to have arisen, probably because intelligence operations were considered in the same category as military operations—a part of warfare, something obviously essential for the fledgling republic's survival. And the perception that intelligence was an adjunct of military operations carried over to the writing of the Constitution. Military and foreign affairs were understood to be national concerns entrusted to the national government. While no specific mention is made in the Constitution of "intelligence activities," the need for "secrecy and dispatch" in the conduct of certain aspects of the nation's affairs was clearly understood. Moreover, the Constitution specifically provides that, in keeping a journal of its proceedings, the Congress shall publish the same "excepting such Parts as may in their Judgment require Secrecy."

The Constitutional Convention itself was conducted under a veil of secrecy that would be the envy of any intelligence official today. The author of *Federalist* Number 64 declared, "So often and so essentially have we heretofore suffered from the want of secrecy and dispatch (in the conduct of our affairs) that the Constitution would have been inexcusably defective if no attention had been paid to these objects." The Framers thus drafted a plan of government whereby both the executive and the legislative branches were given responsibility for military and foreign affairs, with the understanding that the execution of these responsibilities would, in certain instances, require "secrecy and dispatch." Intelligence activities comprise one of these responsibilities, and as such are firmly rooted in the constitutional fabric.

Not surprisingly, the history of American intelligence is poorly recorded. Insofar as the Army is concerned, intelligence did not assume a significant institutional form until the 1880s, and then only as a rather ineffective information-gathering office. When the Army General Staff was created by Elihu Root in 1902, intelligence was accorded a separate and equal position among four general staff sections. Study of European organizations led Root and others to believe it should not be subordinated to operations as was the case in many armies. Even so, Army intelligence was slow to develop. Colonel Van Deman gave it its first real substance in 1917, and one of the most successful operations he launched was in signals intelligence. This activity centered around H.O. Yardley, a remarkable former State Department code clerk, and the cryptanalytic program he built, the so-called Black Chamber. It results proved immensely helpful to national policy makers throughout the war.

In all likelihood, intelligence posed no real legal dilemmas for the first century and a half of this nation's existence because it was almost exclusively a wartime activity. Yardley, however, remained in business after World War I, giving American negotiators at the Washington Naval Conference a great advantage by providing them with the bargaining positions of other participants, particularly the Japanese. When Henry Stimson became secretary of state and learned of the Black Chamber, however, he closed it, remarking laconically, "Gentlemen do not read other gentlemen's mail." Interestingly, Stimson's views changed appreciably over time. A decade later, as secretary of war in the Roosevelt administration during World War II, Stimson was a principal beneficiary of British and American cryptology successes. He is not recorded as having had any negative reaction to these successes and, indeed, presided over much of the enormous growth in American cryptologic capabilities that occurred during that conflict. Nonetheless, it is intriguing to ask just how much more effective U.S. intelligence might have been if the Black Chamber had not been dismantled before the war.

U.S. intelligence activities continued after World War II. Stimson's successors had quite another idea of what gentlemen charged with the national defense should read. The political consensus the country enjoyed for its military and foreign policy allowed the intelligence community to grow and to become an integral part of our national security apparatus. But with the break-up of that consensus, the old problem of making intelligence "legal" in every regard resurfaced. One could not operate and keep Congress basically ignorant of the details, as President Washington had done. Congress had become a partner, a source of healthy funding, and a strong supporter. It was not easy to justify intelligence activities as purely "military operations" when the United States was officially at peace. The idea of a prolonged state of exception did not conform to American experience or attitudes. The truth of the matter, though, was that America was attempting to build a postwar international security order in the face of opposition from a Soviet Union that was legally at peace but politically at war with the United States.

American intelligence remains at war today, even during a period of ostensible peace. While our armed forces train and develop new weapons and doctrine, our intelligence community struggles to learn the potential adversary's capabilities and intentions, while countering his intelligence thrusts. Here lies the basic tension that intelligence officers experience with their law and society. Legally our nation is at peace. For intelligence officers it is at war.

The conduct of this "intelligence war" has created tensions within the government. But these tensions are not "constitutional," at least in the sense that the government's authority to conduct intelligence activities is seriously in question. Rather, they are "institutional." The issue centers on the proper role of the executive and the legislative branches in the management of these activities. For most of our history, the executive branch exercised the intelligence function with little active Congressional oversight. However, as the national consensus on military and foreign policy began to fray and eventually disintegrate during the Vietnam War, a skeptical Congress became increasingly assertive of its prerogatives. This assertiveness manifested itself in legislation like the War Powers Resolution and the

Foreign Intelligence Surveillance Act (FISA)—both Congressional incursions into areas previously reserved exclusively for executive action.

The Congressional investigations of the 1970s into intelligence operations produced not only new legislative controls (such as FISA) but also prompted a series of executive branch measures such as Executive Orders and detailed operating procedures to regulate intelligence activities. These actions reflected not only executive concerns but also an attempt to anticipate and perhaps preclude further statutory intervention. Finally Congressional assertiveness can be seen in its oversight of intelligence activities, now marked by increased scrutiny, inquiry, and at times, policy disputes with the President. Those reforms directed at preserving and protecting the rights of American citizens have been enacted with broad bipartisan support from both the executive and the legislative branches. But where "reform" involved a reordering of the historical exercise of institutional authorities regarding military and foreign policy, a lingering tension exists. Intelligence activities represent the "front line" in the military and foreign policy debate and, hence, are inevitably affected by this tension.

There is no way to resolve the tension fully. It will continue to linger, except for rare moments of strong national consensus on foreign policy. Fortunately, most of our legislators and executive officials support intelligence activities. They see clearly that these are necessary for insuring the common defense. And the public, for the most part, fully supports them as well. So, when confronting the tension on a daily basis, one must keep this consensus, or lack of it, in mind. One cannot overstep it by violating its spirit in operations; one ought not act in ways that evade the constraints its absence imposes; and one must not disappoint that consensus when it does exist and demands effective operational results.

Yet intelligence officials cannot advertise their successes to gain support. They must trust the nation's political leadership to understand their good service and to defend them with the public. Intelligence officers cannot consider either executive officials or the Congress as their enemies. In the difficult times of recent years, Congress and the President have consistently supported the intelligence agencies. When legal limits are set, intelligence officers must adhere to them. They cannot resort to their secret definitions of national interest. They cannot presume to be wiser than the political and legal system. Like military officers, they may argue their case up the chain of command, and they may appeal to the inspector general system, but that is the limit of dissent. Their duty is to secure that system, even if at times its policies appear short-sighted or unwise. Their responsibility is neither to change the policies in secret nor to oppose them by press leaks.

Intelligence has proven its worth. Few people in the government or in the public at large fully understand the war of the reconnaissance regimes that goes on daily among the world's major adversaries. Few people realize the enormity of the intelligence efforts against the United States. Recent incidents, such as the Walker, Whitworth, Pelton and Pollard spy cases have demonstrated vividly that foreign intelligence services are not mythical. These services are both quantitatively and qualitatively impressive. Their efforts tax both our resources and our openness as a society. The numbers of foreign operatives greatly exceeds our capacity to neutralize them, and our open society eases their access both to information and potential spy recruits.

Nonetheless, our intelligence community remains healthy and robust. It contributes as much to deterrence and peace as do our military forces. A Pearl Harbor today is not very likely; a major massing of forces for war probably would not pass our early notice. Nor is our policy community likely to be confused about the diplomatic and military intentions of states in a world crisis, as European leaders were in July and August of 1914. On the whole, today the United States can boast the most wide-ranging and effective intelligence effort the Western world has ever known.

This is not to suggest that there are no intelligence problems. There are. Some, such as the institutional fragmentation and lack of cross-departmental cooperation in the intelligence community, could be solved. Others, such as the lack of adequate resources, have consistently been present in the past and will no doubt continue to persist in the future. And still others, such as the increasingly complex and technical nature of counterintelligence, will require more and more attention.

Perhaps the most difficult problem facing the intelligence community today is the problem of leaks and the publication of information harmful to our intelligence operations. This problem arose in the 1970s, and a rather alarming trend has evolved in the 1980s. The consequences have been not only lost intelligence but also heavy financial costs. Leakers and disclosers with no accountability to the taxpayer have recklessly wasted public funds.

This dangerous trend reflects the break-up of the policy consensus that supported our intelligence operations during World War II and for the two following decades. Leakers spoil intelligence sources presumably to change or support policies. Some have argued that this is the price of doing business in our democratic system, but this view is too simplistic. Few policy improvements or successes have resulted from unauthorized intelligence disclosures. On the contrary, two adverse consequences usually and frequently result when leaks become the major weapon in policy making. First, policy becomes paralyzed. And second, intelligence tends to be discounted and treated as biased. The latter leads to less informed policy decisions and major misjudgments. The inconclusive debate over the growth and structure of Soviet strategic forces in the 1960s and 1970s, the degradation of arms control verification means, and the inability of the U.S. government to cope with terrorist activities are all examples of the harmful consequences of leaks.

The primary source of leaks, of course, is the government, but the press is hardly an unwitting or unwilling accomplice. Many in the media try unrelentingly to pry loose highly classified information. When they succeed, they blame the leakers, refusing to accept any personal or professional responsibility. They are right to criticize the leakers, but they deceive themselves and the public about their role and its effect on genuine national interests that enjoy overwhelming public, Congressional and executive support. When their disclosures are challenged, the media almost automatically invoke the First Amendment.

The media's invocation of the First Amendment invariably includes incantations regarding the public's "right to know." Yet the First Amendment guarantees no such comprehensive "right to know," either explicitly or implicitly. The constitutional system of government under which we live does not envision a "town meeting" approach to the conduct of national military and foreign policy, such that every issue regardless of sensitivity is submitted to the public for resolution. Again, there is the example of the framers themselves whose decision to keep the proceedings of the Constitutional Convention secret reflected their understanding that some issues, even perhaps the most fundamental issues of the day, are of such sensitivity that they cannot and should not be debated openly.

The notion that the media stands as an unelected ombudsman with a constitutionally conferred mandate to extract all information on government activities and to disseminate it to the public has no historical or legal foundation. In asserting such a mandate, the media distort the true meaning and purpose of the First Amendment, while encouraging a fiction that, through repetition, gains increasing acceptance. No court has ever accepted the principle of an unfettered public "right to know," and the media's facile assertion of this illusory "right" inhibits constructive discussion of the need to preserve the secrecy of national intelligence activities.

A second serious problem with the media's First Amendment position is the failure to acknowledge any principle of responsibility or accountability. While the media benefit enormously from the specific and unique protections that the First Amendment offers, as a whole they have failed to perform their function responsibly. Often, reporters recognize the criminal offense being committed by the leaker, yet they perceive no wrongdoing in amplifying the effect of that crime by serving as a conduit for broad and damaging dissemination of that information.

Intelligence disclosures have caused loss of life, sometimes immediately, at other times later, due to a causal linkage that is not immediately recognized. Such breeches of secrecy often result in large fiscal loss to the government due to the forfeited intelligence return on the public funds invested and to the need for new funds to recover sources. The misappropriation or waste of a few thousand dollars in non-intelligence areas begets a huge outcry from the same press that causes the loss of many more dollars by disclosing sensitive collection means. However, for reasons well understood, the media cannot be held legally accountable for its actions. Attorney generals will not invite the wrath of the media, and the media are as notoriously reluctant to criticize themselves as the American Medical Association is to disqualify its own members for incompetence. Other remedies must be sought. Perhaps, if the public were informed of the damage done, the media would be compelled to act more responsibly. But of course, representatives of the media do not inform the public of the harm they have caused, even when intelligence officials can demonstrate it to them.

In all fairness, there are many responsible journalists and editors who indeed try to hold a prudent line on what they publish. They do so at some peril to themselves, because another paper or network may scoop them on information they believe should be withheld. If they refuse to publish what a leaker tells them, the leaker may threaten to go elsewhere with his classified information. In recent years there has been growing recognition in some media circles of the dangers to American security and interests posed by leaks. But, unfortunately, this concern has not produced effective measures to reverse the damaging trend.

It has been extremely difficult to foster public understanding of these problems. However, if this trend of leaks and harmful disclosures is not checked, it may eventually destroy our reconnaissance regime's ability to prevent surprise attacks and policy confusion. The United States may lose the reconnaissance war, and eventually with it, the peace. As the leakers and media methodically educate foreign governments about our capabilities, our adversaries will just as methodically strive to neutralize or deceive our collection efforts.

But this trend can be checked and our intelligence capabilities saved, without endangering First Amendment rights. What is needed is a general realization that in certain situations, national interests can and should limit the unbridled exercise of individual rights. These situations are not always easy to define, but it is quite clear that intelligence disclosures by the media over the last decade have gone too far. Several congressmen, adamant defenders of our laws and rights, have expressed sentiments similar to these. President Ronald Reagan, his cabinet officers, and senior military commanders expounded this same view even more vehemently.

What are we to do? We can begin by admitting that there exists no perfect solution. Then, we should improve our understanding of where the fault lies. First and foremost, culpability lies with the executive branch. Policy makers must set an example by treating leaks as a serious matter and by taking prompt and effective action when they occur. And second, the fault lies with the Congress, although more serious measures have been taken in Congress to stop leaks than is generally recognized.

Finally, we must learn to live with the tensions inherent in the legal basis for intelligence—tensions that stem from the need for a large intelligence effort in peacetime and from the lack of the kind of policy consensus that generally exists in wartime. We cannot return to the conditions which prevailed during World War II, and we cannot operate without oversight as George Washington did. Intelligence officers, for their part, must develop a professional integrity clearly in keeping with their role as protectors of the Constitution. The executive and legislative branches of government must discern and implement a formula for alleviating those legal tensions. And editors and reporters must identify and instill within their own community new standards of responsibility and accountability. When these things have been done, Americans will be able both to protect their national security interests and to maintain a free, open and informed society.

12

The Media and Foreign Policy: A View from the Executive Branch

Robert C. McFarlane

Can the interaction of government officials with the media be modified to improve the level of public discourse in this country about national security affairs? There are strong grounds for skepticism. Competitive pressures in journalism have led reporters and their editors, especially in the electronic media, to place more and more emphasis on éclat than on enlightenment. And these pressures have tended over time and with greater frequency to overwhelm fundamental standards of individual and corporate responsibility and integrity. On the other side of the ledger, there has been a palpable decline in the competence of government officials, at least as compared to the broad standards of an earlier age. Qualification for public office goes beyond an ability to conceive of sensible policy. Those charged with formulating national security policy must be able to explain that policy through the media, and in doing so they must steer clear of iconoclasm and ideological rigidity. Public officials must be aware, particularly when different parties control the White House and the Capitol, that the public interest requires compromise.

This deterioration in both those who make policy and those who report it must be a concern to all Americans. But those who would seek to remedy the problem must be aware of the full dimensions and variety of the forces that have brought it about.

The Responsibility of Government

The decline in the ability of government officials to deal with the foreign affairs agenda has its roots in our very political system. One has only to understand how most of our public officials have come to office: the process through which we elect officials in this country, to the White House and to the Congress, is one in which Presidents, senators and representatives are chosen primarily for their qualifications in domestic policy. This, of course, is nothing new. It has been true for most of our history as a nation. But for most of this period we have been protected by two oceans and, since the late 1940s, by our preeminent economic and military power.

These benign conditions no longer obtain, however. International economic competition has become much more severe; and our economic security more uncertain. Thus the demands upon executive officials and the people's representatives in foreign affairs have grown. Unfortunately, our system is no better prepared to provide qualified leadership than it was before. The country's isolationist habits of mind, born of nearly two hundred years of cheap security, are deeply engrained and continue to express themselves in the election of "domestic" Presidents.

The only way to begin to enlighten an isolationist society about its dependence upon the world abroad—how our jobs, paychecks and welfare, from Des Moines, Iowa, to Graham, Texas, are affected by foreign events—is through systematic education. Only by cranking a generation of Americans through a school system that begins (for a change) to teach things foreign, from language and geography to history, comparative politics and economics, will we begin to produce an electorate that says, "Gee, this is important to me. I should care about the competence of our leaders in these areas."

But even if we were to succeed, after many years of effort, in effecting a sea change in the national attitude toward and understanding of the international environment, there would remain the problem of how foreign policy is made. Even if the executive branch were populated with the most enlightened, skilful and politically experienced people, the relationship between the executive branch and the Congress is so fractious and burdened with non-substantive considerations that the policy process would remain muddled. Without reform within the Congress, and a movement away from the confrontational approach favored in recent years, hopes of producing effective, enlightened national policy will remain dim.

The Lesson of Vietnam

The general indifference of the electorate to foreign affairs, the changes in the international environment that have affected our security position, and the internecine warfare between the executive and legislative branches are all broad problems which can only be addressed in the long term, and are beyond the capacity of most officials in the executive to address in any case.

Executive officials can, however, do more themselves to present fundamental issues of national security policy and planning to the media and, through them, to the public. The most important political and military event in my lifetime has been the loss of the Vietnam War, a war whose outcome was dictated fundamentally, I believe, by the inability of the President to explain his purposes to the American people through the press. There were, of course, many other reasons for our defeat. But this was the core failing. The imperative lesson of that experience was that it is not enough to conceive sensible policies. The other, more difficult half of the problem is to explain them.

As a person involved in that war I resolved that if I ever reached a policy position I would make a substantial commitment to explicating, elucidating and interpreting our policies to the press and to the public. And in fact, as national security adviser, I did not think it unreasonable to spend a fourth of my time explaining national security policy. I regarded this as sensible, and as important to my function as developing effective, credible policies.

Strategic Policy and SDI

The area of foreign affairs in which officials have most clearly failed is in explaining our strategic policies. As a consequence of the failure of the executive branch for more than forty years to engage seriously in promoting public debate and understanding of the issues involved in establishing and maintaining a credible deterrent, our strategic policy is the least understood item on our national security agenda. The consequences of this failure were revealed at the highest possible level in the development and presentation of President Reagan's Strategic Defense Initiative (SDI).

By 1982, when I first entered the White House as Judge William Clark's deputy, efforts had been underway in both political parties for more than six years to restore stability to the strategic nuclear balance. Despite these earnest efforts we had reached a point where the balance in counterforce potential, in prompt hard-target kill capability, had become very lopsided in favor of the Soviet Union, and our own land-based counterforce systems had become very vulnerable. Several sensible concepts were developed by the Carter administration to overcome this strategic imbalance through new missiles and a survivable deployment scheme. But the basing proposals were not accepted. The Reagan administration followed the Carter proposal with three more concepts, an airborne scheme, Densepack, and another—all of which had been defeated by 1982. By the end of 1982 it had become clear that the state of affairs which had begun to develop six or seven years earlier had not changed materially. We had reached a political impasse.

In my view, it was a mistake to attempt to compete with the Soviets quantitatively in land-based missiles. And yet we faced a dangerous situation for as long as our own systems remained vulnerable. If the problem could not be overcome through novel basing schemes and if no other way of compensating for the imbalance was to be found, the only other approach was to have the Soviets reduce the number of their land-based forces. But because the Soviets were unlikely to reduce unilaterally, it would be necessary to find other means of persuading them to do so. It was with this in mind that I came to believe the time had come to review the possibility of constructing defensive systems.

Our advantage in the competition with the Soviets—our technological lead—had been invested almost exclusively in offensive systems from 1945 to 1983. Over time, the possible gains from additional investments in offense had declined sharply. To compete with the Soviets on their terms by deploying missile for missile, I believed, was to play to their strong suit. But if we were to seek other means of exploiting our technological advantage, we might succeed in compelling the Soviets to address a problem of great concern to us, the problem of counterforce imbalance. In short, as an *investment strategy* and a solution to a military problem, SDI was worth consideration.

The President's views of SDI and of its purposes were quite different. His views were and are defensible. The President felt a deep responsibility to fulfill the obligation he had as the chief executive to protect the American people, and from his point of view the notion of doing this by threats of great violence was immoral. In any case, he thought we ought to try to find some other means of defending the country.

The President's views on SDI are well known. What is more telling is that on this central issue the President and his national security adviser were motivated by fundamentally different purposes. The aims of both were military, but the core strategies were fundamentally different. The dilemma this created was profound: how is it possible to promote a policy when the President and the person ultimately responsible for implementing it basically disagree on the nature of the problem and how to solve it?

In the end, the President's March 23, 1983 speech was cast on a "moral" plane, and his appeal touched an emotional nerve with the public. The President decided to present the initiative on these terms in full knowledge of all the complexities of its likely reception from the allies, that is, the issues of its technological feasibility, its potential costs, and its possible effect on strategic stability. He was exhaustively briefed on all these matters. But he believed that there was a higher standard to which we ought to strive, beyond all these political, technological and fiscal considerations. And he believed that by promoting the concept on those grounds it would carry.

The success of the initiative ultimately depended as well upon Soviet belief in our ability to develop the technology to realize the President's vision. The policy dilemma arose, however, from the question of how the initiative was to be presented to the press. Journalists might have understood it well in terms of leverage, as an attempt to use the comparative advantage of the United States in high technology in order to compel the Soviets to deal seriously with our concerns with the strategic imbalance. But such an approach becomes irrelevant, if not misleading, if the apparent basis of your position is different.

In fact, for about a year after the President's speech we attempted to explain the policy in terms of a two-track strategy. We conceded that it was probably infeasible, if not unwise, to attempt to realize the President's vision of a non-nuclear world given the state of the art of verification and given the virtual certainty that the Soviets would not agree to cooperate. But we also attempted to explain that the initiative was basically cast to deal with a military problem, a problem that could be addressed either by building additional defensive hardware of our own or by inducing the Soviets to eliminate some of their offensive power.

Surprisingly, the press took little notice of the glaring disparity between the President's rationale and that of his highest officials. In part, the reason may have been that the press understood that if the initiative were presented as leverage—as a bargaining chip— then its effectiveness would be diluted as soon as it became apparent that this was our intent. More importantly, President Reagan himself dismissed the notion every time it came up. And perhaps it is just as well that the press, like the Russians, ultimately pays attention to Presidents.

Part IV

■

Beyond the Beltway

13
Foreign Policy and the Provincial Press

Charles W. Bailey

It is fashionable for foreign policy professionals, particularly academics, to criticize American newspapers for failing to provide enough thoughtful foreign news coverage. Typical of such complaints was that of Walter Laqueur in the June 1983 *Washington Journalism Review:*

> The quality [of foreign news coverage] is worse now than it was before and just after the Second World War. It is definitely not as good as in most other countries that have a free press.... On the basis of the information and the comment presented in the American media alone, it is difficult, perhaps impossible, to keep well informed on the state of the world, let alone on specific political, economic and military matters.[1]

Another academic critic, Barry Rubin, wrote in 1976 that U.S. newspapers were serving neither "elite audiences" nor "mass readers" with their foreign coverage. He was especially critical of big-city papers: "Particularly serious have been the derelictions of the big-city dailies—in Boston, Chicago, Philadelphia, San Francisco and other urban areas—which have a significant 'elite' audience for foreign news."[2] Rubin's proposed remedies were primarily quantitative. Among other things, he suggested "the creation of special foreign news sections, carrying analysis and longer pieces."

"Long pieces," he added, "providing historical perspective, careful explanation and eyewitness details on a country's political situation or on an outstanding international issue could appeal both to those with little knowledge on the subject and to 'elite' readers seeking detailed data and analysis."[3]

Critics such as Laqueur and Rubin would like American newspapers to resemble the specialized European press—*The Economist*, the *Times* (London), *Le Monde, Neue Züricher Zeitung*, and so on. In this, as in other proposals, they demonstrate their unfamiliarity with the structure and economics of this country's daily press. Here, even what these critics call "prestige" or "elite" newspapers are, in fact, mass-circulation publications; they depend on advertising revenues, which in turn depend on circulation, which in turn depends on attracting and holding the interest of a relatively broad readership. There is, consequently, an air of unreality about Rubin's proposal for special sections devoted to long analytical and historical articles that will appeal to expert and unschooled readers alike.

Such misperceptions are not the sole property of academics. People in government (and even some in journalism) can be equally unrealistic. Most foreign policy makers live in Washington; they regularly read two to three untypical newspapers published either in Washington or New York City. They also spend more time talking to television reporters than they do watching television news broadcasts. In fact, Washington policy makers and reporters probably underestimate the influence of television news programs simply because most of them do not watch these programs. The policy makers and reporters are likely to be still at work when the programs are broadcast. Thus, because the evening news does not significantly shape *their* opinions, they may easily assume that it does not seriously affect public opinion either.

But if foreign policy professionals tend to underestimate the present importance of television in influencing public opinion, they show even less understanding of the changes occurring within the TV news business—changes that will probably reduce television's foreign policy impact. The fact is that even as television becomes the major purveyor of news to the American public, the great TV networks, which for some time have controlled the content and tone of foreign news reporting, are beginning to lose that control. As David Webster pointed out in 1986,[4] the same advances in satellite and other technology that have enabled the networks to bring foreign news rapidly

and vividly into the American living room have also led to the availability of a wide range of competitive news material. Easy access to
such alternative programming allows local TV stations to escape from
network dictation in foreign as well as national and local news. Given
the nature of the subject matter, the inherent limitations of the medium, and the mindset of station managers, the net effect—at least in
the short term—is likely to be a reduction in the quantity and quality of serious foreign news available to the viewers of local TV stations. When such material can readily be deleted from the news programs, it probably will be.

Even when local stations carry foreign news, they are likely to
use the new technology to "localize" it—a process that will probably
also trivialize it, given the way most TV stations cover the news.
Thus, when President Reagan returned from his 1985 Geneva meeting with Mikhail Gorbachev, he went directly to the Capitol to address a joint meeting of the House and Senate. His appearance was
carried live on television. However, on one of the leading Minneapolis TV stations, the narration was provided not by the network correspondents that had been covering the summit and the issues discussed there, but instead by the local station's "Eyewitness News"
anchor team. The station, an ABC affiliate, could just as well have
broadcast the reporting and commentary of Peter Jennings, Sam
Donaldson and George Will. It chose instead to use familiar local
figures with no apparent qualifications to handle the story.[5]

So today the public is receiving a growing portion of its news from
a medium whose broadcast outlets seem likely to devote a shrinking
share of their programming to serious coverage of foreign affairs.
Future viewers will probably spend more time watching television,
but less time being enlightened on foreign affairs by people like Jennings, John Chancellor or Bernard Kalb, because local TV stations
will probably carry less network-produced news.

Good News for the Print Media

The decline of television reporting of foreign affairs offers newspapers an opportunity. The papers have long since lost their position as the dominant mass medium and the prime carrier of late-
breaking news. They still play, however, a very considerable role not
only in reporting international affairs but also in influencing what

television reports. Television remains unsure of itself—at least until its judgments are validated by the papers.

Now, as network television seems likely to lose at least some of its coherence in the foreign news field, newspapers have a chance not only to continue their agenda-setting role but also to buttress their status as the dominant provider of international news to those members of the public who care about it.

More people care about foreign affairs than some in Washington and New York seem to think. There are ample survey data to support such an assertion. Some of the most convincing evidence can be found in a late 1970s Lou Harris poll. The survey reported that even at that time (during the height of the post-Vietnam disillusionment) 41 percent of those questioned expressed a strong interest in international news, while only 5 percent of a separate sample of editors and reporters believed the public had a strong interest. Anyone who has wrestled with readership surveys knows that expressing general interest in a subject is one thing, and actually reading about it is another; but what matters here is the disparity between the public attitude and the journalist's perception of that attitude.

John Maxwell Hamilton said in his 1986 book, *Main Street America and the Third World*, "there is an unwritten rule among journalists that local news is news and foreign news is foreign, and that people want plenty of the former and will tolerate only small doses of the latter."[6] This view has been endorsed by many journalists and by many policy makers. There is some truth in it, but as Hamilton showed in his book, it ought not to be stretched too far. Journalists—primarily those who work for regional or local newspapers—can transform foreign news into local news. And when they do, they find plenty of interested readers. That, in turn, can only enlighten the foreign policy press.

Building Local Interest in Foreign News: The Minneapolis Star and Tribune

The experience of one regional newspaper—the *Minneapolis Star and Tribune*—offers an illustration of how this process works. It is an unusual story, but hardly unique. There are lessons in it for both journalists and officials in the foreign policy community.

The Minneapolis newspapers have been for fifty years one of the most successful of the great regional family publishing enterprises.

John Cowles, Sr., moved to Minneapolis in the mid-1930s from Des Moines, where his banker father had bought a newspaper and made it flourish. In his first six years in Minneapolis, the younger Cowles acquired three separate papers and created a monopoly that soon dominated a four-state region. Today, the product of that monopoly, the *Star and Tribune*, has a daily circulation of over 400,000 and a Sunday circulation of close to 650,000. Though it no longer circulates all the way from western Wisconsin to the Montana line, it still has influence throughout the Upper Midwest region.

When John Cowles moved to Minnesota, it was politically the most isolationist of states. Its international attitudes were reflected in public figures like Charles Lindbergh, hero-spokesman of the America Firsters. As for its newspapers, their stance was typified by this September 1939 editorial in the pre-Cowles *Minneapolis Tribune:*

> The lamps of Europe are going out again, it seems...but the lamps of Europe have been going off and on for centuries and still the world survives. This may indeed be the end of civilization as we know it, yet there are other lamps that may be kept burning and through their light sustain the hope of an ordered world existence....
>
> One such lamp burns today in the United States.... If that lamp ever flickers out, it will be under the stress of war. And if it is ever to light the way to a better ordered world, we shall do well not to leave it while we tend the lamps of Europe.[7]

Cowles was himself a pillar of the national Republican establishment, but he also had traveled to the Soviet Union in the early 1920s. He was a close friend and key backer of Wendell Willkie in 1940, and accompanied Willkie on his wartime trips abroad. Cowles was also a principal early sponsor of Dwight Eisenhower's 1952 presidential candidacy. He was a committed internationalist in a time and place where isolationism was the fashion.

Cowles believed his newspapers should print the news and state their opinions—always on different pages. Nonetheless, he also believed that newspapers had an obligation to educate as well as to inform and entertain. Hubert Humphrey once wrote of Cowles:

> There are times when he just can't resist using his newspapers to tell his readers things he believes they ought to

know, even if these happen to be things they had not asked
to know.... These newspapers were hammering away on the
need for America to become involved in the Far East, before
it was customary or even popular to do so.[8]

To direct his Minneapolis newspapers, Cowles chose people with
extensive experience in reporting and editing foreign news. Executive editor Gideon Seymour had reported for the Associated Press
from four continents; Carroll Binder had been director of the Chicago *Daily News* foreign service before taking over the editorial pages
in Minneapolis. Cowles also was willing to purchase foreign news,
and he made sure that it was printed. He sent staff members (including editors and editorial writers) abroad. He himself traveled around
the world. He hired foreign correspondents long before most regional newspapers did so. And he conceived and cosponsored with the
University of Minnesota an ambitious "World Affairs Program" which
drew thousands of high school students throughout the region into
weekly quizzes on foreign affairs.

From the 1940s to the 1980s, Minneapolis reporters and photographers traveled abroad. The aim was not so much to cover breaking news—the paper's wire services provided enough of that—as to
explore and research situations that might underlie future crises and
wars. In the 1950s, *Tribune* reporters ventured forth from the city
room to the Soviet Union, South Africa, India, Vietnam, and to the
founding conference of the non-aligned movement at Bandung, In-
donesia. In the 1960s they traveled throughout Eastern Europe, Latin
America and Asia. A Washington correspondent covering agriculture
was dispatched to rural regions of the Soviet Union in 1963. In order
to improve his ability to cover the story, the paper's White House
correspondent was detached in 1967 to spend two months in Vietnam, even though the *Tribune* already had someone stationed there.
In the 1970s reporters and reporter-photographer teams took long
looks at Mexico, Northern Ireland, the Middle East, Iran and sub-
Saharan Africa. One team traveled through half a dozen of the world's
poorest nations to investigate and report on the causes and effects
of world poverty. More recently, the paper's roving correspondent
has left Minneapolis for long visits to Ethiopia, Sudan, the Philippines, Central America and the Middle East.

The Minneapolis papers are by no means typical in their sustained
attention to foreign affairs, but they are not unique, either. The

Chicago Tribune, once the most isolationist of newspapers under Colonel Robert McCormick, has done much similar work, as have other regional papers.

Results and Lessons

There is no precise way to measure the long-term effect on public opinion of the kind of news coverage the Minneapolis papers provided their readers. Nonetheless, rough estimates can be drawn from public-opinion surveys. In 1944, the first year of the *Minneapolis Tribune's* Minnesota Poll, two out of three adult residents of this once-isolationist state favored U.S. membership in a postwar "council of nations." That figure rose to four out of five by July 1945; and by 1953, despite the Korean War, 70 percent of Minnesotans were in favor of continued U.N. membership.

Internationalist sentiment was strong in other poll measurements. In 1953, 71 percent of those polled were against cuts in U.S. defense spending; 85 percent were for continued U.S. membership in UNESCO; 55 percent were for continued economic aid to Europe; 64 percent were for continued overseas donation of surplus foods; and more than half were in favor of continued economic aid to India and Pakistan. Furthermore, on the most painful issue of the period—the Korean War—Minnesotans' support for U.S. involvement never fell below 40 percent. By May 1953 that support had actually risen, despite the bitter 1952 presidential campaign, to 52 percent.

The lesson to be drawn from the Minneapolis experience is not simply that a newspaper can heavily influence public attitudes if it devotes substantial space, money and energy to covering international issues. A critical element in the Minneapolis situation, and in similar but smaller efforts by other regional papers, was constant attention to *relevance*. What does this story mean to the people who read *this* newspaper, who earn a living in *this* community? How is this news connected to *this* church, *this* business, *these* jobs, *this* farm co-op?

Because most of the Minneapolis reporting was done not by Washington or overseas-based correspondents, but rather by reporters who lived and worked among their readers, it was easier and more natural to keep in mind such questions of relevance. The foreign affairs writer in Washington, D.C. and the foreign-based correspondent usually report for a national publication, or for a news service with clients in many parts of the country. Sometimes, as in the case of correspondents for the *New York Times*, the *Washington Post*, the *Los Angeles Times* and Knight-Ridder newspapers, they report for both.

The reporter from the Minneapolis newsroom will have less prior expertise than these foreign affairs writers, but that reporter will also know a lot more about the news interests and needs of a specific readership. Satisfying specific needs and interests is the best way to insure high readership and maximum influence. Of course there is no substitute for experience in a foreign assignment, and the kind of locally based reporting described here must be an adjunct to the continuing work of foreign-based experts—not an alternative.

In terms of educating the public on foreign policy and national security issues—an important concern of policy makers—locally based reporting also pays dividends. The reporters involved find themselves much in demand for speaking appearances and college campus talks back home. And because they are part of the community they are addressing, these journalists should have greater credibility than nationally known media representatives.

This might sound humdrum, and certainly the slide-show talk at Kiwanis is a long way from Washington, D.C., let alone Beirut or Beijing. But it is interesting to note the State Department's decision in 1986 to create a new post in the Deputy Secretary's Office specifically for the purpose of increasing domestic support for U.S. foreign policy. The department's spokeswoman said the position was established "to market the foreign affairs budget."[9] The kind of reporting favored in this essay is the journalistic equivalent of that State Department post, except that the aim is not to sustain budgets, but rather to increase the public's understanding of foreign affairs. Given the importance foreign policy officials attach to this goal, it should logically follow that locally based reporting deserves media and government encouragement.

Building a Local Media Base

Representatives of the major media and the government must begin to think differently about their work and their audiences. Primarily, they must remember something easily forgotten when one works for a long time in Washington or abroad: "foreign news" can be defined in many ways, comes in many forms, and has many constituencies.

John Hamilton's book is the best available source on the many ways of reporting "foreign" news at the local level. "There is no question," writes ABC anchorman Peter Jennings in the foreword to that book, "that much of [the] improvement in understanding and reporting can and must take place in American communities. For while there is no substitute for foreign correspondents, there is also no substitute for the powerful impression the local angle makes in revealing the impact of foreign relations."[10]

One example of those "local angles" is the domestic economic impact of international developments. Hamilton's book explores the many ways in which local businessmen, farmers, bankers, retailers—indeed, almost everybody in some communities—are affected by exports, imports, Third World debt, joint ventures and so on. This is precisely the kind of reporting that is useful to a State Department trying "to market the foreign affairs budget," and—much more important—is relevant to local readers.

And just as the local angle's crucial role in stirring the public's interest in foreign affairs must be recognized, so too must the advent of new international news constituencies. Many of these, such as the post-Vietnam grassroots groupings, have interests totally unrelated to economic concerns. Moreover, some of these new foreign policy constituents—such as Lutheran and Catholic overseas social service and famine relief organizations—can be quite valuable, even if unconventional, as news sources. For example, Minneapolis reporters visiting places as varied as Ethiopia, Sudan and the Philippines have been plugged into information networks and introduced into remote areas they could not possibly have reached without the personal help of people in their home communities.

Finally, foreign policy professionals must take account of the new levels of governmental involvement—at the state and local level—with issues such as sanctions against South Africa, sanctuary for Central American refugees, and a variety of nuclear matters. This involvement may seem irrelevant, or even offensive, to foreign policy professionals, but it demonstrates the widespread popular interest in certain foreign issues. And it does highlight promising subjects for the journalist seeking ways to expand his audience for international affairs reporting.[11]

These subjects are about as local as you can get, but they truly are "foreign news." Making the connection for the reader is the key. A significant number of "local" stories have foreign connections. In Florida, for example, these stories might include trade, citrus canker, drug trafficking, AIDS, illegal immigrants, and the price of dozens of products Floridians buy.

Of course, it works the other way too. Much news that seems "foreign" has obvious local impact. The current trade dispute between the United States and the European Community can be reported in broad, abstract terms, or it can be described in terms of higher prices for *Beefeater* gin and French cognac, or in terms of feed grains piling up in the local country elevator because they can no longer be sold to Spain. The reporter must make that connection if he wants his readers to pay attention to what he writes.

When such connections *are* made, newspapers in all communities can play a greater role in shaping public attitudes on foreign policy issues. Newspapers will have to expand their commitments—in terms of money for reporters' travel, news space devoted to additional coverage, time taken by reporters and editors to learn new subjects, and so on. And the Washington foreign policy professionals, both in government and in the press, will have to accept a new idea: that a great deal of the most useful reporting on foreign policy and national security can best be done from outside the Beltway.

Notes

1. Walter Laqueur, "Foreign News Coverage: From Bad to Worse," *Washington Journalism Review*, June 1983, 32.

2. Barry Rubin, *International News and the American Media* (Washington, DC: Center for Strategic and International Studies, 1976), 65.

3. Ibid., 66.

4. David Webster, "What's to Become of Network News," *Washington Post*, September 9, 1986, A-24.

5. William Drummond, "Is Time Running Out for Network News?" *Columbia Journalism Review*, May/June 1986, 50.

6. John Maxwell Hamilton, *Main Street America and the Third World* (Washington, DC: Seven Locks Press, 1986), 1.

7. Quoted in Bradley Morrison, *Sunlight on Your Doorstep* (Minneapolis: Minneapolis Star and Tribune Co., 1966), 36.

8. Ibid., Foreword.

9. *Washington Post*, January 7, 1986, A-19.

10. Hamilton, op. cit., x.

11. For a longer discussion of this, see Michael H. Shuman, "Dateline Main Street: Local Foreign Policies," *Foreign Policy*, no. 65 (Winter 1986/87), 154.

14

The Norman Conquest: Freedom of the Press in Britain and America

Harold Evans

On a very important and contentious foreign policy issue, a senior member of the executive branch deliberately deceives the legislature and the citizens. The deception is discovered and exposed to public scrutiny. What happens next in a well-run democracy? More than likely, an investigation would ensue. The degree of deception would be established, the truth promulgated, and the deceiver arraigned and punished.

This is indeed what happened in the course of the National Security Council (NSC) staff's efforts to raise money and other aid for the Contras. Lying to Congress is a felony. In this case, Robert McFarlane, the former national security adviser, and the prosecutors settled for pleas of guilty to the lesser charge of a misdemeanor.

In what type of democracy would the results have been different? Surprisingly, one answer is—in the type of democracy found in Britain. For in Britain, there are no penalties for deceiving the people or Parliament. Rather, punishment is meted out to those who dare expose the deception.

Take, first, the case of Clive Ponting. Ponting was a senior civil servant in the Department of Defense during the Falkland Islands conflict between Britain and Argentina. A significant body of British opinion believed that the dispute was diplomatically resolvable and judged the sinking of the Argentine cruiser *Belgrano* to be

189

provocative and cruel. The position and apparent intentions of the cruiser were crucial in the escalating policy controversy. Consequently, Ponting was ordered by the minister of defence to prepare misleading answers to Parliament's questions concerning the whole incident. He did so involuntarily, and at the same time, wrote to one of the critical British members of Parliament (MPs) and exposed the deception.

Subsequently, Clive Ponting, not the minister, faced trial. The government summarily dismissed Ponting and sought to have him jailed under the Official Secrets Act, which makes any unauthorized disclosure of official information a criminal offense. The minister of defence ended up facing hostile questions from the Opposition, but it never occurred to anyone to prosecute him for deceiving Parliament.

Then there is the case of Sarah Tisdall, a junior clerk in the ministry of defence. She sent to the *Guardian* newspaper a document that revealed the minister's public relations strategy for the missile deployments. She did not disclose any national security secrets; her case involved simply a question of conscience about deception. At the government's request, however, a court ordered the *Guardian* to surrender the document. Tisdall was thereby identified and prosecuted under the Official Secrets Act, ending up in jail for six months. Ponting was acquitted, but not before, and perhaps because of, an extraordinary summary by Mr. Justice McGowan. He directed the jury to decide against Ponting on the grounds that state interests and government policies were ipso facto identical. According to this reasoning, no public interest could outweigh the importance of fidelity to government policy.

The only commendable aspect of the Ponting case was the jury's judgment. It displayed a better appreciation of British constitutional theory, if not practice, recognizing that the sovereign state of Britain comprises more than simply the Crown or the executive. Indeed, it encompasses the Crown in Parliament, and Parliament consists of the Queen's ministers *and* Her Loyal Opposition. Thus, Ponting, in talking to an MP, was talking to a member of the sovereign state.

The government's defeat by the jury gave it second thoughts but not about the wisdom of conducting government by secrecy and deception. Rather, the defeat led the government to reconsider the methods of enforcing secrecy, so that it never again would risk the common people's verdict. Before delving into the government's change of mind, however, an analysis of Britain's political structure and the role of the media within it is necessary.

Britain, America and Press Freedom

Such is the feeling of communion between the British and the Americans, in blood ties, in political heritage, in the culture of a common tongue, in the comradeship of modern history's closest wartime alliance, that they often think of themselves as one society of common values. This creates a warm but misleading sentiment. For today, there exists between Britain and the United States a profound and accelerating difference, one from which both can learn.

The differences in political structure are conventionally regarded as embroidery on two different systems of representative government, based on respect for the rule of law and human rights. Britain's unitary parliamentary democracy, sustained by tradition and convention, and with the state's continuity vested in a constitutional monarchy, obviously contrasts with a democratic federal republic with a written constitution. These differences, and others, have never deterred anyone in the last century from equating the two countries' devotion to freedom.

Indeed, some distinguished American public servants, such as Douglas Dillon and Lloyd Cutler, have advocated a conversion of the U.S. Constitution to a quasi-British model. They argue that such a change would make government more effective in the dispatch of foreign and domestic policy while preserving essential human rights. And there are others who have been attracted to the British way of dealing with questions of secrecy and national security. The U.S. *Naval War College Review,* for example, has called for a War Press Act, based on the British Official Secrets Act, as a way of legitimizing the exclusion of reporters from events such as the invasion of Grenada. Max Kampelman, before he took to arms control, used to argue that citizen liberties are "as well preserved" in Britain as in America, despite the existence of press-restraining laws.

There is a fundamental misunderstanding at work here. The conflicts in the two countries between government and the press may be over similar issues. Both British and American governments have accused the press of sustaining terrorism with the oxygen of publicity. Both would prefer to conduct foreign policy without scrutiny. The issues that provoke charges of irresponsibility and countercharges of censorship are similar in all the political democracies.

But the similarities end there. The British political system is parliamentary with executive predominance. Indeed, in the words of the former Lord Chancellor Lord Hailsham, it has been developing into an elective dictatorship because of the power of the Prime Minister to dismiss ministers and to dissolve Parliament. There is little practical restraint from the cabinet's "collective responsibility" and less from the majority of the legislature whose members observe party discipline in a way unfamiliar to Capitol Hill. There is also in British political and social life a San Andreas fault—an underlying philosophical crack in the country's approach to freedom of the press. Britain has a half-free press and the ruling elites find nothing objectionable in that. A review of British law supports this assertion.

Official Secrets

The nomenclature is suggestive. Britain has an Official Secrets Act that punishes any unauthorized disclosure of official information. The relevant statute in the United States is the Freedom of Information Act, which stipulates that all federal government records must be provided on request to anyone unless one of nine specific conditions apply. These conditions mainly concern national defense, privacy, privileged or confidential trade secrets, and the regulation of financial institutions. The Official Secrets Act, on the other hand, makes the giving and receiving of *any* official information an offense, irrespective of whether the public interest would benefit. The British government resisted all efforts to allow a public interest defense when a "reform act" was passed in 1989. This new legislation still allows the suppression of whatever official information the government chooses to keep secret. The information may be suppressed for legitimate reasons or simply because the government finds it politically inconvenient to tell the British people what they ought and have a right to know.

The Official Secrets Act in the past has been put to both shameful and silly uses. In the 1960s it was used to conceal a series of scandals involving atomic radiation hazards. The Home Office permanent secretary warned the *Daily Express* about reporting a radiation leak at Windscale. The newspaper, fearing prosecution, refrained from disclosing the information—of indisputable immediate importance to public health and long-term nuclear policy. The public was kept unaware that the Atomic Energy Authority as constituted was incapable of ensuring the elimination of radiation leaks, an inability shown up in the 1980s revelation that the same Windscale plant had wantonly spilled plutonium into the North Sea.

Successive governments have tried to misuse the act's provisions and could certainly misuse the new act. Jonathan Aitken and the editor of *The Sunday Telegraph* were once prosecuted for reporting information critical of the Nigerian federal government's military capability during the Biafran war. The Crown opened its case in dramatic tones claiming that major military secrets had been revealed. Two days later, after some cross examination, it was shown that every military fact Aitken reported had already been published. Moreover, it was learned that the British defence attaché, upon whose leaked document the report had been based, had himself read it out at a press conference on an unattributable basis. Halfway through the trial, therefore, the Crown was forced to concede Aitken's innocence.

The D-Notice

Just as governmental abuse of the Official Secrets Act has served to destroy its usefulness, so has official abuse of another device, the D-notice, served to undermine it. The D-notice is a wartime relic, a voluntary system whereby government defence and security officials, working with media representatives, agree on what subjects are off-limits to the press. In principle this makes sense. Nobody in the responsible press, even in the silly British popular press, inadvertently wants to disclose important secrets to a potential enemy. But, on the other hand, neither does anyone want to be conned into suppressing information that is really a matter of politics and not a matter of security.

The D-notice works in the following manner. There is a committee of civil servants and editors, who meet at the ministry of defence. There, the committee discusses what subjects may properly be identified to the press as sensitive and hence placed on a D-notice. Once this committee reaches agreement, the rest of the press is notified and encouraged to seek guidance from the Secretary of the D-notice committee before publishing anything covered by the one-line references in the D-notice. Editors may still choose to disregard a D-notice but they do so with the knowledge that government prosecution is likely.

The D-notice is, in effect, an institutionalized way of doing what is done in the United States through informal government-press contacts. Recently, for example, the late director of the CIA, William Casey, enlisted National Security Adviser John Poindexter and President Ronald Reagan in a successful effort to persuade the *Washington Post* to remove some information from a story on National Security Agency analyst Ronald W. Pelton. Pelton had sold the Soviet Union secrets about electronic interception techniques.

Editors who have served on D-notice committees say that it can work well. Much depends on its permanent secretary and on the government of the day. There has to be trust and fair play. As editor of national and regional newspapers, I have both obeyed and defied D-notices. In the 1960s, I obeyed a D-notice not to reveal the secret places where the British government would locate in the event of a nuclear war.

In another case, I took no account of a D-notice specifically reissued in a belated attempt to discourage *The Sunday Times* from reporting on the Kim Philby affair. The notice forbade the publication of anything regarding the past and present security service members. I disregarded it because, as the British government well knew, *The Sunday Times* had spent more than a year investigating Kim Philby and we were about to reveal the fact that he was a major Soviet spy who had been head of Britain's anti-Soviet section of espionage.

The Philby investigation had necessarily led to the interviewing of many security service members—a feat unheard of at the time. I did decide to withhold the name of an intelligence operative serving in Singapore who came into the Philby history, but I continued with a series of articles on Philby's treachery and the cover-up. I did so because I was convinced that all of the information was already known to the Soviets and that the D-notice was simply an attempt to prevent the embarrassment of certain civil servants and politicians. The series revealed appalling negligence on the part of MI6 (the British foreign intelligence agency), the betrayal of operations in Eastern Europe, the leakage of atomic information from the United States, the suborning of the press, lies to Parliament, and much else. Because of this the rather excitable foreign secretary of the day, Mr. George Brown, denounced me as a traitor—essentially on the grounds that my newspaper's revelations would weaken American confidence in British intelligence. The Central Intelligence Agency was, of course, already well aware of the damage Philby had done and so were the Soviets.

The D-notice system is still operative in Britain, but any residual trust in it was destroyed by Mrs. Margaret Thatcher's actions against the proposed radio program, "My Country Right or Wrong." In the wake of the *Spycatcher* book sensation, this program interviewed former security service operatives. Donald Trelford, editor of *The Observer* and a member of the D-notice committee, judged it to be an anodyne program, no more than a cautious review of the issues. The committee heard tapes of the program before its release, and the committee's secretary proclaimed that the security service had no objections to it.

Mrs. Thatcher, nonetheless, sought and obtained a court injunction which banned the program along with a similar one on television. The ban was enforced not on the grounds of national security but on the grounds of confidence: the officials who had spoken had broken their lifetime confidence guarantees.

Law of Confidence

In other cases, the law of contempt of court and an obscure common law of "confidence" have been deployed to limit press freedom. Both devices circumvent the jury system. In national security cases, as an English High Court judge observed, the government's use of these means established a doctrine of absolute confidentiality unknown this side of the Iron Curtain. In the 1974 Granada Guildhall lecture, when I characterized the British press as half-free, I suggested that the law of confidence would develop as a powerful suppressor. At the time, I thought I was indulging in a little journalistic license; my audience probably thought so too. But today, the law of confidence that was then a tiny cloud on the horizon now darkens the entire landscape. Numerous enemies of the press have resorted to it and most of the judges who have ruled on it have succumbed to the doctrines of executive power. They have argued that ministerial decisions are prerogative acts which preclude judicial review. This is the dangerous path.

There is not yet a law of confidence in the United States, but it is not inconceivable that one could develop. Thus, in order to prevent its realization in America, it is worth describing how the law developed in Britain.

The first seeds of the law of confidence were sown in 1849 when a man called Strange acquired some copies of Queen Victoria and Prince Albert's privately printed etchings. He proposed publishing a descriptive catalogue of them. The laws of property, copyright and contract had no relevance to the case, because all that was at issue was raw information, so the judges obligingly argued a law of confidence to stop Strange from publishing the catalogue on the grounds that the information was the private property of the Prince. This marked the first use of an injunction to withhold information, as such, rather than information in a unique form of words. Over the years the judges developed this precedent in commercial law to protect formulas for patent medicines, glue, and designs for winches and brassieres. Eventually, these commercial principles were applied to social and political cases, and consequently, property rights, rather than personal rights, became the decisive legal issue.

It was in *Fraser v. Evans* that the contemporary law of confidence entered the jurisdiction currently affecting the press. In 1967 *The Sunday Times* was about to disclose that the Greek colonels had bribed a British MP, when a judge ordered the story retracted. The following week the newspaper lost in the High Court: the document on which *The Sunday Times'* report was based was judged the confidential property of the bribers. On appeal the newspaper won only because the bribers, the Greek government, made the mistake of not having someone in court.

The law of confidence has been used to prevent exposure of a crooked laundry, a property racket, and the hazardous effects of the drug thalidomide, which has maimed hundreds of mothers and children. Vice Chancellor Wood remarked once that the law of confidence could not be used to prevent disclosure of an "iniquity." But hardly anything is judged iniquitous enough to satisfy British judges. In the thalidomide case, Mr. Justice Talbot ruled against *The Sunday Times* and argued: "Negligence even if it could be proved [against the drug company] could not constitute an exception to the need to maintain confidentiality."

The result of all this is that the attorney general is now able to argue that the common law of confidence applies to domestic political information as well as to glue and drugs. The first time the government chose to rely on this law in a case of domestic politics was when Harold Wilson's administration tried to prevent publication of the diary of his former cabinet minister the late Richard Crossman. The trial involved the same legal principles as the Pentagon papers case, with the exception that public interest arguments were not allowed. The Lord Chief Justice accepted this radical extension of the law of confidence. As it happened, he chose not to apply this extension in the case of the Crossman diaries, regarding them, incorrectly, as too stale to be relevant. Nevertheless, the endorsement of the law of confidence was a little-recognized disaster for the press. I wrote at the time that the Lord Chief Justice had given to the government a powerful new weapon—one that would be used sooner or later to suppress matters of public interest. Mrs. Thatcher did exactly that in the *Spycatcher* trials, where the law of confidence, argued before a judge alone, proved more convenient than the Official Secrets Act with the need for inconvenient press.

Consequences

The Official Secrets Act, the D-notice, the laws of contempt and of confidence are laws that have become more wide-ranging than is commonly understood, and affect many matters of public health and happiness not even remotely associated with the national security. The uncompensated victims of the drug thalidomide had to suffer for twelve years due to the blanket of secrecy imposed by contempt and confidence laws. The Franks Committee identified sixty-one other statutory provisions which served to conceal information of public interest. For instance, Section 26 of the Clean Air Act makes it a criminal offense to disclose that a criminal offense has been committed. Consequently, the owners of a factory emptying cyanide into a river face a maximum penalty of £100, while the river inspector who mentions the results of his analysis to the public risks three months imprisonment. These examples (and there are plenty more) are cited to demonstrate how suppressive laws get out of hand.

The result of the British panoply of laws can be dramatized simply by demonstrating that the American media never could have exposed the Watergate scandal if it had had to operate under the British legal restraints. From the moment the famous five were charged on June 17, 1972, as from the moment of private litigation in the case of the thalidomide children, the certainty under British regulations of prosecution for contempt of court would have prevented the kind of press inquiry that occurred. Nobody knew then that the trail of wrongdoing led to the President, and even if someone did, no public interest argument would have been allowed to affect a case before a court. Even if the press had inquired, contempt law would have prevented publication of any of the results for years as indictment followed indictment. Under British law, revelations such as the promise of government help for companies who contributed to Richard Nixon's campaign funds would never have occurred. More than likely, the law of confidence also would have been invoked to gag the press. Woodward and Bernstein, it will be recalled, were able to acquire and investigate the membership list of CREEP (the Committee to Re-elect the President). In Britain, that would have been stopped in the twinkling of a judicial eye by the mere mention of the *Prince Albert v. Strange* case. The names and addresses, not merely their copyright expression, would have been "a confidence."

Some leading politicians want Britain to incorporate the European Convention on Human Rights into British law. That would be an excellent move, for it would give personal rights, such as free speech, a guaranteed hearing. It will not happen in Mrs. Thatcher's reign. A Freedom of Information Act also stands no chance with Mrs. Thatcher's parliamentary sheep and with a body of lawyers in Britain that is reactionary on free speech issues. In the United States the American Bar Association played an important role in the passage of the Freedom of Information Act. It is unthinkable that British lawyers would do likewise.

Different Philosophies

At the heart of the differences between Britain and the United States is a distinction, insufficiently appreciated, between opinion and fact. In neither country is the coercive power of the state often brought to bear against the utterance of an opinion. The teachings of Milton, Locke and Mill are embedded in everyone's consciousness. At Speaker's Corner in Britain, a beaming policeman protects hecklers who, within earshot of Buckingham Palace, incite the violent overthrow of the monarchy. And in the United States, the lawns opposite the White House are saturated with effigies of the President and banners denouncing his administration. Indeed, in both countries politicians, judges, corporate leaders, and, of course, editors pay sonorous tribute to the value of free speech. Yet, despite these similarities, significant differences exist, and they rest upon a fundamental philosophical distinction.

In America the prevailing philosophy, though it is not without its enemies, is that, in Madison's words, a popular government without popular information is but a prologue to a farce or a tragedy. The law obliges government agencies to disclose official information.

The First Amendment says, significantly, "Congress shall make no law abridging the freedom of speech *or of the press* [emphasis added]." In other words, Congress should not constrain the institution which provides the facts. In Britain the comparable philosophy regarding press freedom was formulated by the great jurist Blackstone: "The liberty of the press is indeed essential to the nature of a free state; but this consists of laying no previous restraints upon publication. Every freeman has an undoubted right to lay what sentiments he pleases before the people; to forbid this is to destroy the freedom of the press." Note the word "sentiments."

As Britain moved from monarchy, to aristocracy, to oligarchy, and finally to mass democracy, the assumption remained that the facts on which to base an opinion were available. This was always a risky assumption, but perhaps bearable in a society with very small conglomerations of power. Certainly, it was as tolerable as the classical economists' assumption of a free flow of goods and services in a perfect market. In recent periods, however, the citizen's access to knowledge has failed to keep pace with the vast expansion of state and corporate power. Yet there has been no change in the philosophy. In the thalidomide case hearing in the House of Lords, the late Lord Reid, thought the greatest judge in the land, ruled that *The Sunday Times* was entitled to publish an opinion but not the facts on which the opinion was based. This ruling, banning the thalidomide articles, had the support of all the other Law Lords.

Two attitudes seem to underlie Britain's restrictive practices. First, information is frequently considered by judges and politicians as the property of the government and not of the people. Second, in cases where free publication has been challenged, the British courts have fallen back on common law precedents rooted in property rights. There is no Bill of Rights to place personal rights in the balance. A Bill of Rights is rejected on the grounds that it would limit Parliament's supremacy. Consequently, Parliament is no longer either an effective monitor of the executive or a reliable defender of individual rights.

Today, there is substance to Jefferson's conviction that in Britain the Tory or Norman concept of rights is dominant: they are grants from the Crown. This is distinct from the Whig or Saxon concept, which holds that rights are natural to the people and that the Crown has no powers except those expressly granted. Jefferson believed that the American people's idea of popular sovereignty had its origins in the fact that their Anglo-Saxon ancestors held their lands and property in absolute dominion until the Normans came. Jefferson blamed Norman lawyers, rather than William the Conqueror, for lumbering the Anglo-Saxons with the feudal burdens which blotted out their ancient rights.

Thus, Britain and America are two societies that have diverged in questions of government and freedom in ways more significant than political structure. To miss this point and to impose British methods on the American system would be disastrous as well as unconstitutional.

In the United States there have been, of course, abridgments of the First Amendment—for example, the Sedition Act, the Espionage Act, and the Smith Act. There have been periods hostile to political dissent and fact finding. Nonetheless, the First Amendment remains a foundation of American freedom. It has been a restraining influence on the adjudications of the courts and an emboldening influence on the conduct of the press. Hence Americans should not tolerate any weakening of the First Amendment, even on the grounds of national security.

At the same time, one must recognize that no right is enhanced by its irresponsible exercise. Alexander Hamilton was wrong to doubt the value of a Bill of Rights, as history has shown, but he had a valid point when he wrote that "whatever fine declarations may be inserted in any constitution must altogether depend on public opinion and the general spirit of the people and government."

The press must behave responsibly. But it must also be cautious of gypsies bearing gifts. There are risks of confusion and contamination in seemingly helpful laws concerning journalist privilege, such as shield laws to protect sources. These seductions should be spurned because they lead to constant fiddling by the lower courts and legislators and because, as British experience demonstrates, they increase the risk of hazardous precedents that work against the public interest. Exceptions to the First Amendment have been proposed, for instance, to protect information that would cause "grave and irreparable damage to national security." This sounds reasonable enough, but portentous phrases are not a substitute for real patriotism. And real patriotism invariably requires that people who bear the sacrifice should weigh the risk. With language as vague as that regarding national security, who knows what room would be left for fact finding and debate on precisely those grave issues where they are needed?

Secrecy is sometimes essential in operations and in new technology, but where policy is concealed from public scrutiny, it is commonly the handmaiden of disaster. The invasion of the Bay of Pigs, Laos and Cambodia; the fake oil sanctions against Rhodesia; the ill-controlled nuclear test explosions; the supply of arms to Iran and the diversion of funds to the Contras—were they all issues better left unexplored and undebated? As Justice Gurfein once said: "Security is defended not on the ramparts alone but in the values of a free society." America, arguably the best template for a free—and secure—society, embraces a certain set of values which find their clearest expression in the First Amendment. Even in the face of the most eloquent "patriotic" appeals, that amendment must never be sacrificed.

15

The Italian Press and the Moro Affair

John L. Harper

On the morning of March 16, 1978, Aldo Moro, president of the
Christian Democratic party (DC), and his plain-clothes escort were
ambushed at the corner of via Mario Fani and via Stresa, near Moro's
home in northwest Rome.[1] In less than five minutes, a nine-member
"commando" team blocked the Moro party's two automobiles, killed
or mortally wounded Moro's five body guards, seized the party president, and sped him off to a secret "people's prison." The gunmen
(and one woman) were members of the Red Brigades (*Brigate Rosse*
or BR), a clandestine left-wing organization whose aim was to overthrow the Italian state.

So began the extraordinary "Moro affair," a drama that consumed
the world's attention until, after fifty-five days of soul-searching,
pathos and suspense, it ended, as it began, in violent death. Moro's
body, containing eleven bullets, was found on May 9 in the rear com-
partment of a red Renault-4. The car was parked in via Caetani, a
small street in central Rome, near both Christian Democratic and
Communist party headquarters.

Aldo Moro was Italy's most important political leader. Now, more
than ten years after his kidnapping and murder, these events can
be seen as a turning point in Italian postwar history. Moro's disap-
pearance marked the beginning of the end of collaboration between
the DC and the Italian Communist party (PCI) that Moro himself had
promoted. It also provided the shock that led the political system
to mobilize its resources decisively against a left-wing terrorist

assault. Finally, the Moro affair sparked an inconclusive but fascinating and instructive debate about the behavior of the Italian information media during a serious terrorist incident. The Italian printed press played an active role during what was both a major national emergency and a compelling news event.

The unfolding story, although peculiarly Italian, raised a series of more universal questions: First, should the press, by reporting the event and the captors' demand, provide a platform to terrorists? Second, who is the enemy and what does that enemy really want? Third, how much credibility should be given to the prisoner, particularly if a statesman, once he has begun to lobby for his life? Finally, can the state negotiate with terrorists without conceding political recognition to criminals and encouraging future terrorism?

Both the press and the state grappled with these questions at different points throughout Moro's captivity. That period can be divided into three phases. From March 16 to March 30 the main concerns were the behavior of the press itself, the nature of the BR, and the issue of negotiations. Following Moro's first letter on March 30, which called for an exchange of prisoners, attention shifted to the hostage himself, and the discussion of negotiations intensified. Between April 20, when the BR issued its ultimatum, and the affair's tragic conclusion on May 9, a full-scale debate emerged between two clearly divided camps.

In time the two sides became known as the *partito della fermezza* (the party of firmness) and the smaller but articulate *partito della tratativa* (the party of negotiations). The former opposed dealing for Moro's life and tended to deny the moral and intellectual autonomy of the prisoner. The latter opposed the sacrifice of human life on the altar of an abstract "state," or in the name of an unholy alliance between the dominant political elites. Their view that Moro was a lucid man fighting for his life anticipated the argument of the Sicilian novelist, Leonardo Sciascia, in his vitriolic attack on the "regime press" and political establishment (the DC and PCI), published later in the year, *L'affaire Moro*.

The newspapers covering the crisis, it should be noted, saw themselves as protagonists, not merely passive observers. This is because privately owned Italian newspapers have traditionally engaged more heavily in partisan debate and controversy than their counterparts in the United States. They are also subject to greater pressure from the political parties themselves. Italian political parties use manifold channels of influence, including the control of certain kinds of financial credit, of inside information, and of the regulatory framework within which the press operates. There is direct control in the case of the official party press, for example *l'Unità* (PCI), *Il Popolo* (DC), and *l'Avanti* (the Italian Socialist party or PSI). Each of these papers had a role in the affair, as did influential independent papers such as *Il Corriere della Sera* and *La Repubblica*, and to a lesser extent the widely read *La Stampa*, *Il Giornale Nuovo*, and *Il Resto del Carlino*.

The First Stage: March 16 to March 30

"Luck helped us out. Actions like that almost never go right the first time, but that morning everything fit together smoothly." This observation was made years later by Valerio Morucci, one of the gunmen at via Fani on March 16. Indeed, the apparent "Teutonic" efficiency and ruthlessness of the operation stunned the country and cast a lingering spell over the entire affair. The contrast between the efficiency of the BR and the impotence of the Italian state, embodied in its slain policemen, had a lasting and contradictory effect. For a large majority, the patent weakness of the state demanded an extraordinarily strong response, if only to do justice to the five policemen. For others, however, via Fani raised the question of whether the Italian state was defensible or really worth defending now that its institutions appeared unable to protect its most important servant.

The March 17 headline of *Corriere della Sera* of Milan, "Moro kidnapped.... Country rejects blackmail," accurately captured the reaction of most readers. The next day Eugenio Scalfari, editor of *La Repubblica* of Rome, called a hypothetical exchange "not only impossible but not even proposable." Scalfari cited the case of the Genoese magistrate Mario Sossi whom the BR had kidnapped in 1974. No deal had been made in that case, and Scalfari maintained that Moro could not be treated differently from any other citizen. Controversy immediately erupted over the defense of the state and the origins of the BR. The *Corriere* and *La Repubblica* harshly criticized not only the state security apparatus but also the position of *Lotta Continua*, a widely read paper of the extra-parliamentary Left that described itself as "neither with the State nor with the BR."

Worse still, the *Lotta Continua* line appeared to have tacit support from two leading novelist-intellectuals, Alberto Moravia and

Leonardo Sciascia. On March 20, Moravia published a long article in which he declared his "painful extraneousness" from the entire business. Sciascia, who had failed to make a ritual statement of support for the state, was denounced by the communist-owned *Paese Sera* of Rome. Sciascia replied that he was "sick and tired of having his views distorted by the ignorant and the imbeciles." In fact, Sciascia was disgusted by what he later called the "melodrama of love for the state," a situation in which papers and politicians were trying to outdo one another in a hypocritical "game of intransigence."

On March 20, a phone call from the BR alerted the Rome paper, *Il Messaggero*, to the distribution of the BR's first communiqué, along with a snapshot of the prisoner. The message announced the "trial" of Aldo Moro, calling him a central actor in the current transformation of Italy into an "imperialist state of the multinationals." The BR advised the public not to trust the "regime press" (the daily papers and television) and stated that they would publicly communicate the trial's findings. But the BR were themselves dependent on the "regime press" to reach the mass public and evidently sought to use the papers to impress what they saw as a vast constituency of sympathizers. All the major papers printed Moro's picture, taken with a Red Brigades flag in the background, and reproduced (with the exception of the Communist *l'Unità*, which carried an edited version) the full text of the BR communiqué.

The arrival of the photo shifted public attention to the plight of the prisoner, while the BR's message (the first of nine) raised the issue of the press itself. Anticipating Sciascia's critique, the semiologist Umberto Eco observed in late May that the press had created two images of Moro during the kidnapping, neither corresponding to reality: Moro the superman, heroically resisting, and Moro the letter writer, tragically broken and manipulated. Indeed, DC sympathizers calling for firmness tended initially to build up Moro, and the photo lent itself naturally to that purpose. The prisoner's appearance was haggard, yet the composed, melancholy countenance was unmistakably that of Moro under more normal circumstances. Viewers could therefore assume the prisoner must be resisting the BR and providing a lesson to the state and to the public at large.

Although some observers detected a certain wishful thinking and self-delusion in the press's initial treatment of Moro's imprisonment, publication of the Moro photo and the subsequent discussion fostered the image of an ideal prisoner-statesman—resolute in the face of adversity—and therefore reinforced the press's initial, essentially reflexive, call for *fermezza*. Aside from the inherent merits of this line, the press could not henceforth reverse itself without admitting a serious initial miscalculation.

Of the press's decision to publish the BR communiqué Umberto Eco later observed, "For the last two months the press has done nothing but discuss its own situation, its own possibilities, its own responsibilities, its own conditioning." This is especially true of March 21–23 when a series of articles tackled the question of terrorism and censorship. On March 21 the *Corriere* carried an interview with the Nobel prize-winning poet and occasional journalist, Eugenio Montale, under the title "A Case for Our Consciences." Montale agreed with the decision to publish the photo but not the communiqué, which conceivably could "feed the fantasies of the young." On March 23 the *Corriere* offered an interview with the proverbial expert on mass communications, Marshal McLuhan. McLuhan favored a reduction of coverage, even a total blackout. The terrorists, he declared, were in search of a self-image, "a new identity," and used the media for their purposes. A total blackout of all news, including television, would restore "a sense of reality," at least for a time. McLuhan then proceeded to reverse himself, saying that there were no automatic rules of behavior under such circumstances.

For most, however, a blackout policy was simply not practical in Italy, and there is no evidence that the government ever considered it seriously. The head of the state television network RAI, Paolo Grassi, spoke for many when he said on March 25: "Ours is a country that has to be guided by persuasion, not with military orders." For a clear majority, government censorship would have been a step toward the sort of repressive regime sought by the BR themselves. In the event, almost all of the newspapers printed Moro's letters, which began to arrive after March 30.

The decision by the major papers to give massive coverage to every detail of the case, thereby acting as a forum for the BR, reinforced the *fermezza* line of the papers themselves and, presumably, public opposition to negotiating for Moro's release. The importance of the rigid *fermezza* line to the Communists and the Christian Democrats (especially with administrative elections scheduled in some cities for May 14) became quickly evident. At the time, the PCI was particularly sensitive to the threat of destabilization of Italian democracy by a combination of inside and outside forces. The party had formulated its "historic compromise" strategy with the 1973 Chilean coup in mind and saw itself as a main target of the BR and their presumed "manipulators." The Communists also admitted that the BR had genuine support in some factories and drew strength from a popular reaction against the PCI's revisionist tendencies. Indeed, the BR had made no secret of wanting to appropriate the emotional symbols, resistance tradition, and base of support of the PCI. The PCI leadership's animus toward the BR was all the more visceral and intense as any hint of deviation from *fermezza* would surely invite charges of duplicity from such anticommunist observers as the *Corriere's* popular columnist, Alberto Ronchey and from critics of "Eurocommunism" in the United States and elsewhere. By the same token, the PCI's defense of the Italian state was seen as a sort of "rite of passage" by nonparty sympathizers. Ugo La Malfa, president of the Republican party, and one of the most authoritative supporters of a government role for the PCI, observed in April that the Communists' unbending stand proved that he, and Moro himself, had been correct to trust them. And even though Moro was their most important, and probably indispensable, interlocutor, the Communists saw no choice but to resist a deal to save Moro's life in order to safeguard the PCI's new role in the political system that Moro himself had helped to make possible.

A majority of the DC leadership was as concerned as the PCI to avoid any semblance of compromise because it was sensitive to charges that the DC itself was mainly responsible for the state's weakness and because it did not want to take second place to the PCI in its dedication to *rigore*. The DC feared a backlash from the public and the police that might stem from a deal to save Moro. Pressures on the DC from the United States and West German governments are hard to document but undoubtedly also played a role. Public opinion appeared to back the DC line. A poll taken in early April said that 77 percent of the population opposed a deal with the BR. Finally, aside from the calculations of those in the party whose positions might potentially improve with Moro's demise (for example, Prime Minister Andreotti), or those who argued that Moro's political line was safer without Moro after March 16, his friends, including party secretary Benigno Zaccagnini, argued in good faith that *fermezza* was an expression of Moro's own political message.

Clearly there was considerable pressure from politicians and the party press on the independent papers to back a policy of firmness.

L'Unità and *Il Popolo* outdid each other in single-minded dedication to the hard line. One may even conclude that a more or less unspoken understanding existed from the start that there would be no real effort to control the press and that information about the case would be made available as long as the press did not compromise the government's position. The popular commentator Giorgio Bocca went further in asserting: "The papers and mass media put themselves in a disciplined and servile way under the orders of the political parties." Yet such accusations overlooked other, more subtle motives for the press's behavior, including the sincere conviction of many that there was, indeed, no alternative to firmness. Despite their rejection of censorship, the papers were visibly pained by the image problem and moral dilemma connected with providing a forum for the BR, and coverage of the Moro affair continued amid serious ambivalence on the part of the press itself.

Essentially, once the press decided, in effect, to exploit Moro's plight to the fullest to sell papers, and to provide free publicity to the Red Brigades in the process, it became all the more unthinkable for most editors to support the idea of negotiations. In addition to the other factors that tended to reinforce *fermezza* during the early days of the affair—the stunning impact of the operation itself, the interpretation of the photograph, the inevitable political pressure—*fermezza* also reflected the press's concern with its own public image and in some cases probably represented a bargain editors and journalists had struck with their own troubled consciences.

The Second Stage: March 30 to April 21

The next phase of the ordeal began with Moro's letter to Interior Minister Francesco Cossiga, calling for negotiations on March 29. The question of the authenticity of Moro's letters became the most controversial and bitterly divisive feature of the affair. More than ten years later it seems clear that Moro's letters were essentially his own, though many believed at the time that they had been extorted or ghost-written by his diabolically clever captors.

After all, the hallmark of Moro's political approach had been the search for dialogue with the Left, a patient, tenacious attempt to divide the opposition by co-opting its reasonable elements and isolating the extremists. That Moro should have seen the BR as a political, not a criminal, phenomenon, that he should have tried to reason with and divide them, was as natural as his desire not to become a martyr to what he saw as some theoretical and un-Italian model of the "state."

Later accounts by Moro's captors indicate that Moro had quickly grasped who the BR were and what they were after as the price for his life. In addition to the liberation of their comrades in prison, and to the information in Moro's possession (or so they thought) on DC financial scandals and links to right-wing terrorism, the BR sought the sort of political legitimacy implied in direct negotiations with the state (or the DC) for the exchange of "political prisoners." Accordingly, the idea of a first letter appears to have been Moro's attempt to open a secret channel through which to mediate between the BR and the state. That it was to have remained secret is clear from passages of the letter itself. One can imagine Moro's reaction when the BR decided to cash in on the letter's presumed propaganda value and made it available to the public. (The BR subsequently observed Moro's wishes that certain letters remain secret.)

The letter went quickly to the heart of the matter. Moro explained that he faced

> the risk of being called upon or induced to speak in a manner that could be unpleasant and dangerous in determinant situations.... The doctrine that says kidnapping should not bring advantages is debatable enough in common cases where harm to the victims is extremely probable. It does not hold up in political circumstances where sure and incalculable damage is provoked not only to the person involved but to the State. The sacrifice of the innocent in the name of an abstract principle of legality, while an obvious state of necessity should induce one to save them, is inadmissable.

Given the prevailing image of Moro, the letter's publication produced a considerable shock. The *Corriere* demanded to know, "Who wrote this letter? Aldo Moro, president of the DC and statesman...or was it written by a man with the same face...but reduced to impotence by a cruel imprisonment?" *La Repubblica* saw psychological torture as probable and expressed disbelief that Moro would sacrifice his reputation in return for his physical salvation. The *Carlino's* front page the same day showed a drawing of Moro's hand holding a pen, with the hand emerging from a barrel of a gun. An editorial in *l'Unità* entitled "Fermezza" dismissed the letter's authenticity and, significantly, that of any future letters that might emerge from the BR's "people's prison."

The press had scarcely digested the Cossiga letter when a copy of a second letter, this time to party secretary Zaccagnini, arrived at the Milan office of *La Repubblica* on April 4. The letter, along with communiqué number four, appeared in most papers the next day. Moro now made no attempt to hide his resentment.

> I am a political prisoner placed in a unsustainable position by your brusque decision to close off any discussion relative to other detained persons.... I would like to clarify that I say these things in full lucidity and without having suffered any coercion to my person. At least as much lucidity as one can have in an exceptional situation with no one to console him, who knows what awaits him. And in truth, I also feel a little abandoned by all of you.

The second letter produced an official DC statement claiming that such words were not "morally ascribable" to Moro. *La Repubblica's* editor, Eugenio Scalfari declared that although the BR had failed to gain significant revelations from Moro, or to use him to divide the DC, they had successfully reduced "a man to the status of a puppet." Montanelli had no doubt that Moro had been coerced, although he conceded, "We don't know what means they used to extort it from him, whether torture, drugs, or a pistol to the neck." Finally, the *Osservatore Romano* pronounced Moro's "values and principles" unrecognizable in the Zaccagnini letter.

Moro's second letter referred to conversations held several years earlier with party colleagues, in which he had supported the principle of bargaining with kidnappers. One of the colleagues, Luigi Gui, confirmed Moro's words, but another, Paolo Emilio Taviani, denied them. On April 10 the papers received a long memo from Moro painting a sarcastically worded portrait of Taviani's political career. Moro implied that Taviani, while defense and interior minister, had been a creature of the Americans, who, Moro suggested, along with the Germans, were perhaps behind the current refusal to negotiate.

Moro's public attack on his own party was the last straw for many, and announcements of his political demise came even before a BR communiqué on April 15 declared the end of Moro's trial and the sentence of death. Gianfranco Piazzesi now argued that even if Moro were to return, "In no case will he be the DC leader of greatest prestige and authority." Sandro Viola observed that Moro had revealed nothing new but that what came out was the "fall of Moro the man." In an article called "Political Requiem," Montanelli declared, "The one whom the BR are holding and forcing to speak is no longer the president of the DC. We hope with all our heart that Moro will be restored to his family, but as a political figure he disappeared on March 16." Among the few voices with a kind word was the *Carlino* of Bologna, which noted that if the BR had managed to extract from Moro only a harmless polemic with Taviani, Moro's "moral fiber" must be stronger than that of his captors. In fact, the BR later admitted that the prisoner had been unwilling or unable to provide any new, sensational information.

It was only natural that the most rigid backers of *fermezza* should give the least credence to Moro's calls for negotiation and suffer the greatest disappointment at the prisoner's behavior. It was equally natural that those who had stressed the extraordinary capacities of the BR should see the letters not as Moro's but as part of an elaborate mise-en-scène. But such logic was hard to swallow for those who had been suspicious of *fermezza* all along, and the death sentence announcement served to intensify the debate. Enzo Forcella, a journalist with ties to the PCI, rejected the "official interpretation" and found Moro's call for an exchange perfectly consistent with his Catholic conception of politics. Meanwhile, Giovanni Guiso, a lawyer for the Red Brigades on trial in Turin told the press that Moro could still be saved and that the true "problem [was] the recognition of a political status of the BR."

On April 19 the papers printed the famous "false communiqué" number seven, announcing that the BR had carried out the sentence and that Moro's body could be found in a mountain lake, snowbound and frozen over at the time. Opinions were mixed as to the document's authenticity, and the discussion continued while helicopter-borne police searched the lake. Skeptics were vindicated the following day when the BR dispatched a photo of Moro holding a copy of the previous day's *La Repubblica*. For the first time the BR demanded an exchange of "communist prisoners" and an answer within two days.

The headlines on April 21 reflected the sensation that the climax of the story was approaching. The *Corriere's* editorial proclaimed, "The Republic will not be bartered." For Scalfari, there could be no compromises: "Either sacrifice the life of a man or lose the Republic." But the paper also quoted an ex-president of the Constitutional Court (Italy's highest judicial body), Giuseppe Branca: "The protection of the presumed prestige of the State is not worth the life of an honest man." In another interview, the priest-historian Gianni Baget Bozzo observed, "To deal would not be giving in, but [would be] an act of dignity by a State whose constitution has made the primary value of human life one of its final ends.... You cannot talk about absurd principles that belonged to a Jacobin liberal State that no longer exists."

An appeal for "necessary and formal" steps to liberate Moro had appeared in the left-wing paper *Lotta Continua* on April 19. Though deliberately vague on the question of an exchange, the statement was signed by seventy prominent "Friends of Moro," including theologians, artists and intellectuals. The Italian Episcopal Conference (of Catholic bishops) issued a similar appeal the same day. On the evening of the next, a second letter to Zaccagnini arrived, the contents of which filtered out over the next several days:

> I will say it clearly: for my part I will not absolve or justify anybody...it is above all to the DC that the country turns, because of its responsibility, because of the wisdom always shown in adapting reason of state to human moral considerations. If it were to fail now it would be for the first time. The party would be swept into the vortex and would be finished.... My blood would fall on you, on the Party, on the country. Think about it carefully, my dear friends. Be independent. Don't look to tomorrow. Look to the day after tomorrow.

On April 21, the day after the arrival of both the letter and BR communiqué number seven, Bettino Craxi met with top party colleagues in Rome. Craxi had been confirmed as Socialist party secretary at the recent party congress in Turin and had been in contact since then with Giovanni Guiso, a Socialist and defense lawyer at the BR Turin trial. On April 21 Craxi received the green light from his party to try to save Moro. His initiative marked the real emergence of the "party of negotiations" and the beginning of the final stage of the affair.

The Third Stage: April 21 to May 9

Different people supported *fermezza* for different reasons, ranging from political interest to concern for the stability of the system, or some combination of the two. By the same token negotiations attracted people for a variety of emotional, religious and political reasons. After April 20 it was only natural that there should have been frantic efforts to find some alternative to doing nothing and formally recognizing the BR. On April 22 the papers published Pope Paul VI's handwritten appeal to "the men of the Red Brigades" for Moro's release "without conditions." Three days later the BR (in their eighth communiqué) named thirteen prisoners for exchange, including the BR's founder Renato Curcio. The next day an appeal to the BR from United Nations Secretary General Kurt Waldheim ran on television and in the newspapers.

Craxi was prepared to go further, and his reasons were fundamentally political. Craxi's goal was to make his Socialist party the decisive third force in Italian politics. He was searching for ways to distinguish the PSI politically and ideologically from the DC and especially the PCI. Craxi's medium-term goal was to return to a coalition with the DC, thereby forcing the Communists back into opposition. Thus, he was looking for ways to break the logic of "national solidarity," that is, to split the DC-PCI alliance. Persuading the DC to depart from *fermezza* was an obvious way to do this. Craxi calculated that he would garner favorable publicity whether he succeeded or not. He also counted on winning friends in the right wing of the DC, with whom he hoped the PSI would eventually ally (and did in early 1980). Finally, Craxi was apparently convinced that there was somebody bigger behind the BR. If an outside manipulator could be identified during negotiations and turned out to be—as Craxi suspected—from the East, then so much the better for Craxi and so much the worse for the Communists.

Craxi knew the public did not want a straight prisoner exchange and was careful to speak of a "humanitarian solution" or "unilateral initiative." On April 28 the PSI privately suggested to the DC the idea of offering grace to several terrorist convicted on minor charges (or the release of untried prisoners in poor health) and improving conditions in the special prisons where terrorists were held. Although the details of Craxi's plan became available only on May 3, the public debate intensified on the question of a deal.

Moro himself reentered the debate on April 24. In a third letter to Zaccagnini, he once again hammered away at the consciences of his Christian Democratic friends and linked his salvation to the higher interests of the state. By refusing an "exchange of several prisoners of war" the DC and the state, in effect, reintroduced the same death penalty that had been abolished after the war as "a first sign of authentic democratization," he argued. "With its inertia and holding back, in the name of reason of State, the state organization [that is, the DC and the police] is issuing, without real thought, a death sentence in order to defend a preeminent state of imprisonment [of captured BR leaders]. This is something enormous." Moro ended with a request that no government or party officials be present at his funeral, "Only the few who really cared about me."

By the last week of April a debate raged between those who continued to press *fermezza*, and denied Moro's authorship of the letters, and those who sought negotiations with the BR, and insisted the letters were authentic. On April 25 *Il Popolo* published a statement signed by fifty "longstanding friends of Aldo Moro," including many clergy and Catholic intellectuals: "The Aldo Moro that we know, with his spiritual, political, and juridical vision...is not present in the letters to Zaccagnini that have been published as his." Baget Bozzo was one of the few who not only accepted Moro's letters as Moro's but endorsed the Moro-esque line of reasoning the letters advanced. It was true that to negotiate with the BR implied a kind of political recognition of terrorists, but the BR also represented a certain political constituency. He asked, "Does the State benefit from a certain politicization of the BR, or is it better that they be pushed back into the ghetto of violence?"

On April 30 the papers printed a long letter that turned out to be Moro's final public message. Once again Moro bitterly attacked the DC's failure even to discuss seriously the possibility of a nonviolent solution. He was "profoundly saddened" that old friends had attributed his own arguments to the BR: "There is not the slightest similarity of views between myself and the Red Brigades." According to what logic, he asked "can one deduce that the State will go to ruin if, once in a while, an innocent man survives, and to compensate, another person, instead of going to prison, goes into exile? The entire question is right here."

Craxi and others saw a gleam of hope in Moro's reference in his latest letter to an exchange for "another person" rather than thirteen as indicated by the BR on April 24. In a tense, stormy meeting with DC leaders on the evening of May 2, Craxi proposed a unilateral gesture of clemency by the president of the republic for a convicted terrorist (not one on the BR's list of thirteen), in effect a one-for-one exchange. Craxi reportedly exploded at one point in the meeting: "There's somebody in here who wants Moro dead and I'm going to tell it to the *piazzas.*" There was, by now, tremendous pressure within the DC itself to shift in Craxi's direction. Zaccagnini rejected Craxi's bid for an a priori gesture by the state but suggested in an official statement that the government would show mercy in response to the release of Moro and other behavior (unspecified) by the BR that indicated a renunciation of violence. This stance was too much for Prime Minister Andreotti, who saw that Fanfani, an important party leader who like Craxi opposed Communist–Christian Democratic collaboration, was now moving to support the Socialists. On May 3, Andreotti issued a statement reaffirming strict *fermezza* on behalf of the government. In the end, all of the major papers rejected Craxi's initiative.

Though the papers reported that a meeting of the National Council of the DC would not take place until after the May 14 elections, the directorate of the party convened on May 9 to schedule a meeting of the council (which would address the Moro case). Moro was shot the same morning.

Conclusions

No event in postwar Italy has raised such fundamental questions about the role of the press, or sparked such intense debate. Critics have charged that the papers allowed themselves to be manipulated both by party politicians and by the Red Brigades. Both of these criticisms are exaggerated. Because they were sensitive to both charges most newspapers made an effort to avoid the pitfalls of either servility to established power or service to the terrorists. The reasons why most newspapers supported the government line were varied and complex. They no doubt included genuine conviction and the fact that the public itself, by and large, was seen to back *fermezza*. Undermining the "hard line" in any event became unthinkable once the papers had made the initial decision to give full coverage to BR actions and communiqués.

At the same time, most of the independent papers gave ample space to opponents of *fermezza* and were harshly critical of the government's failure to produce results. Though the press ultimately rejected a news blackout or self-censorship as impractical and undesirable, the decision was taken after a brief but intense debate on the subject. The controversial issues of the BR's origins and of Moro's lucidity were also fully aired, analyzed, and agonized over.

What of the opposite charge that the papers did the bidding of the Red Brigades? There is no evidence that publication of BR communiqués won them new converts or sympathizers. On the contrary, from beginning to end the BR's actions managed to generate only revulsion and helped to set in motion a campaign that led to the capture and conviction of most of the Red Brigades during the next several years. Their failure to rouse a revolutionary proletariat, like their failure to wring sensational confessions from Moro, merely illustrated the "lethal imbecility" (in Sciascia's words) and isolation from reality that distinguished the Red Brigades.

Perhaps the heavy coverage had other more subtle, and unintended, effects. Certainly portions of the press endowed the BR with greater efficiency, inflexibility and cunning than was in fact the case. This build-up may have affected the BR's image of themselves, leading them to overestimate their leverage and to delay the discussion of terms until after the *fermezza* line had firmly set. The eventual rigor of the hard line, promoted by and reflected in the press, no doubt took the Red Brigades by surprise. It may ultimately have induced the BR to harden their own position and to kill Aldo Moro in a gesture of anger, frustration and defiance.

The press's treatment of Moro himself and of his letters certainly did not enhance the prisoner's efforts to mediate a solution to the case or to make what was presumably one of his basic, though for obvious reasons unspoken, points—negotiations might divide the BR; hence dealing with them might serve the interests of the state. Yet the press's declaration of Moro's political death after his April 10 letter may (if he was aware of it) have affected Moro's own calculations: once he had discounted his future as a statesman, he may have become less inhibited about pleading for his life. His apparent political demise may also have inclined the BR to strike a deal on the grounds that his return would only sow dissension within the ranks of the enemy.

It seems clear that Moro's strategy to save himself was eventually linked to the knowledge that the papers would print his letters and to the hope that publication might win public and political support for his arguments. This was a costly miscalculation. Remaining silent, however, would not necessarily have improved his chances of survival. It is hard not to feel great sympathy for Moro in his tragic isolation. The Red Brigades themselves later acknowledged his dignity and intelligence and that he essentially refused to play their game by providing useful or embarrassing information.

In the final analysis, the lessons one draws from the case and one's judgment of the press's conduct are difficult, for Italians virtually impossible, to separate from one's judgment of the *fermezza* line itself. Today most agree that the sacrifice of Moro's life—for that is what it amounted to—contributed to the disintegration of the Red Brigades and to the strengthening of the constituted political order. As for Moro's political strategy, "national solidarity" seemed destined for defeat in any case, although with its architect alive it might have lasted past early 1979, when the PCI pulled out of the coalition.

This is not to say, however, that an exchange of prisoners would have hastened Italy's slide into chaos, as some proclaimed. Nor can one conclude that refusing categorically to negotiate with terrorists is a wise or practicable policy. But the press, like most of the public, quickly grasped that the Moro case was sui generis. Moro could not be exchanged precisely because he was who he was—not an ordinary citizen—and because of the appalling circumstances of his kidnapping. Moro embodied more nearly than anyone "the heart of the state," a state that was vulnerable and unesteemed and therefore had to be defended with exceptional, and as some argued at the time, rather un-Italian, firmness.

Note

1. An expanded version of this essay appeared in the *SAIS Review*, vol. 8, no. 2 (Summer/Fall 1988).

16

New Communications Technology and the International Political Process

David Webster

Predicting the effects of technological change is an inexact business. One need only recall the British government official who, quite reasonably, opined that the electric telephone would never catch on in England, there being a plentiful supply of inexpensive messengers. It is difficult today to gather a group of people to discuss the media's impact on the political process without someone, either in a hopeful or disparaging tone, raising the problem of television. A long and rather ragged conversation then follows about the vast, but ill-understood, effects of this mass medium. Given that this is a new and rapidly developing subject on which most peoples' views are conditioned largely by anecdotal evidence, this confusion is not surprising.

One thing is clear—we are experiencing today only the initial impact of the new forms of international electronic distribution and the creation of a 'populist diplomacy.' National leaders, more and more, appeal directly to constituencies in other nations. This international political discourse, often including players unauthorized by officialdom, exists alongside traditional and controlled intergovernmental transactions.

219

Already, the tension between these two forms of communication causes a great deal of unhappiness and demands significant adjustment in the way in which we attempt to manage our foreign affairs. In a sense, strictly "foreign" affairs no longer exist. Drawing the line between domestic and foreign policy issues is becoming increasingly more difficult as the information constituency expands and becomes influenced by transborder streams of less and less filtered information.

These electronic distribution systems take many forms, speeding up and increasing the information interaction on an individual and mass public level. Without a doubt, one of the most important of these forms, particularly for the public, and therefore for the political process, is television. Thus, the focus here is on television. Understanding what television does to nations now is essential if one wishes to contemplate what it may do to the world in the future.

The Television Revolution

Whenever one talks of the growing importance of cross-border television, someone is sure to ask why its impact should be different from that of older technology such as shortwave radio, newspaper dispatches, the electric telegraph of Samuel Morse or the Reuter pigeons. The answer is that television's influence would not be all that different were it not for the fact that it is part of a process which has now reached critical mass. Consequently, it revolutionizes, rather than merely continues, the process.

Most of the technology that is changing national political campaigns today in the United States already existed in 1984, but it was in the 1988 campaign that it was first extensively used—and its full potential has yet to be tapped. In modern consumer marketing terms the introduction of new technology usually experiences a time lag of at least twenty years before it begins to have a significant effect. This has been true of television, of video cassette recorders and of satellites.

Television on a national basis both in the United States and in Europe probably began to assume a really significant role in the domestic political process in the 1960s. We are now witnessing its effects on the international process and will become vividly aware of them during the 1990s. The extreme turbulence on Wall Street in late 1987 should have made everyone painfully conscious of the existence and significance of round-the-clock global trading, stimulated by the development of computer technology and satellite transmission. Similar developments are starting to take place in the world's political life. We are aware of international finance's nervous system with its instant transactions, but not quite so cognizant of its diplomatic and political equivalents. As usual, the moneymen are ahead of the curve.

We are now so accustomed to the pervasive presence of television that it is quite difficult to remember the world in which it did not exist. Fifty-three years ago, in 1936, Franklin Roosevelt defeated Alf Landon by a landslide, fascist rebels began the siege of Madrid, Somoza was on the verge of usurping power in Nicaragua, and, in England, Edward VIII was about to abdicate. None of these events was conditioned by television, or reported by it. In that same year, a Portuguese surgeon, Dr. Egaz-Moniz, developed the first techniques of prefrontal lobotomy, and, in an apparently unrelated development, the world's first regular television service was opened by BBC and seen by a select few on primitive and expensive equipment.

Television now transcends all classes and borders. By creating an instantaneous transborder imagery difficult to assess and impossible to control, it has added to the complexity of international relations. Not only factual but also fictional television is creating the world's shared icons and common imagery and providing the broad cultural context in which complicated political messages are correctly and incorrectly decoded. In the view of some traditional diplomats, the choppy waters of world politics have been whipped to a frenzy by television's intervention. According to the televisers, however, television has served to inform the people. The tone in which TV does its job and the underlying motives are beside the point. Politicians and government officials will have to learn how to navigate those choppy waters, just as in earlier days the generals of the Crimean War had to adjust to the presence of William Howard Russell and the strictures of the *London Times*.

Some of the likely long-term effects of living with television can be identified. Likewise, one can analyze the impact of the unprecedented growth of transborder communications on countries where television was previously regulated and a comparatively scarce commodity.

A small but useful example is the island of Bermuda, which finds itself within the transmission cone of the United States' low-powered satellite system. The people of Bermuda, by and large, are well off, and many of them have bought satellite dishes in order to receive a multitude of signals not actually intended for them. One result has been the erosion of the economic base of Bermuda's indigenous television system. From this may flow a number of unintended consequences, both social and political. Canada, whose main markets are within reach of normal U.S. television signals, has struggled with this problem for years. Now with satellites changing traditional ideas of distance, the rest of the world has become, in a manner of speaking, Canadian.

Among the possible benefits of television is that it has given many people a wider perspective on the world. Some doubt, however, must be cast on the quality of that perspective. As compared with print, it is non-linear, non-rational and inherently impressionistic. Even when television does deal with serious subjects, it is preoccupied with imagery and is seldom as reflective or organized as print. Our leaders come to rely on pictures rather than argument. Their thoughts are expressed in sound bites or in sharp political advertising. Rational discourse is avoided. Information is moved, but rarely analyzed or explained. This national problem becomes more severe in the international cross-cultural Babel of misunderstanding.

Another primary characteristic of television is decontextualization—time and space, particularly in the era of satellites, have been annihilated. The discontinuity inherent in the process initiated by Samuel Morse and the electric telegraph has reached its maturity in the television age. In many respects, watching television differs from reading. The eye cannot scan the television set as it can the newspaper, sorting out items of interest from those of disinterest; it cannot linger on an interesting thought—should there be one.

Television news just hops through, and the viewer is its prisoner. Many anchor persons nonsensically read the end of one item into the next with no pause or change of inflection, lest the viewer slip from their grasp. Many people, especially self-styled serious people, believe television is at its best as a broadcaster of worldwide news. The problem is that television insists on telling us things that we did not ask about, and for which we have no response. We can all have opinions, but no power. Continually being informed of problems that one feels impotent to affect must leave its scars. Our attitude becomes either anguished frustration or more likely, defensive insulation. Even Ethiopian famines are likely to lose their impact or interest.

The attempted transmission on television of complex information and argument is nullified by the relentless drive of most other television content, and by the nature of the medium itself. Moreover, even in its fictional forms television has great difficulty in dealing with ambiguity, for, in many countries, it has trained its viewers to expect constant simplification, stimulation and hype, and the simple resolution of human dilemmas. These values unfortunately have spilled over into our politics. Show business has come to influence significantly our news judgments. Consequently, those issues which do not easily lend themselves to the pizazz and flair of showbiz—and probably the two most pressing ones, arms control and the deficit, do not—are given scant coverage.

Another national and international effect of television involves amplification. Stories, issues and trends both nationally and internationally seem to be exaggerated by television. At the same time, however, television's memory often is a little faulty. Dramatic stories charge across the screen for a night of so and then disappear, sometimes without being concluded. This interacts with another factor, the acceleration effect. Information moves faster and people react faster. Instant response and instant interaction help to generate those choppy waters in the sea of international politics. The immediate turbulence of television's constant action and interaction is real and must be dealt with, but it *can* be misleading.

The Revolution Comes to Europe

In Europe during the coming decade the effects of this rush of information are going to be even more dramatic than in the United States, as the role of paternalistic, highly regulated public service broadcasting is diminished. (The United States has never experienced this paternalism.) Brash newcomers will enter the European market using a variety of transmission systems to carve out their share. Players with names such as Murdoch, Maxwell, Berlusconi, Hersant, Bouygues, Turner and Mohn will wheel and deal, some becoming the new tycoons of this great global game.

The newcomers will be riding on a wave of deregulation. Gone will be the restrictions and public obligations of the old broadcasting establishment. In order to stimulate high-technology industry, Europe is breaking down the old order and bringing to its television services new money and new energy. Ideological inclinations have shifted, and elitism is no longer fashionable. The market will deliver, the thinking goes, and those assumed 'social goods' previously encouraged by the regulated system will just have to take their chances. This is a revolution of great political significance. In one sense it will mean more freedom of choice, but no one yet knows what may be destroyed in the process.

The European Commission estimates that by 1990 Western Europeans will have approximately ninety satellite and cable channels, both public and private. These would be in addition to the existing networks. While these figures are extremely suspect and may not bear very much commercial reality, they, nevertheless, do make quite clear the fact that there will be more and diverse television. It will be less regulated and less national. The funds being invested in cable transmission capability are indicative. West Germany, for example, is investing about $10 billion in cable television, and France another $12 billion. In Britain, billions in private money are being gambled on the Direct Broadcasting Satellite.

The Commission of the European Community expects many millions to be spent on direct satellite television program services as well as on high-powered satellites. All this is an attempt to form a united broadcast market of 320 million people spread across twelve nations speaking nine major languages and with different laws.

By 1992 the European Commission plans to develop a single market for all goods and services, including broadcasting. Some national regulations governing broadcasting will, therefore, be redundant or illegal. However, this applies only to intra–European Community trade. As far as television programming is concerned, some of the Commission's work (under pressure from the French) is aimed towards protecting Europe from the United States.

The Commission's directive also stipulates that the nations of the European Community adopt common program and advertising standards, and proposes that where possible a majority of its television programs, except those covering news and sports, should be made within the European Community. It calls upon broadcasters to invest heavily in interpretation and dubbing systems so as to allow programs to be broadcast simultaneously in several languages. The Commission also seeks to encourage European co-productions.

The concerns behind the Commission's attempts to build a European industry and to protect European programs from American competition are both commercial and cultural. If you rapidly multiply the number of channels, you clearly have to be free to import programming at marginal prices in order to fill that capacity. Because its original costs are amortized in its huge domestic market, American programming is marginal in price. While in France an hour-long drama costs at least $500,000 to make, an episode of something like "Dallas" can be bought for not much more than $30,000. Furthermore, no matter what reservations some European people and politicians might have about cultural identity, there is no denying the attraction American programs hold for European viewers. Europeans, consequently, will first want to develop their own product base, but realize that multiplying distribution channels is a comparatively simple task when compared with generating the capacity to make good programs. The fact that delivery systems are more likely to be subsidized, for reasons of industrial policy, makes this realization all the more apparent.

This soon-to-be worldwide problem of preserving cultural identity in the global television age is seen most clearly in Europe, because it is in Europe that the most dramatic impact of new delivery systems will be felt. Most of the less developed countries will not experience the same change because they cannot afford the necessary transmission systems and are not yet an attractive enough market. (Some of these countries, however, do fall within the satellite transmission cone of services directed at other markets, and for these countries the results could be devastating.) The United States, for its part, will probably not experience such an obvious impact because it has never had the same degree of regulation, the same restrictions on television outlets, or the elitist cross-subsidization of product.

In Europe, however, this fundamental shift in the structure of mass communications, and its release from traditional geographic confines due to satellite and cable technology, will have far-reaching political implications. The recognition of this can be seen perhaps most clearly in France. While the struggle in other European countries may be less vivid, it is no less real. In Britain, for instance, Margaret Thatcher appears to be attempting the impossible. A passionate believer in deregulation and market forces, Thatcher is seeking to stop broadcasts of which she disapproves—a difficult position to sustain, particularly when many of the signals will originate from other sovereign nations.

Throughout the world, technology and entrepreneurial ambition will spur rapid and ragged change. The familiar institutional landmarks may not survive. The spread of cable and the proliferation of other local delivery systems, when combined with satellites capable of delivering signals around the world, will confuse both the markets and the viewers: What are we watching? From where did it come, and to whom does it belong? Copyright lawyers will become both busy and wealthy.

The Political Impact

The international political process will also be affected. Already, there exists a professional, global news-gathering electronic system, and within the last few years, live television from the ends of the earth has become commonplace. Now, the dissemination of this information to the world public is expanding significantly and is becoming less filtered. Television shows little concern for national boundaries or for traditional geography. Satellite economics are not distance-sensitive; everything is next door. Transmission costs are going down as labor costs go up. There may be less discretionary editorial authority. As a result of all this, international discourse will become more complex, more populist and more difficult to manage. We are witnessing the departure of the gatekeepers.

Due to the convergence of key technologies, national governments are losing control over their national communications. Satellites make nonsense of traditional geography and notions of distance; cable multiplies the local delivery systems and sucks in distant signals; videocassette recorders give to individuals the ability to retain and replay the signals; computers process information; and the downsizing and demystification of video technology allows its use by ordinary people. These technical advances have been accompanied by a fashion for deregulation and privatization—ideology and technology in a marriage of convenience.

Within certain nations, old-fashioned network television historically has been a cohesive factor, a shared national experience. This situation is now disappearing, because technology is creating both commercial opportunity and danger in fragmented international markets and because the major networks are losing control over television schedules and, consequently, over consumers. Of course, some barriers will remain—market, cultural, regulatory and language. As well as those (sometimes quite deliberately set up for protectionist reasons) of different technical transmission standards. Any country which really wants to protect and isolate itself from the world information economy will be able to do so by running its national communication system on standards severely incompatible with those of other nations. The price, however, will be considerable.

Just over the horizon are a number of new developments that will affect the international scope not only of television, but also of newspapers, radios, telephones, and other things. The arrival of optical fiber systems will dramatically increase transglobal links. Particularly in Europe, a new generation of satellites will deliver high-power signals directly to consumers with small receptors. Other satellites in development will have a cone of transmission covering both the eastern United States and Western Europe. The capability for onboard switching of signals will exist.

There will also be significant advances in the use of remote satellite imaging—the spy in the sky. The effect of these advances and of the increasing availability of this particular technology on world affairs will be significant. Remote satellite imaging is already a factor in arms control, and as some of its advanced capacity ceases to be the exclusive preserve of the intelligence community, it could play a crucial role in the management of natural disasters and in news gathering. Its impact on international law and commerce could also be considerable.

Predicting the exact impact of these technological changes on the world's nervous system is tricky. All we can be sure of is that familiar ground will shift. The combination of satellite overspill and the VCR technology will, for example, make all societies more porous.

The dominant characteristic of what we are now experiencing is private rather than governmental. It is the drive for future markets and profits that is producing technical innovations and breaking down institutional and governmental controls. These market forces have their own political power and in many countries complement government policies that view electronic information industries as vital to the nation's economic well-being.

In an age of mass media and growing transborder signals and unfiltered information, publicly available information and popular impressions increasingly condition the conduct of international relations. Woe betide the politician who underestimates the power of images to affect radically the views and moods of his constituents. Due to the new communications technology, the reach and the impact of these images can be enormous. We now live in a world of populist democracy. And to borrow the words of Ronald Reagan, a man of the image, "you ain't seen nothing yet."

Neither Hero
nor Villain

Simon Serfaty

An adversarial relationship between the executive branch of the U.S. government and the news media is neither avoidable nor deplorable. As Walter Lippmann wrote, American Presidents "announce, proclaim, disclaim, exhort, appeal, and argue. But they do not unbend and tell the story, and say why they did what they did, and what they think about it, and how they feel about it."[1] Telling the story is what journalists in the United States do best—probably better, and more, than any other group of journalists in the world.

Lippmann's complaint, written a few weeks after America's entry in World War II, appeared to encourage the American press to continue to challenge the official interpretation of events, even, or especially, at a moment of national emergency. This was not considered unusual, much less improper: such had been the tradition of the press for more than 150 years. By war's end, however, the inherent adversarial relationship between the media and the executive branch had been progressively muted, and power and truth often followed their separate ways. "It was routine practice," recalled President Eisenhower of his years at the White House, "to deny responsibility for an embarrassing occurrence when there is even a 1 per cent chance of being believed."[2] Policies developed by the executive branch on the basis of the coolest calculations of interest were easily justified with a self-serving (and even, at times, deceptive) rhetoric that was accepted uncritically by most journalists and, for that matter, by most scholars too. With the press inclined to view itself as the government's partner, official denials were usually taken at face value: in Korea, Guatemala, Lebanon, Cuba and elsewhere, the covert or overt use of U.S. force rarely provoked the debates that have accompanied similar actions in recent years. These were years of near-indoctrination during which America's role became enshrouded in myths.

In the 1960s, the Vietnam War shattered many of those myths, and modified profoundly the terms of the relationship between the press and the executive branch as that relationship had evolved during the previous decade. Yet the role of the press throughout the war was hardly consistent: neither a hero or better, nor a villain or worse, the press seldom deserved either the credit or the blame it widely received for bringing the war to an end. From 1955 to 1965, the scope and the intensity of the U.S. intervention in Indochina escalated steadily; but all the while the U.S. press remained generally indifferent, or even favorable, to the war. By late 1965 most newspapers held editorial stands that supported the administration's policies in Indochina, and even an escalation of the American involvement. Calls for a negotiated withdrawal were vague in substance and few in numbers. Said the *New York Times* in April 1965, as the President was committing the nation to major combat in Vietnam: "No one except a few pacifists... are asking for a precipitate withdrawal. Virtually all Americans understand that we must stay in Vietnam at least for the near future." With the flow of information from, and even access to, the source managed to a significant degree by the administration and the military, many American journalists appeared individually inclined to support the war effort. "Vietnam is a legitimate part of the [U.S.] global commitment," wrote David Halberstam, "perhaps one of only five or six nations in the world that is truly vital to U.S. interests.... It may be worth a larger commitment on our part."[3]

In the end, it was not an adversarial press that precipitated the U.S. failure in Vietnam. Rather, the mounting evidence of failure precipitated and exacerbated the hostility of the press whose coverage grew in intensity and improved in organization *after* American opinion began to shift against the war.[4] To be sure, because it was the conduit for such evidence, the press played an important role in facilitating that shift. The conduit was especially decisive in the case of television, whose images of the war—from the rice paddies of Vietnam to the streets of Chicago—had an unprecedented impact on public perceptions. But opposition to the war found its catalyst elsewhere: in the open criticism of the administration's policies by congressional leaders and former officials who, over the years, had inspired and supported not only the U.S. intervention in Vietnam but also the policies that had helped cause that intervention and shape its expansion.

In any case, during and after the harsh and protracted debate over Vietnam, a more skeptical attitude emerged throughout the country toward America's role in the world and the policies devised by the executive branch to fulfill that role. Perhaps the United States was ill prepared by history to cope with the side effects of its rise to power. Democracy has little tolerance for secrecy: hence the forceful and even emotional public reaction to revelations of the fact or even perception of deception. Thus while the Gulf of Tonkin incident reflected far less intent (if any) to mislead deliberately, at least at the top, than popularly believed, the widespread conclusion that the Johnson administration had willingly deceived its people (and leaders in Congress too) reflected a pervasive erosion of public (and congressional) trust. And the impact of that discovery was felt even more deeply because it took place at a time when the highest representative of the government—the President—lacked the credibility enjoyed by his immediate predecessors.

Both Lyndon Johnson and Richard Nixon appeared to share a penchant for deception that deepened the skepticism provoked by their respective actions. As institutional trust eroded, the press and the administration relied increasingly on a more covert relationship, based on the innuendos of leaks and plants. The earlier presumption of a collective "We" gave way to a fractured multitude of narrower groups and constituencies (including vastly expanded congressional committee and subcommitee staffs) that increased substantially the number of points of entry into the policy process.

The impact of these divisions—within the executive and the legislative branches of the U.S. government as well as between them and in the equally divided general public—cannot be overstated. In Congress, the indifferent acquiescence of earlier years gave way to a fierce challenge to the administration's day-to-day conduct of diplomacy. The bitterness of the debate between the executive and the legislative branches of the government added to the public confusion over the nation's interests and role in the world. The passions first revealed during the latter years of the Vietnam War continued to shape the foreign policy disputes that beset, in different ways, every administration from Nixon to Reagan. Predictably waged over absolutes, those disputes lost sight of the need for nuances and the play of linkages which often condition success or failure in foreign policy.

Increasingly, over issues that ranged from arms control to Central America, any group hostile to the policies or the views of another found in the press the best way to be heard and to influence policy.

To be sure, there had always been in the manner in which America conducts its foreign policy an open invitation to struggle for the undisputed privilege of directing it. But now, the struggle was waged most vociferously in and by the press whose adversarial coverage of official policies grew accordingly, even though most of the leaks upon which such coverage was based came mostly from the executive branch.

Yet the resulting perception of the press as the cohesive embodiment of an opposition party whose invisible hand helped shape public attitudes that undermined national policies can be easily exaggerated. Journalists do not make American policies in the world: they merely bring these policies, and their impact in the world, to the attention of the American people whose reactions, then, determine the measure of support or opposition received by the administration. In the 1960s, confusion over the effectiveness of the methods used to fulfill the country's goals in Vietnam, however those might be defined, was translated into general doubt and reappraisal of America's goals, methods and effectiveness, not only in Vietnam but anywhere in the world. It was as if the country was now intent on pursuing two foreign policies, one of limits and disengagement and one of absolution and renewal, thereby introducing images of vacillation and confusion that persisted and increased after the end of the Vietnam War. Perhaps the most significant sin of the press was to attempt to give some order to such confusion. For, in a sense, reporters came to resemble scholars whose attempts to reconstruct and interpret events, decisions, policies and legislation usually impute a cohesion and coherence that rarely existed at the time when events unfolded, decisions were made, policies were launched, and legislation was passed. But, in so doing, the press built no unified agenda of its own, and, when a consensus did emerge over any one issue, it was rarely conditioned by a preordained bias.

Although they are linked by the bitter debate over the Vietnam War, the recent debate over the role of the media in foreign policy and the traditional debate over America's role in the world should not, therefore, be confused. Leaving aside criticisms that are focused on specific policy issues, or are motivated by ideological preferences, an assessment of the role of the American press in foreign policy points to three broad conclusions, which are all made relative by the limits of the nation's consensus on these issues as well as by the limits set for the press by the interests of their audiences and, especially in the case of television, the very nature of the medium.

First, competent coverage of foreign news is abundant and may even be increasing.[5] Such coverage has helped illuminate the dark areas of public ignorance which, in the past, shaped America's general indifference to world events. Crises abroad are brought into our living rooms, almost instantaneously. It started with Vietnam, of course. But, since then, a sophisticated use of steadily improving technology has facilitated the live coverage of international events. Over the years, images of peace and war, humiliation and pride, hunger, hope, despair, violence, and renewed hope have shaped the country's exposure to foreign policy, and populated its collective memory: the TWA pilot with a terrorist's gun at his head at the Beirut airport, and the disappointment on the face of Secretary of State George Shultz as he reported on the final outcome of the summit at Reykjavík; the young man standing up to a tank in Beijing; the older man standing on top of the Berlin Wall and smashing at it with hammer and chisel—all these images and many more remain penetrating visions of the world that continue to be be carried live in the citizen's mind for years to come. They have all expanded the scope of public sensitivity to dangers and opportunities around the world, even as they tested, often and in a most tangible manner, the boundaries of the real.

As polls and studies demonstrate, Americans do not know much about the world, and they may not even care to learn more about it. But this has not prevented them from gaining ample—and, yes, at times intelligent—access to whatever information was available whenever a crisis increased demand for such information: about wars worth fighting or ending, aid programs worth launching or avoiding, defense expenditures worth assuming or reviewing, and so on. In hindsight, the record of the American press in bringing the world home, and that of the American people in responding to the world, are not bad—and those records are even better when compared to those of other industrial countries in Europe and Asia.

Certainly, there remain insufficiencies in the scope, diversity and use of press coverage. With most American correspondents based in just a dozen countries, foreign reports still tend to emanate from a small number of places that leave immense areas of the world largely ignored beyond the ephemeral headlines necessitated occasionally by a sudden crisis. Moreover, advances in the foreign coverage provided by the leading national newspapers have been more than balanced by the retreat from such coverage in the smaller and more parochial newspapers that are read by the majority of Americans. There, editors often fail to put to good use the news reports made available to them by wire services and other supplemental services, on which they usually depend for their foreign news. That such would be the case is all the more deplorable as the increased relevance of foreign policy news to local concerns should be an inducement for more and not less foreign policy coverage.

The case for more information, not less, is valid even in the controversial case of terrorism—and even if, in the process, excesses are likely to occur. For instance, an unsavory agreement made by NBC News to keep secret the whereabouts of a terrorist in exchange for an interview proved all the more distasteful as he seized that opportunity to threaten action against specifically named Americans within U.S. borders.[6] Similarly, during the TWA hostage crisis, one of the networks apparently chartered a plane to follow possible troop movements at a time when military intervention was being considered seriously by the administration: its reports may have tipped off the terrorists to an impending strike.

These examples, among others, make it possible to concede that there are limits to the coverage of issues with life-threatening consequences or high national security content. Yet granted the necessity—and even the desirability—in principle, of some limits to what can or should be reported in such instances, who holds the authority to define those limits specifically, and, perhaps more important, how can such limits be enforced, by whom and against whom? There is no clear-cut issue of right and wrong here—of a bad press and a good government, or vice versa. On either side, there may be a few malevolent individuals—perhaps the source of a deliberately or costly leak (assuming the unusual case of a single source) or the author of a willfully damaging report (assuming the uncertain case of an author who explicitly understood the potential for damage). But these are exceptions that, however disturbing any one incident may be, do not warrant the imposition of rules designed to structure a relationship that is inherently unstructurable. In short, in relaying information, the press should remain its own watchdog in determining what is fit to print and what is proper to see.

Second, the coverage of foreign news is generally good and getting better. This is even true of television, where reporters and producers are learning to overcome the inherent limits of the medium. These limits are well known, and condemn much of what is seen on television to a shallow and over-dramatized presentation of reality. Television, David Gergen writes elsewhere in this volume, "loves sagas where someone wins and someone loses. It abhors long, tedious, complex stories and will usually ignore them if possible." There, as David Webster adds, "thoughts are expressed in sound bites.... Rational discourse is avoided. Information is moved, but rarely analyzed and explained.... It cannot linger on an interesting thought." And how could it be otherwise when a "long" news item rarely exceeds two minutes that amount to about 320 spoken words?

Yet, with all three major networks now devoting more than half of their news time to international news (as much as two thirds in an average broadcast of ABC's "World News Tonight"), producers deserve credit for providing coverage that may well exceed public demand. Moreover, in an attempt to bolster substance, the networks have achieved better reliance on words as a useful addition to pictures (including the words of outside academic experts called upon to provide background analysis) or even as an effective substitute for pictures. As Peter Jennings observed following the sweeping press restrictions on the press imposed by the South African government in November 1986: "However important is the picture...there are lots of things we are learning to do without the visual."[7] In the case of South Africa, television coverage was sustained, however temporarily, through various methods of illustration, including the use of high-tech graphics and interviews with witnesses, to convey scenes that cameras could no longer record.

The power of the image can never be replaced, however: as the picture fades from the screen so does the impact of the words that continue to be said on television or written in the press. And conversely, as long as the picture remains on the screen its impact cannot be easily eroded. In the 1960s the televised rendition of repression in the American South and atrocities in Southeast Asia shaped the public revulsion that led to congressional action to change the nation's laws at home and the nation's policy abroad. These pictures then entered the nation's living rooms from other settings—starving children in Ethiopia, racial repression in South Africa, indiscriminate beating in the Occupied Territories, raw violence in Central America,

democratic fervor in Eastern Europe. There and everywhere television cameramen gave the reporters' words a reality and a poignancy
that transformed the impact of the media in foreign policy, in particular on the use of force.

Of course, this dependence on the visual, and the related need
for action and pathos that are an intrinsic part of television, can distort the reporting and create a bias of its own. The effects of this
bias are not always predictable, however. Television coverage of SDI,
for example, was uneven, but by and large appeared to convey more
skepticism about the President's vision than support for it. Yet, because of their emphasis on animation over description, television
reports on SDI were, more often than not, tied to the presentation
of successful tests, or even graphics, which fed the viewers' imagination and seemed to confirm the President's spectacular evocation
of a defensive system that would herald the obsolescence of nuclear
weapons. The cumulative impact of those images made the coverage
of SDI somewhat more favorable on television than it was in the written press, and may even help explain why public support for SDI remained generally high over the years. Accordingly, even as it argued
against SDI, Congress—generally a good judge of public sentiment—
tended to give the President's requests for funding relatively favorable treatment.

Another limit to media coverage, on and beyond television, has
to do with the reporters' familiarity with the issues—not only the
immediate substance of those issues but also their context in time
and in space. As it is now, reporters may be overwhelmed by the
pace of events. Pressed to attend to a steady flow of stories that compete for front-page space, they are denied the time needed to gather
or absorb the required background for each. Tokyo or Tehran provide the dateline, but the story may still be written in a void of adequate knowledge of the language or prior exposure to the culture.
In due time, these may be acquired, and the reporter may stay in
a foreign bureau long enough to qualify for the assignment. Meanwhile, faced with so many breaking stories, the general public starves
for more analysis: what does it all mean—for me at home, and for
us around the country and even the world? As Michael Mosettig has
suggested, the public is left with "a front page without the perspective of back pages."[8]

Although these shortcomings, too, need not be exaggerated, leading newspapers and magazines around the country would be well

advised to devote additional resources to the training of their reporters before sending them to the field for permanent or semi-permanent
assignment. Foreign Service officers usually receive this training at
the Foreign Service Institute, with substantive seminars and language classes; journalists, too, but also editors and even headline
writers, could use such training from a "Foreign Press Institute"
that would help substantiate their qualifications before assuming
responsibility for new assignments.[9] At their best, journalists are the
scholars of the present even as, at their best too, scholars are the
journalists of the past.

Third, government access to the media remains generally open
and the flow of information generally free. An adversarial relationship need not entail confrontation and does not prevent cooperation.
Examples of "strategic deception" are few, and lessons drawn from
specific examples are often exaggerated precisely because they do
not abound. As Bernard Kalb once put it so very aptly, "Faith in
the word of America is the pulsebeat of our democracy." Yet it is
because that faith is commonly respected by policy makers that the
mere perception of disinformation (such as that which prompted
Kalb's resignation in October 1986) creates so much attention and
stirs so much emotion. In 1986 the so-called "disinformation campaign" reported to have been launched by the Reagan administration over Libya found its way in a front-page story in the *Wall Street
Journal* because of the reporter's own "errors" and not as the result of the administration's deliberate efforts to deceive, "or even
of a few officials peddling lies on their own."[10]

No less than the media, the executive and legislative branches
of the U.S. government, too, need to put their respective houses in
order if there is to be an improvement in their mutual relations as
well as in their respective relations with the press. As Representative Les Aspin has observed, "Every administration wants to have
it both ways—to keep its secrets, and to reveal them whenever doing so is useful for their politics and policies." The manipulation of
disclosures for policy gains or political advantage—whether in the service of ideological conviction or personal ambition—is a flagrant deviation from the guidelines that should serve as the basis for briefing
of the press: "no lies, no misleading, to be as forthcoming as possible
within security constraints." Here, too, it is a two-way street: even
as the administration and Congress carry out their obligation to police themselves, the news media also face the obligation to exercise

restraint or at least caution, especially in relying on anonymous sources in their day-to-day reports.

Reliance on covert relations between the press and the government is damaging to both, and tends to increase rather than allay mutual as well as public suspicion. If journalists are presented with two versions of the fact, one on the record and the other on background, some ambiguity in their reports should come as no surprise. In the Reagan administration, for example, with many high officials "explaining" differently the President's different declarations on SDI, the debate grew increasingly confused. In short, an administration that wishes to be understood consistently should seek to make itself consistently understood. As Robert McFarlane writes in this volume, "Qualification for public office goes beyond an ability to conceive of sensible policy. Those charged with formulating national security policy must be able to explain that policy through the media, and in doing so they must steer clear of iconoclasm and ideological rigidity."

Viewed in broader perspective, the adversarial relationship between the media and the executive branch of the government has been relatively salutary, providing ample access to international events and producing a reasonably well-informed body politic. That journalists would find themselves at odds with the government as they carry out their responsibilities according to their own lights follows a normal pattern of American political history. Too collegial a relationship between the two institutions would serve neither the national nor the public interest well. And the controversies that periodically surround the role of the media in foreign policy should not be allowed to obscure the fundamental triumph of the American system in reconciling freedom of speech with effective policy. If there is a "problem," that problem is more manageable than the proposed cures. This is hardly a dramatic conclusion. But de-dramatizing the state of relations between the media and the government may go a long way toward improving those relations.

Notes

1. The *New York Herald Tribune*, January 29, 1942. Lippmann's column is reprinted in Clinton Rossiter and James Lare, eds., *The Essential Walter Lippmann* (New York: Vintage Books, 1965), 470.

2. Dwight D. Eisenhower, *Waging Peace, 1956-1961* (Garden City, NY: Doubleday & Company, 1965), 551.

3. The *New York Times* editorial and David Halberstam are both quoted in Norman Podhoretz, *Why We Were in Vietnam* (New York: Simon & Schuster, 1982), 81-2.

4. See Clarence R. Wyatt, "Paper Soldiers: The American Press in Vietnam," *Conflict Quarterly* (Summer 1989), 21-40.

5. Stephen Hess in David M. Rubin and Ann Marie Cunningham, eds., *War, Peace & The News Media* (New York University: Conference Proceedings, March 18-19, 1983), 166.

6. At the time of his interview in an unnamed Arab country, Abbas was sought by American, Israeli and Italian authorities on charges that he had orchestrated the *Achille Lauro* ship hijacking. The propriety of the arrangement was criticized by some members of NBC News, among many others. The *New York Times* was reported to have rejected a similar offer from Abbas.

7. Quoted in Peter J. Boyer, "South Africa and TV: The Coverage Changes," *New York Times*, December 29, 1986.

8. Michael Mosettig and Henry Griggs, Jr., "TV at the Front," *Foreign Policy* (Spring 1980), 73.

9. Admittedly, in large news organizations journalists do get such training, especially for posts, such as Moscow, where language is crucial. But the practice deserves to be extended further.

10. David C. Martin and John L. Walcott, *Best Laid Plans: America's War Against Terrorism* (New York: Harper & Row, 1988), 380.

In the Gulf:
The Wars of the Press

Stephen S. Rosenfeld

Iraq should have been, as wars go for the press, an easy war. By and large, it was a popular war at home. This spared the media any real repetition of the split that developed in Vietnam between the military, which fought the war, and the press, which reported the war, as always reflecting the sources and strains in the larger society. Saddam Hussein was no Ho Chi Minh: In his person and performance, there was little that even a minority of Americans could respect or defend or, at the least, sympathetically understand. There were almost no circumstances to mitigate the judgment of Saddam's sheer malevolence on which George Bush had moved to war.

Moreover, it was a winning war. Prewar anxieties about the result, or more precisely about the likely costs, especially in casualties, evaporated as the air war began on January 16, 1991 (Washington time) and the ground war on February 23. One hundred hours later, it was all over on the battlefield, and any pretense of press detachment from the event being covered was smothered in common relief and patriotic exultation. Those pathetic Iraqi soldiers who, waving white flags, actually surrendered to unarmed journalists unwittingly caught the essence—that, to most intents and purposes, the press was on the official side.

How ironic, then, was the onset of what might be called the wars of the press in the Gulf. Odd as it seems in retrospect, as the war unfolded after Saddam Hussein's seizure of Kuwait, a hard-edged discussion of media roles and responsibilities became a fixture of the scene. The shared premise was that for good or ill, the media were in conflict with the military and that the issues lying between them were real and urgent enough to address even while the war raged.

241

No one in the media anticipated this development or desired it. All the media wanted to do was cover the war according to supposedly familiar professional routines. Suddenly, however, the media found themselves on their own lesser front line, having to defend themselves not so much against the Iraqi authorities, who were acting in the manner expected of a hostile authoritarian government at war, but against the American authorities and plenty of other people back home—a strange and uncomfortable reversal.

The simple explanation for this turn was Vietnam. True, many other events in the culture aggravated trends that surfaced in the Gulf. But Vietnam convinced many in the military that although they had done well in battle and could claim to have accomplished their mission, they had been undercut by a liberal, elitist national media establishment, which was untutored in war, sensationalist, anti-war, and, in fact, a second culture. This group of journalists with its private agenda (starting, it was pointed out, with avoiding military service) was said to have undermined domestic support for the military as an institution and the Vietnam War as a national policy. The Tet offensive, in which the Vietcong were decimated in an operation widely depicted in the United States as a Vietcong victory, was cited as a leading case.

The many journalists who have been invited to take part in countless encounter sessions with military officers over the years will have a sense of how deeply embedded in their psyche is antagonism to the media. This is so even of younger officers who did not see duty in Vietnam. The typical journalistic response would be that the press was only doing its job and that it was not the press that undercut support for the war, but the war itself and especially the casualties. Despite the truth in this assertion, this can sound like brittle and defensive special pleading. The Gulf War showed just how indigestible the Vietnam element has remained.

The Grenada Invasion

U.S. wars are typically public wars: The American public demands that their purposes express U.S. ideals and their conduct bear up under scrutiny. However, in his invasion in 1983, President Reagan applied some of these one-sided lessons of Vietnam with a vengeance. It was a historic departure from traditional media participation. Although the first shots fired in the American Revolution had been "heard round the world," at Grenada, the Reagan administration ensured that the shots it fired would not be heard, except at its own later discretion.

The model the Reagan administration followed was the far-reaching control that Margaret Thatcher had imposed on the (far more quiescent) British press in regaining the Falklands the year before. Instead of keeping in civilian hands the essentially civilian responsibility of balancing the military's need for secrecy with the public's right to be informed, the Reagan team delegated this responsibility to the military. Taking revenge for real and imagined press excesses in Vietnam, the military proceeded to treat information as just another operational commodity. In Vietnam, journalists had official patronage to go almost anywhere their initiative or instinct took them. (It is "never crowded at the front," said Colonel Harry Summers.) In Grenada, the official edict prevented journalists from covering the operation until it was virtually over.

In an unhappy indication of what was to come, the public indicated its support for the military's muzzling of the press at Grenada. Perhaps more important, the press—still somewhat off balance from its Vietnam passage—was slow to realize how its own institutional position was being undermined—a lapse that bears directly on the unhappy situation in which it found itself in the Persian Gulf. The media's complaint in Grenada was that it had a right and responsibility to cover the news and that it had been prevented from covering an important story. But here the collective press analysis broke down: Instead of defining the problem as an excess of government control, it defined it as a denial of media access. Thus, it was but a small step to the situation in which the military's role in providing or denying access was legitimized.

After Grenada, neither the White House nor the civilian Pentagon leadership—rightly the responsible parties—but, instead, the chairman of the Joint Chiefs of Staff appointed a commission on combat coverage. It was headed by the retired chief of army information, Major General Winant Sidle, who took some newspeople aboard. The commission did not demand that the secretary do the right thing and open up the next war. It requested the military to take the press into better account. In short, the Sidle Commission, ostensibly a commission dedicated to reform, in fact replicated the civilian Pentagon's Grenada error when it let the military make the rules. It did so with the general complicity of the press corps, which participated in its work and generally accepted its principal recommendation to set up a military-controlled media pool.

This is how a new, unlovely, and largely unremarked phenomenon came to American journalism: a willingness by the media to accept government regulation. Important journalistic organizations accepted the unprecedented official requirement to register, to be "responsible" in their coverage, and to countenance sanctions (loss of pool accreditation) for breaking the rules. Indeed, they accepted the very requirements that, when presented in a foreign country, journalists properly denounce as the abridgments of a totalitarian or Third World order. The principal flaw that journalists identified among the new procedures was that they might not always be guaranteed a place in the pool.

The new rules were tested in the Panama intervention of December 1989. The press grieved, but, as the military intended, the pool worked as an instrument of control.

The Gulf War

On August 2, 1990, Saddam Hussein invaded Kuwait, and American forces were dispatched to Saudi Arabia. A huge American and international press corps began to gather in the region, with another contingent working back in Washington. The rules of Grenada were immediately put into effect. In Saudi Arabia, the chief source of daily information was the daily briefings conducted by American, British, Saudi, and other military officers. The opportunities for journalists to collect information by their own enterprise were regulated by the now-familiar pools.

Expert, informative, and crisp as most of the briefers were, the briefings were never enough for the journalists—especially for correspondents for whom Vietnam had taught that the truth is available only with the troops out in the field. To many of these journalists, it seemed unprofessional and unworthy to be sitting in a tent in Saudi Arabia, hundreds of miles from military action, covering a briefing that the whole rest of the world was watching live on Cable News Network (CNN) at the same time.

Moreover, international viewers could also see the officially released videos of smart bombs landing precisely on enemy targets. These images became the signature and, to many, the glory of the air war. Certainly they dominated the impressions of the war as

conveyed in the war's initial air stage, and they made footnotes of
the reports most correspondents, broadcast and print, were filing.

It was not only that correspondents were getting scooped by the
briefers and overshadowed by videos. The public could also see journalists asking questions at the briefings, and here a fissure began
to open. The journalists were right, although not always smart and
skillful, in pressing questions. But a public largely unaccustomed to
seeing journalists practice their craft was disturbed by a method that
sometimes seemed to tread on reasonable security concerns. A
"Saturday Night Live" sketch of a briefing in which reporters asked
insensitive questions ("Where would you say our forces are most vulnerable to attack?") drew a sharp presidential reproof. To hear members of the media complaining that they were being denied information that the public had a right to know was too much for many
members of the public. Back home on talk shows, in letters to the
editor, and in other forums, an anti-press tide began to flow.

Press complaints about the pools also failed to elicit a response from
the public. Pool rules were restrictive, and the public felt they were
meant to be. They required the chosen few (100 or so out of 1,000 or
more) journalists to travel in assigned groups, work under the eyes and
ears of their official escorts, share their findings with colleagues not
assigned to the pool, and submit their reports to military officers for
a security vetting—although, at the end of an appeals procedure, the
journalist or the parent news organization would have the last word.

Some experienced correspondents found nothing much to gripe
about. Said David Lamb of the *Los Angeles Times*: "The security
review is just common sense review. It started off very restrictive,
and they boiled it down. Now it's just basically not talking about anything that would endanger allied troops, which is basically the same
restrictions we had in Vietnam. I don't find that's an obstacle to working here at all." In "boiling down" guidelines, which was done by
the Pentagon in consultation with journalists, one of the rules dropped
was a ban on showing wounded American soldiers in distress.

Others correspondents with Vietnam credentials were disgusted.
Malcolm Browne of the *New York Times* said the pool system was
turning journalists into "essentially unpaid employees of the Department of Defense." To a true war correspondent, being denied the
opportunity to experience the sights and sounds of war—that is, being forced to see the war through the prism of an official briefer far
behind friendly lines—is death itself.

At one point, 820 pool reports had been approved and of the five cases in which the military had suggested revisions and newspeople had appealed, four had been decided in the media's favor and in the fifth case, the news organization was persuaded not to publish details of intelligence gathering. By itself, this does not suggest profligate censorship.

Still, the journalists, I feel, had a point. It was not that grievous American shortcomings and embarrassments were being concealed from them as in Vietnam, but, rather, that legitimate news was being held back. The mechanics of the pool system were onerous: too few pool reporters, too much restriction on their movements, too much favor supposedly shown to select journalists, too slow and cumbersome a procedure for relaying and clearing their reports.

It is little wonder, then, that some frustrated and enterprising reporters slipped off to cover the news on their own. For their pains, a number of them were detained, searched, and threatened with expulsion by American and Saudi authorities. At the battle of Khafji in January, however, reporters and photographers who got there on their own provided vivid accounts. Some of the best film of the ground war came from a few intrepid souls who broke away from the pools. These forays were not cost-free. CBS correspondent Bob Simon and crew were picked up in January by the Iraqis, interned, and terrorized for 40 days. Another 40 international journalists (11 Americans) were caught by the Iraqis as they headed for Basra after the fighting stopped. These journalists experienced tense passage before being safely returned.

Twenty-seven American correspondents hit the beach at Normandy on D day, filing their reports on the action that same day and making their deadlines. No American correspondents, however, were assigned to the Gulf's "Normandy" or could file a similar first-hand first-day account. Secretary of Defense Richard Cheney suspended briefings at the outset of the offensive. No daily pool reports, no briefings: a news blackout unprecedented in American history. Only because a few journalists then risked the military's wrath did Americans learn in a timely fashion about the capture of the country that the allies had been trying to free for almost six weeks.

It is wearisome, but probably necessary, to contest the notion that journalists are scoop chasers, falling over each other in ignorance and arrogance to spill military secrets on troop movements, battle damage, and the like. No doubt there are fools and knaves among us. But the military, being always the source in these matters, knows well how to keep secrets that must be kept. It can keep the press in the dark or it can coopt with offers of trust and promises of bigger stories to come. It was rumored by the Pentagon during the war that some reporters were in fact keeping some real secrets. Still, the military's Vietnam reflex, its instinctive wish to maintain control, beats strong.

Reporting from Baghdad

The ground war was relatively short, barely four days. The air war was relatively long, almost seven weeks, and perhaps the most meaningful part of it could be covered only in the country being bombed. This put extraordinary importance on the reporting emanating from Baghdad, which is to say, reporting of Saddam Hussein's peculiar view of the world.

Saddam has long had a fascination with the Western press. The expression of this fascination was as an inclination to blame the media for his political troubles and to situate the media at the heart of the supposed imperialist Zionist conspiracy, which was responsible for Iraq's woes. No doubt that somewhere in this nexus of shrewdness, suspicion, and hopelessly poisonous myopia and bias lies the explanation for his celebrated discussions of the media with foreign interlocutors.

One of these discussions, with Senator Alan Simpson of Wyoming, had Simpson assuring his eager listener: "I believe your problems lie with the Western media, and not with the United States Government." Then there was the dialogue that Saddam conducted on the eve of his invasion with the American ambassador, April Glaspie. He complained of "the media campaign" against him, and Ambassador Glaspie replied, according to a later Iraqi text: "I saw the Diane Sawyer program on ABC. And what happened in that program was cheap and unjust. And this is a real picture of what happens in the American media—even to American politicians themselves. These are the methods the Western media employs. I am pleased that you add your voice to the diplomats who stand up to the media. Because your appearance in the media, even for five minutes, would help us to make the American people understand Iraq. This would increase mutual understanding. If the American president had control of the media, his job would be much easier." Again, one can only speculate on how these remarks affected the way Saddam approached the media during the war.

In the period following August 2, Saddam applied an Iraqi version of *glasnost*. Showing a notable and, it turned out, unwarranted confidence in the appeal of Iraq's cause and in his own personal persuasiveness, he invited some American TV personalities and friendly public figures to interview him. This initiative dissipated, however, because of the worldwide loathing that greeted his attempt to exploit the foreigners he had detained as human shields. His interaction with the brave five-year-old English boy, whose head Saddam patted, was the last straw for viewers.

In this period, Saddam also let a complement of foreign journalists stay and work under strict censorship in Baghdad. Perhaps he wanted to have some credible witnesses on hand against the possibility that the allies would begin bombing "downtown Baghdad"—eyebrow-raising words that Air Force Chief of Staff General Michael Dugan used in the September interview that cost him his job.

With the start of the air war, Saddam drastically cut back the ranks of the foreign press. One figure, CNN veteran Peter Arnett, became at once the most acclaimed and most vilified journalist of the war. And, he was acclaimed and vilified for precisely the same things: for staying in place in dangerous circumstances and for providing, within the limits of what the Iraqis let him see and broadcast, clinical eyewitness accounts of bombing damage. His admirers, thought he was performing with aplomb the classical journalistic mission of reporting from behind enemy lines.

His detractors—and this attack quickly became both exceedingly personal and nasty—argued along two lines. One view held that it was intrinsically harmful and even unpatriotic for a reporter to be behind enemy lines at all because his reports could only further the propaganda purposes of his hosts. The other held that Arnett himself was committing professional lapses that lent some credence to Saddam's propaganda. His report on the bombing of what Iraqi authorities claimed was a baby milk factory and what American authorities said was a biological weapons plant became a cause célèbre. Likewise, his account of the hundreds of civilian deaths in an American raid on a Baghdad air raid shelter, which the United States said was being used as a military command bunker, drew similar fire.

A number of Western news organizations passed up the opportunity to keep a correspondent in Baghdad on grounds that, under the circumstances, professional work could not be done. I would argue that adequate work, if not work at a full professional level, could still be accomplished. All the proper disclaimers about propaganda, censorship, and Iraqi control were constantly being made by CNN and other broadcasters. It was important not to leave Saddam in sole and uncontested possession of the version of reality coming out of Baghdad. Valuable reports on Iraqi morale were made by correspondents who came in during the air war and saved their full stories for delivery from Amman, Jordan.

As for Arnett, my impression is that, in the end, he brought the allies less in obloquy for careless and unacceptable civilian bombing than in respect for the relative precision and purposefulness of the aerial campaign. That made its own contribution to the allied cause. A *Washington Post*-ABC News poll of February 16, 1991 found that 8 of 10 people questioned said Saddam and his government were most to blame for the Baghdad bunker bombing. Similarly, according to that poll, the level of support for the decision to go to war with Iraq remained at the high level it had been two weeks earlier.

A widely cited poll conducted by the Times Mirror Center for the People and the Press on January 30, 1991 gave the press good marks for covering the war. But 78 percent of those surveyed also said the military was telling the public as much as it could under the circumstances, 79 percent said censorship was a "good idea," and 57 percent said that if given a choice between military control of information or leaving it up to news organizations, they would favor greater military control. In the *Washington Post*-ABC poll, 62 percent of those polled said that, with warning, the United States should bomb the Baghdad hotel—also reported to be an Iraqi communications center—where foreign correspondents were staying. Five percent favored bombing the hotel without warning.

Finally, Senator Herbert Kohl of the Governmental Affairs Committee organized a congressional hearing on February 20 to provide a forum for discussion. Pentagon Spokesman Pete Williams followed the faithful defense-limitation strategy of admitting to small fault in the implementation of controls, even while insisting on their high necessity. "It is only the slightest form of exaggeration to suggest that the U.S. military is also at war in the Persian Gulf with the news media," declared Cragg Hines of the *Houston Chronicle*. If the hearing proved anything, it is that Congress has no role in adjudicating or even defining military-media differences.

Performance of the Media

The media's first role is always to tell the story. Because of the media's general unfamiliarity with the history and politics of the Gulf, journalists, too, with some honorable exceptions, were hardly more attuned to the perils of Saddam Hussein than the Bush administration before August 2. The press missed almost the whole story; for example, it failed to cover of the deep and lengthy pre-war tensions between Iraq and Kuwait. What the press subsequently learned from its daily work and from specialists in the field fell largely to the area of "catching up." One might rashly say that the collective unreadiness of the media for a Gulf War may have cost readers and viewers considerably more in timely collective understanding than what the Pentagon subsequently took away by news management. Unfortunately, it is often easier for journalists to complain about government lapses than their own.

In reporting the military buildup and the conduct of the war in Saudi Arabia, the media were energetic and comprehensive within the limits of allied military censorship. At least some of the daily errors inevitable in a fast-breaking war story were caught—such as the reported first-day "decimation" of the Republican Guard and the reported first-night gassing of Tel Aviv. Through no fault of their own, journalists were permitted only a glimpse of Iraq at war and no firsthand look at all at Kuwait. In the ground war, from the start the media were held at bay by their own side.

In their second role of sorting out the multiple political messages of the combatants, the media's performance was mixed. There was good pursuit of Saddam Hussein's intents and maneuvers, but the press was probably less effective in laying out the policies of the Kremlin and even of the White House. The situation lying between them was unusually complex. But how was it that we were never quite sure just why the United States entered the war? This bore directly on the results expected and the manner in which these might be reaped.

All this raised the further question of what it takes to produce the best journalism, particularly in a war context. Notwithstanding the wars of the press in the Gulf, in no other conflict since World War II have the American media been readier to accept official statements and purposes, to use the patriotic "we" in describing the war. Much of this came from the transparently villainous character of

Saddam Hussein, another part from the skills of President Bush, who wrapped the war in a corona of high purpose, national consent, international approval, and, finally, success.

Most journalists did not need to be persuaded of the rightness of the war. Journalists found the conduct and costs of the war bearable and the restrictions on coverage burdensome, but not venal. It took the American Civil Liberties Union (ACLU) and some peace groups, for instance, to protest in a suit the Defense Department's closure of the Dover Air Force Base mortuary; the department acted ostensibly to protect the privacy of military families, making no claim that national security was involved. None of the big American news organizations joined a second suit in which 13 publications and writers—including the *Nation* and the *Village Voice*—brought against the Pentagon for its restrictions on news coverage.

What did matter, however, was that two of the kinds of journalistic stimulus that were provided in all too ample measure by the Vietnam War were missing this time around. After the war began, there was no skeptical and aroused public, and we did not have to cope with the pain of American casualties. There was another missing element, too. "Trust me," General Colin Powell, chairman of the Joint Chiefs of Staff, had implored the media early in the air war; the evidence shows that most of the media did.

Evidence is also clear that the military and civilian commands learned something important from Vietnam, as well, and they practiced no grand deceptions as in the old model. At least none had surfaced by the time the war ended. The most controversial decisions—to hold back from negotiations with Saddam Hussein, to raise the troop levels in November, and to move to war—were taken by the president, not the military, and were taken in public view where they could be discussed and criticized. The situation that had generated deceit in the Vietnam War—when presidents were squeezed between dissent at home and frustration in the field—simply did not arise in the Gulf War.

A third role of the media is to encourage a broad and enlightened public debate on policy. Particularly in the long months before the United States joined Saddam's war, the press (both print and television) gave considerable space and time to a range of qualified and articulate people from outside daily journalism. Recall, for instance, the informative multimedia duel of Henry Kissinger and Zbigniew Brzezinski. Military strategists were brought into the discussion, turning all of us briefly into armchair generals. Some of the specialists found themselves saddled with forecasts that later provided the only comic relief of the war.

The debate that took place in the media came to center mostly on the mainstream political alternatives of embargo or war. This focus on the center is the strength and weakness of American political dialogue. Nonetheless, whatever the flaws of American policy, they could not be blamed on lack of adequate outside ventilation.

The performance of the American media has a flip side. How did the American government employ and exploit the media? Here it is useful to look beyond the military's use of the press in protecting security, convenience, operational flexibility, and self-esteem. There is the more manipulative purposes of bolstering American public support for the war and of helping to deceive Iraq, both by civilian and military officials.

At home, the administration was determined to maintain public confidence that the war was going well, but not to raise expectations to levels that might create credibility problems. General Thomas Kelly, the Pentagon briefer, who initially said the United States could beat Iraqi troops "in short order," changed his approach the next day to "in good order." "In a very masterful way," said (Democratic) media consultant Frank Greer, "they released information always showing American forces exceeding expectations, while always cautioning against overconfidence." The president and the war's media star, Allied Military Commander General Norman Schwarzkopf, had the happy task of coping with a success that the media could report, but not deny.

The media, especially television, carried the stunning message of American technological mastery—the smart-bomb footage. Because most of the large numbers of Iraqi casualties (civilian and military) did not get covered on camera as was the case for the few American casualties, the grisly images that American policymakers most feared never occurred. Anti-war protest—another big and controversial Vietnam story—never grew to the proportions necessary to kindle heavy debate about the media's coverage of the protest. "Chance" ensured that the first accounts of the ground campaign emanated from TV correspondents accompanying Arab troops—a reminder that American troops were not bearing the whole load. Bad news, such as friendly-fire deaths and the Baghdad bunker bombings, were quickly smothered in extra detail.

"Some people say the media is the enemy," a senior army officer told the *Wall Street Journal*, "but in fact the media is really a battlefield, and you have to win on it." Without ever stating specifically that the Marines were going in over the beach, the Pentagon dangled that possibility. Full press coverage of Marine amphibious maneuvers followed, and on this feint so crucial to the eventual success of allied strategy, Saddam bit, to Schwarzkopf's delight.

The general also hailed what he later called exaggerated early news accounts of the U.S. troop buildup in Saudi Arabia. In actuality, so few forces were on the ground—the command was withholding numbers—that they would have been vulnerable to Iraqi attack. Many citizens might see nothing wrong and much right in instances like these of the military's use of the media as a tool of strategy. Many journalists might go along on the basis that the cause was good, the government was not actually and actively lying, and journalists should not whine when they are bested in the daily duel of figuring out from official sources what is really going on.

Had the war gone badly, the press might now be fending off the usual double reproof: that it had undercut the rightful powers that be and that it had been too cozy with power. With victory, however, inside and outside the press, the general inclination seemed to be to let grievances of the press and grievances against the press subside.

Many people would conclude that the wars of the press were less about great issues than about small irritations. The public did get a lot of timely news, and the press did not really alienate the military or alter its conduct of the war. The questions that did arise about the interaction of media and military tended to be more or less at the margin. Journalists like to feel that their concerns are the center of the universe. However, they should not be surprised when the rest of the crowd wants to move on.

The war provided a snapshot of where the press stood with the culture: in an uncertain and ambivalent place, attended and distrusted at the same time. In sharp contrast, the military's contribution, reputation, and values won unconflicted acclaim. If Vietnam was in a sense the media's war, Iraq was the military's. Broadly speaking, the military met the demanding standard set by General Dwight Eisenhower, who knew whereof he spoke, in World War II: "The commander in the field must never forget that it is his duty to cooperate with the heads of his government in the task of maintaining a civilian morale that will be equal to every purpose." That the war was short and successful eased the military's task on this score, but should not deny it the appropriate rewards in public regard and self-esteem.

Journalists should not worry about their ranking in the polls, but they should worry about whether they are doing a job commensurate with their constitutional privilege and their professional purpose. Their job, after all, is very different from the military's charge to "maintain civilian morale." It is to independently pursue the truth of war.

It seems self-centered of the press to keep harping on arrangements for combat coverage. The specific ground rules of security, numbers, and logistics are always arguable. But when the press is excluded from covering events of great importance, the character of the relationship between those who govern and those who are governed subtly changes. Diminished, if not lost, is the people's opportunity to gain the materials essential to a timely and detached judgment of the use of power. Diminished, too, is the chief executive's opportunity to gain a useful check on the information flowing up to him from his own soldiers and bureaucrats.

This argument seems overly theoretical in the midst of wartime activity. The fact remains that, in a democracy, information policy bears on the most sensitive and fragile interior relationships, the ones that define essence. If journalists are not prepared to understand their own best case, and to make it, they forfeit their claim to complain.

But not only must the press understand its role, it has to do its work well. This is its first responsibility: not to take one attitude or another toward public policies or public authorities, but to be competent and conscientious—competitive but not irresponsibly so—in tracking the news and the meaning of the news. The First Amendment does not absolve journalists of the moral dilemmas of citizenship, and the issue of patriotic duty will not be easily resolved. Yet journalists should puzzle no less about their professional duty. On this crucial point, I quote from a letter received from a knowledgeable army colonel during the war:

> Military reporters in the major media are usually youngsters with Ivy League grad school backgrounds in politics or foreign affairs—useful in reporting arms control issues but little else. It has been my observation over the past five years that they check what they learn by the congressional route commissared

by the likes of anti-technologists . . . and the politically correct reform caucus. No wonder the Iraqis assumed we were a Keystone Kops army, the gang that couldn't shoot straight. Sad.

As one reviews military reporting over the past 10 years, one sees very little attention has been paid to the changes in our forces or the complete renaissance in our thinking since Vietnam. It is interesting to me and surprising to most that in this war the generals are fighting the right war—right weapons, right tactics, right training, and the right troops. In comparison, the press, the protest movement, and our politicians—and even Saddam—are trying to refight Vietnam. Shame. The reason for our success may be because, of these groups, only the military lost status, power, or political capital in the post-Vietnam era. The others were ascendant. Remember, power and status corrupt.

I am not ready to say the press is corrupt. There was much that was excellent in coverage of the war on the home front and in the battlefield, too. But I think that members of the media must be as open to criticism and self-examination as what is demanded of other elements of society. The best ending to the wars of the press in the Gulf would be a reflective cease-fire.

Index

257